CALLS OF DUTY

E

CALLS OF DUTY

Thirty Years in Telecoms

RAPHAEL CHANNER

Matador
9 Priory Business Park,
Wistow Road, Kibworth Beauchamp,
Leicestershire. LE8 0RX
Tel: (+44) 116 279 2299
Fax: (+44) 116 279 2277
Email: books@troubador.co.uk
Web: www.troubador.co.uk/matador

ISBN 978-1783065-516

British Library Cataloguing in Publication Data.
A catalogue record for this book is available from the British Library.

Printed and bound in the UK by TJ International, Padstow, Cornwall
Typeset in 11pt Bembo by Troubador Publishing Ltd, Leicester, UK

Matador is an imprint of Troubador Publishing Ltd

To the memory of my parents

Contents

Foreword

The events described in this book all either happened to me or took place around me, and I have endeavoured to recount them as truthfully as possible. I did not keep a diary, but have found the process of recollection remarkably productive.

I have no great understanding of the workings of the human brain and its capacity for memory, nor of the role of psychology. I have nonetheless concluded that our ability to recall precise details of passing events, momentary feelings and fleeting acquaintances, is advanced by our participation in activity of some lasting worth and purpose, which indelibly sears itself to our very being. It becomes part of us. We are thus defined, at least in that part, by what we have done.

If that is correct, then what follows is not simply the story of how I spent the past thirty years, but also of how I became the person I am today.

RC, July 2014
Ithaca, Greece.

Introduction

British Telecommunications plc came into being in the autumn of 1984 when it was privatised by the UK government and overnight went from being the telecoms department of the national postal operator to become one of the largest publicly quoted companies in Europe. The reasons behind the move were numerous, with political and ideological considerations clearly major drivers. In addition, UK governments had been running budget deficits for almost a decade. In that financial climate, there was deemed to be insufficient public money available to fund a national programme of investment in the new electronic telephone exchanges then coming on stream. So a compelling commercial case lay in the argument that with the bow wave of technological developments then foreseen, the only means of guaranteeing the flow of capital necessary to deliver a thriving telecoms market was to place the organisation in private hands and liberalise the sector.

Today, thirty years on, few would query that analysis, or the outcome. The UK now has one of the most competitive telecoms markets in the world. BT is unrecognisable from the staid, state-run behemoth which ran an army of a quarter of a million people and had fallen into disrepute with a significant section of its subscriber base. It needed to change and it needed to improve. I joined the company just days after the initial share sale, and saw myself in the vanguard of that change, the transformation that was so obviously necessary and which was made all the more feasible by the opportunities thrown at it by endless technological advance.

This book follows the evolution of the company through the eyes of someone closely involved in the commercial projects and challenges that arose from these technological developments, throughout that entire three decade period. The narrative chronicles those tumultuous ebbs and flows, a personal and organisational white knuckle ride driven off the back of economic and business cycles, market euphoria, flights of capital, flights of fancy, delusional grandiose schemes and blood curdling efficiency drives.

★

Thirty years is a long old stint and from an economic and strategic perspective it is possible to describe and understand how the wider canvas over time determined our priorities and plans for achieving them. Specifically, I worked through three ten year business cycles, the beginning, middle and end of each indelibly shaping our business mindset and thus the trajectory of our objectives.

I began work in the early 1980s when the economy of the UK was emerging from a deep and disruptive recession. There followed a five to six year upswing and growing prosperity, fuelled by privatisations, financial liberalisation and tax cuts. These helped to foster a positive and risk taking climate that would transform the UK's prospects for twenty years. The bubble of excessive asset prices subsequently burst and led to the hard landing of the recession of the early 1990s, which prompted widespread corporate introspection, a reduction in risk taking and a retrenchment to core businesses. The first cycle was complete.

The release of the pound from the ERM straitjacket prompted calls for new, investment-led growth and, together with growing liberalisation in major European markets, this created the next wave of opportunity. The dovetailing of these factors with the gathering dot.com boom and its subsequent bust created an investment landscape that within the space of five years went from nirvana to dystopia. The second cycle came to a nasty juddering halt.

Down but never out, euphoria would inevitably return, based on fundamental competitive and technological advantages, as accelerating global developments and transformational cost saving opportunities in newly emerging economies drove a third tidal upswing through the mid-noughties. This time around it was all ominously compounded by continuing deregulation, excessive debt and spiralling technological advances which were themselves accelerating in their impacts on daily life, to no greater effect than in their culminating ability to bring the world to its knees with a financial crash and credit crunch that is still grinding out its debilitating effects to this day. The third cycle cast the longest and darkest shadow yet.

That then is the backdrop to what follows. Part One is a reflection on life in a new organisation slow to find its commercial feet; Part Two the story of globalisation and transformation and trying to run before we could properly walk; Part Three is what happened after someone pressed the reset button: a fixation with basic improvements that had never been made, and a more measured, incremental and mature approach to change. Part Four ruminates on evolutionary aspects of the company's thirty year journey and how these have ensured its survival.

★

Above all, this is my story. No colleague underwent the same set of experiences, so it is unique in that sense, as any working life is. But the very novelty of my own set of experiences, and the number and range of them, would also mark it out as uniquely fortunate, compelling, even cavalier.

For almost thirty years, I worked on some remarkable assignments: I experienced at first hand the initial commercialisation of mobile phones, the internet, cable television, broadband, globalisation and digital television, through my involvement in a series of ground-breaking strategic projects, both here in the UK and overseas. These initiatives ranged from product developments to market launches, from acquisitions and joint ventures to disposals and buyouts. Through a variety of operational, project and management roles, which took me to three continents and over twenty countries, I was able to work with a galaxy of stimulating, challenging and commercially astute individuals and organisations who brought their own perspectives and contributions to this festival of opportunity.

My tenure coincided with the generational development of my employer from monopolistic telephone provider in the UK to a global communications business supplying everything from corporate IT networking to digital television platforms, wifi and mobile internet services, sports television channels and web services, via optical fibre, wireless technologies and networked devices which would have been, indeed were, unthinkable to the layman as commercial and technical propositions when I fetched up in 1984. Little did I realise then what lay ahead of me and the role I would play in making so many of them happen.

My developing expertise in business planning and financial analysis, strategic investment and corporate development meant that I was able to spend, out of personal choice and business need, almost my entire career at the telecoms frontier. I witnessed the good, the bad and the unlikely. The ridiculous and the sublime; it was all there. And given the stretch of time in question, there are few others who can say they saw it all too. I would contend, and believe few would dispute, that telecoms has undergone transformation so manifold and significant that no other area of commercial enterprise would have provided such diverse and challenging opportunities as those I and my colleagues alighted upon during that time. This book is a testimony to that contention.

★

A personal memoir, the following chapters each relate a particular episode of change, through the story of a project or initiative which grabbed our collective imagination and stretched to the limit our mental and at times physical capabilities, while enduring the infuriating bureaucratic and political machinations that inevitably pollute all major corporations at some time or other.

While the nature of the commercial projects I worked on would evolve in the wake of technological developments, there were other notable factors which together formed the backcloth, script and drama of my working life: the state of development in my own career and aspects of my own life; the interplay and relationships with and between colleagues, partners and clients; the nature of the market and our abiding business objectives; the overall economic and political environment. Into this mix, there was the growing commercialisation and professionalisation of the organisation as it continued its emergence from its public sector embodiment and progressively took on the appearance and approaches of what one would expect from a "normal" company striving to operate competitively in the private sector.

It is interesting that only now, in retrospect and through undertaking an analytical account such as this, do I fully realise how meaningfully these factors were changing and how they were affecting my day to day working experience. What is perhaps most striking of all is the increasing level of seriousness with which we all as an organisation were taking ourselves and our activities. This is not to say that we had ever been flippant and reckless, nor that we would knowingly have ever presented plans and undertaken projects that would have jeopardised shareholder value and undermined our strategic intent. But as time passed it became clear that we were having to keep a wider and more sophisticated management caucus apprised and convinced of the value of the projects and that this would involve an ever deeper and more searching examination of risk. While this merely betokened the encroachment of normality and the realities of an ever tougher world, it would make life far harder and eventually drain it of the sense of adventure I had so easily come by and had for so long taken for granted.

It was a rollercoaster ride, and thirty-odd years of it was quite enough. Drained by it, and unprepared for another spin on the switchback, I collected my final pay cheque in January 2013. I wanted to do something else with my life. But I thought that writing a book about it all would be a good idea. It will be for others to judge if it was.

PART ONE

A Lumbering Giant

1984 – 1993

Westenders

The privatisation of BT in the autumn of 1984 had been widely trailed through the British media for several months and it had a further, if unintended consequence in that it persuaded me to apply, on spec, for a job in their finance department. I had spent a couple of years after graduating from university in a series of temporary positions in the Civil Service, then as a research assistant in Oxford and latterly with an accounting firm, but none of them had particularly floated my boat. Now these dazzling televisual images with their explicit message of a future of ubiquitous, superfast communications struck me not just as a cash investment opportunity but as an invitation to come and play a part in the coming revolution itself. I got hold of a graduate trainee application form and sent it off. It was February, and nine months later I received a reply: could I attend an interview the following Monday morning? I was so stunned I decided I would indeed attend, if only to complain about their staggering inefficiency and totemic arrogance.

The interview took place first thing the following week in an unprepossessing office block at the northern end of Drury Lane in London's Covent Garden. I arrived to find two rather prim middle-aged gentlemen seated behind a desk. And they were very gentle men, apologising profusely for getting me in at so early an hour, and would I like a cup of coffee and some biscuits, and was my seat comfortable? They were like a couple of cheesy men's outfitters from the 1950s, and were so patently decent with it, that I decided to forestall my fulminations. They asked me some initial, lowball questions about myself, then together showed me to another desk in the corner where I was invited to carry out a short paper exercise on a basic problem in business finance. Having completed this, I stood at a rudimentary flipchart and presented my analysis and recommendations to them. They sat there smiling widely and nodding. It was all immensely civilised and after some closing pleasantries and handshakes I was shown out. I walked down Drury Lane in a state of bafflement and was even more baffled to arrive home that evening to a message on the answer machine from one of my inquisitors, saying that he was very pleased to offer me a role in BT as a finance manager. There would be no need for me to follow a graduate induction programme. I think my face had just fit.

And so it was in late November 1984, that I arrived at a BT office on Shaftesbury Avenue on my first day, and reported to the sixth floor. My new boss, Alan, was there to meet me and showed me into his office. He was a bearded, rather weasely type in a shabby, ill-fitting suit and I was not exactly overwhelmed with confidence. After a few minutes of form filling, during which time I signed the Official Secrets Act (although I am possibly legally bound not to disclose that), we moved on to meatier matters. My university. My degree. My school. My parents. I wasn't sure if this was related to my having just signed the OSA – did he now have rights over mine? – or if it was simply the result of his chippiness. I decided it was the latter; I must have looked reasonably good on paper, and this strange little man was sizing me up as a potential threat. I was relieved when he moved to the white board and drew up and began to explain BT's byzantine organisation structure.

It transpired the company employed at the time over two

hundred and forty thousand people. The majority of them belonged to a vast operation known as the Local Communications Services Division, which looked after the UK's telephone network and serviced a base of some twenty five million residential and business subscribers. This division was broken down into regions, of which ours was London, and thence into districts, of which ours was the West End. Other, far smaller divisions looked after international satellite links, some overseas assets and the company's renowned research laboratories, based out in Suffolk. A small corporate function based in the City of London looked after finance, strategy and product development. I noted with interest there was even a chief economist. Plainly nothing was being left to chance. Our district was run by an executive board, which was headed up by the general manager and included the chief accountant, three operational heads and a personnel manager. He, Alan, reported to the chief accountant. The GM reported to the director for London. It was all highly structured and everybody clearly knew their place.

Our finance department, under the chief accountant, consisted of some twenty souls and was charged with producing monthly financial returns for the corporate and regional units, and a set of management reports for our local executive board. Two of my colleagues had their hands full with the new financial reporting strictures that came with being a newly privatised business, while my job was to take on the management reporting. Alan showed me to my desk, and then effectively left me to it.

The job title of finance manager implied, it seemed to me, that I had undergone at least some basic training in BT's financial methods and procedures. This was far from the case of course, but since BT's approach to financial management at that time was at best formative, I would bluff for a while and prove my aptitude for the job through applying my innate analytical and quantitative abilities, and a little psychology. So I dressed like a finance manager, in a dark blue suit with grey pinstripes. I appeared like a finance manager, with my dark-rimmed spectacles and black briefcase. I spoke like a finance manager, with a developing technical vocabulary and a growing proficiency in the proliferation of three letter abbreviations which seemed to turn every conversation into an exchange of code. I followed a simple premise; if it looks like a duck and sounds like a duck, then it obviously is a duck. Nobody questioned my suitability for the role, or asked for my qualifications. I had applied as an economics graduate for a trainee financial management position. I had ended up a couple of notches further up the hierarchy. Who was I to argue with that?

My very first task that week was to pull together a profit and loss statement for the West End's telephone box "business". It was described to me as such, although the merest inspection revealed this as grand overstatement, since it was more realistically speaking a collection of several hundred rank and festering kiosks, just starting out on their latest phase of existence as advertising hoardings for the local population of prostitutes.

However, since this era predated mobile phones, the call boxes were still being regularly used for their intended purpose as well. The cash takings were collected each day and taken to a counting centre in west London; daily cash reports were produced and sent over to our office every four weeks. I had had the latest of these thrust into my possession by one of my new colleagues at pretty much the moment I walked in on my first morning, so clearly he wanted rid of it right away, no doubt having deemed the entire exercise a hellish chore.

Coopers and Lybrand, a "big six" accountancy firm and BT's then auditors, had recently produced a report which identified, allocated and apportioned a set of costs notionally attributable to the phone box business. I now had a copy of this to hand as well, and worked my way diligently through their methodology in order to come up with a total cost figure. Subtracting this from the cash receipts gave me my total profit; not exactly rocket science, nor necessarily a precise accounting exercise, but as good a sense of the financial position as we were going to get.

I wrote up my phone box report (which showed a reasonable profit margin) and was then keenly escorted by a colleague to get it typed up by something quaintly called a typing pool. This was his excuse to leer at its handful of nubile females, as he dusted off his well rehearsed repertoire of salacious remarks. How cretinous he sounded. I went on my own in future, if only to emphasise my disassociation from the older, cruder order. How prissy I was.

I duly circulated my report and a few days later received a request from the chief accountant's secretary – no PAs then – to meet with him later that afternoon. It was to be my first encounter with him and I made my way anxiously along Shaftesbury Avenue towards (I kid you not) Dial House, where the district board members' offices were located. I was ushered into his empty office and took up a leather chair across the massive hardwood desk from his own imperious seat. The room reeked of tobacco and cologne. I thought of salesmen in Ford Cortinas, and furry dice, and there came the question: what on Earth am I doing here?

This bout of self-doubting introspection was thwarted by the sound of guffawing from the corridor. The door flew open and in through a cloud of cigar smoke strode Roger. "Aah – my lad!" he exclaimed, "Good to see you. Welcome aboard!" I was obviously expected. Roger was a lovely Yorkshireman who took me under his wing from this day on. *A propos* of nothing, he launched into an anecdote concerning time he had spent working in Africa, where he arrived at work one morning to find his boss slumped dead over his desk, with a spear in his back. "Ya see lad, they don't bother choppin' their 'ands off when they catch 'em with t' fingers in t' till." Was that a warning of some sort? I clearly had much to learn, and I wanted him to teach me.

"Word of advice, son – be commercial." And he went on to explain how in the new world, as he saw it, he would need a whole slew of financial reports and that I was going to assist him and the district board in understanding the true financial position of their multi-million pound business. This was the future, ya see lad, product profitability, and could I start off by having a word with Marigold from marketing, regarding the handset business. Then his phone rang, he took a deep puff on his cigar, winked, and lifting the phone, jerked his head to dismiss me. We hadn't even touched on phone boxes. I was clearly going to be kept busy, and off I went to find Marigold.

So my next task was to put together a profitability report on telephone handsets. Our marketing colleagues, under the aforementioned Marigold, were responsible for buying in various handset products, showcasing them in department store concessions around town, producing promotional fillers to accompany telephone bills, and tracking the sales and rental volumes. My task was to calculate the total revenues this brought in, cost up the inventory and the marketing activity and then report on the margin generated. Straightforward enough in theory and so it proved in practice, with some light relief thrown in. It would prove impossible to compile the report without convulsing with laughter at the comical nature of the phone models now on offer as the company sought to act commercially. I clearly did not share the earnest, humourless diligence of my product management colleagues who would debate the relative market performance of, amongst others, our Disney character phones – Donald, Goofy and Mickey all featuring luridly – without cracking a smile. It was with a tinge of sadness that I recommended we shut down this hideous loss making range and concentrate instead on basic black and silver handsets.

★

In the same way as the wealth, pride and self-esteem of a country can be assessed from the nature and quality of its roads, so the same can be gleaned of a company from its portfolio of office buildings. And by that token BT West End was pretty pleased with itself. The main offices were housed in a monolithic eight-storey redbrick block on Shaftesbury Avenue, just around the corner from Cambridge Circus. My own desk on the sixth floor overlooked the whole of central London, from Covent Garden down to the Thames and beyond, and I relished this magnificent, commanding view even on the gloomiest of days; my city, laid out before me. The executive board were enthroned in their imperious art deco edifice, hewn from fine Portland stone, while the BT London regional office was housed in a slum down near Vauxhall station, leaving little doubt as to where the power lay in that relationship. We were the West End swells and we lived like them, the kings of our patch.

The office-based work environment and experience in late 1984 was little changed from that of the post-war period. Throughout the sixties and seventies, American and Scandinavian influences had taken hold in certain quarters, desks had become more streamlined and chairs appeared in rainbows of nylon and plastic, but the sturdy grey filing cabinets, and desktop regime of buff and manila, foolscap and treasury tag remained as essentially British trappings from another, distant administrative age. And for my first few months in BT this would remain the case.

We were aware of computers as things that were beginning to run our networks, and as mainframe beasts that housed our subscriber records and churned out batches of bills. But that was it; they were part of an invisible infrastructure that sat elsewhere. None of us had ever actually seen one or knew how they worked. I had a letter published in our local in-house magazine Westenders, beseeching the editor to adopt laymen's terms when describing software drops, data warehousing and other arcane features of coming computer systems. "Saw your letter," said Alan. "Very good." Sensing my curiosity, he sent me on a course; his stock response to any slither of initiative.

Things were to change momentously, if rather prosaically, one morning soon after I returned, when a man with a trolley arrived on our floor with a large cardboard box. Sensing destiny perhaps, and seeing something was afoot, we watched in awed fascination as he produced from inside it something resembling a large diver's helmet, together with an array of subsidiary features which he proceeded to plug into the back of it. And lo, it was a desktop PC. And he didst turn it on. And the screen, it didst flicker. And it only bloody worked.

And not only was it a desktop computer. It had "email" too, admittedly an early prototype, for use between BT's various finance units. But here it was. The future. Well, a bit of it, as there was only one, to be shared for general use. Up stepped our financial accountant, appropriately named Sony. History was upon his shoulders as he fired up the first programme and created and sent our first file. How had he managed that? We applauded generously. Over the coming months more of these boxes arrived, and gradually we all acquired them, and set about becoming experts in Supercalc, MSdos and Telecom Gold. They were treated like toys rather than tools, their magical transcendental quality removing any traces, any pretence of actual work. In a strange way, we loved them.

Keith, an otherwise underemployed finance colleague, had placed himself in charge of organising and meeting our computing requirements. While he amused himself ordering and installing our PCs, he had also found time to get his hands on some even more revolutionary kit for himself. It was cutting edge stuff, at the very frontier of "convergence", where computing met communications. Branded the Tonto, it was also possibly the clumsiest piece of desktop equipment ever designed. It looked like a PC with a telephone screwed onto the side. Actually, in retrospect, that is precisely what it was. We cooed and aahed nonetheless, and wondered what other delicious novelties lay ahead.

Slowly but surely, and with the aid of our gleaming new toys, we worked our way through the design and production of dozens of financial performance reports. If it moved we measured it, and if it didn't measure up, we canned it. I made a name for myself locally as something of an axe man and as the new financial year hoved into view, Roger had a plan for me to cause a little more disruption.

As a company BT would have at any one time hundreds of millions of pounds worth of stock tied up in its many and various warehouses around the country. This unproductive use of capital had been targeted by our corporate financiers for more auspicious applications, and so a number of projects were launched to drive down the volume of operational stores to more efficient and affordable levels. Yawningly, I was sent away for a week to learn all about the new computer-based stock management systems that would be implemented across the country. London would be in the first wave, and I and my counterparts from across the region were the first into the sheep dip.

I did ask Roger why I was being tasked with this, after all I was not in charge of finance systems, nor had I any experience of them. "That's t' bluddy problem. Nobody has, now that Adrian's gone off again." He then went on to describe the highly unconventional working life of our systems manager. Adrian, a heavily set and forbidding looking Chinese, was a part-time actor occasionally called upon for film and television work. He had recently landed himself a role, and was required to be on set, outside London, for the coming month. He had been granted unpaid leave and had left the previous week. The year before, he had played the part of a SPECTRE agent in the James Bond picture Never say Never Again. A critical scene in Blofeld's lair would be lessened without Adrian's evil Sino grin, which betrayed his evident self-satisfaction at evading the latest revamp of BT's accounting procedures. The future of his contrasting twin careers had thereby been assured, and it was now my turn to pay the price for it.

I arrived back in the office to find Roger had arranged a meeting for me to explain to our three operational heads how this system would be introduced in our district, what the purpose of it was, what was expected of their people and how they would be trained to use it. Through the use of charm, humour and no little grovelling, we got them to agree to pilot the system for twelve months. Moreover, it was my thankless task to train and guide their operational teams in the use of a computer system for the first time in their working lives.

Now I have a lot of time for the engineering manpower at BT; I have spent time with many of them during "back to the floor" exercises in management condescension, and can vouch for their exceptional technical skills, while their sense of humour is on a par with that of members of the armed forces, gruesome and unrelentingly hilarious. But when it came to getting them to sit down at a computer screen to place an order online for their kits and components, let alone to return and account for unused items, it was like training kittens to walk in a straight line. Their technical prowess reverted to that of chimps, and their humour soured sharply. Their morale fell through the floor and the levels of productivity went with it, while our stock levels were actually rising. I got a kicking from Roger and told to drop all other projects until this was fixed.

Soon after, I happened to watch Apocalypse Now on television and had a moment of revelation part way through the film, when the Jane Fonda lookalike turns up in the jungle and dances and sings for the GIs. She has them in the palm of her hand; they would do anything for her. It occurred to me then that this was what I needed for my GIs at BT; a Jane Fonda.

And by a stroke of luck that was what I got. Well not exactly Jane Fonda, but a lovely Irish technical assistant called Miriam who appeared, out of the blue, in the IT office one morning the following week, on special dispensation for three months after injuring herself in the field. She was a bright spark, a quick learner and wanted to "get into computers". I spent a morning training her up and then let her loose on the operational teams.

Her teasing, sisterly manner, feminine wiles and warm self-deprecating humour were more than a match for their laddish attitudes and cantankerous behaviour, and she soon had them wound round her finger; Jane Fonda indeed. I could never have found the patience, the even temper, the sheer humanity required to persuade somebody to do something they really had no intention of doing. I learned a lot from Miriam, mostly about what I wasn't, and what I would never properly do.

★

I was progressively being subsumed into the culture of the

company. This worked on a number of levels and in various ways. I found myself gradually becoming closed off from the outside world in BT. Sure, there were those pesky residential subscribers, companies and government departments, who all depended on our copper and satellite networks for their telecoms requirements. But our time was spent talking to other BT people, other BT businesses, other BT organisations. We didn't have time to look outside and see what was going on in the world, we had big BT to look after. And if we did that, then big BT would look after us. And we certainly did get looked after. My salary almost doubled the day I left the accounting firm and joined BT. In my first couple of years, it virtually doubled again, with pay rises each year on my birthday and on the anniversary of my joining, as well as annual increases to compensate for inflation. This was extraordinary; I was able to afford a mortgage on a London flat at the age of twenty four.

There was a sizeable, subsidized staff bar on the top floor of Dial House, open to employees Monday to Friday lunchtimes, early evenings and on certain nights when it hosted particular events or parties. But by and large it was simply there as somewhere to go on to in order to finish the drinking that would commence at the end of most meetings, when trollies would be wheeled in, groaning under the weight of vast quantities of alcohol.

The culture of drinking was everywhere. I was a relative novice but was happy to undertake a crash course. It was a hugely enjoyable place, and half the time it really didn't feel like being at work at all. Taken to the limits this could have led to the height of irresponsibility, but it did remain largely sensible and a means of sustaining a fond sociability that has disappeared almost entirely with today's po-faced, supercilious rectitude. I recently went with a handful of younger colleagues to an Indian restaurant on a Friday lunchtime. Arriving five minutes before the rest, I ordered a beer. They subsequently trailed in, some of them glancing warily, others uncomprehendingly, at my drink as they shuffled into their seats, before ordering their obligatory cokes and mineral waters. The conversation remained as cool and strained as their sense of occasion.

I had noticed when working in temporary jobs, that I never felt a part of the culture, the nature of my contract with the organisation delineating our mutual relationship. I remained at arm's length, from both the perspective of the established employees, and from my own point of view. There was a distance, a safety margin. This dissipated now I had become a fulltime member of staff, and was absorbed into the tribe. I was regarded differently; in a sense I was now fair game, to be assessed and treated the same as everyone else. This applied to both the formal aspects – performance assessment and reward are two obvious areas – and to the informal aspects too: as a trusted colleague, say, or as a mentor to younger members of staff; and even, let's be honest here, as a player in the hormonal merry-go-round of office-based sexuality.

I was becoming aware of an undercurrent of eroticism around the office, a phenomenon I had never experienced before. There were a number of women about, not all obviously attractive in a physical sense but, certainly, womanly. In contrast to the females who had populated my university life and early adult social scene, who formed part of and conformed to a broader, earnest unisexual culture, the women at work seemed different, more feminine, more alluring. I had no great desires towards any of them individually, but I enjoyed the overt flirtatiousness of the group and some of our interactions, and gave as good as I got.

Some of the conversations I was party to over the years would have made a porn baron blush. The more senior your position becomes, the less likely these are to occur, if my own experience was anything to go by. There is less opportunity and scope for badinage; relationships become more formalised. So it was an aspect of office life that gradually disappeared as my career developed. I do, however, look back fondly on some of the more salacious verbal interplay with selected female colleagues. How we ever got on to some of the subjects we covered I no longer recall, but the advice and guidance I came away with remained quite clear in my mind, and underpin aspects of my technique, range and prowess to this day.

Another complete novelty to me was my responsibility for managing two members of staff, Dennis and Abdul. To this day, I do not know what their actual responsibilities were when I first arrived, nor indeed do I recall having much interaction with them at all. They would arrive each morning, say hello and then disappear for the rest of the day. I would occasionally bump into Abdul in the stationery office, where he would be humping boxes around and shuffling documents, while Dennis might cross the office floor with a cheery wave on his way to God only knew where. My experience of staff management then consisted more of a pastoral than operational responsibility. As long as I could see they were happy, looked purposeful and appeared in good health, that would suffice. I had no use for them, nor they for me. In time they would each move on to new assignments, though you would barely have noticed it. I would still come across Abdul up to his knees in photocopier paper, and exchange a passing thumbs-up with Dennis.

Prior to December 1984, I had had no previous experience of an office Christmas party. Preparations for this longed-for event had been in full swing since the day I first arrived, with meetings convened to plan the richly layered tableau of debauchery and dissolution. Or so it sounded, judging by previous functions so fondly recalled by my glassy eyed colleagues. I awaited the moment feverishly.

Came the day, the floor of the general office was cleared of furniture, a sound and light system was installed and trestle tables appeared bearing colossal consignments of booze. All was set. Bang on time, the music began, bottles were breached, and bodies surged onto the floor. It was extraordinary, a sea of shirtage, bobbing heads, and wide eyes and grins. They didn't need to tell me what was going on, I could see quite plainly; they were all picking up precisely where they had left off the previous year. It was seamless: the same drinks, the same songs, the same couples coming together. And for four hours it continued, a carnival of merriment and good humour. No depravity or hedonism, just an explosion of communal, seasonal bonhomie. It would follow the same pattern for the next two years; an off-the-shelf celebration as formulaic as it was fun. For it was the sameness that was the thing; it was theirs, untouched, and would remain so. How they loved it. As did I, never experiencing anything comparable for the next twenty five years. In the days before bonuses and in the wake of Wakes Weeks, this was the occasion when the workforce took their due. More importantly, it put the "happy" into Christmas.

★

Somewhat out of the blue, a visit to a local telephone exchange was arranged for me. It was located just off of Tottenham Court Road and was home to some fifty-odd engineers and operators. It is easily forgotten that at the time BT was almost entirely comprised of engineers and operators; we so-called commercial employees, those charged with generating and marshalling the cash, were in a distinct minority.

I was guided into and around the building by the senior engineer. "You must have friends in high places," he assured me mysteriously. "Don't get too many of your lot down here." I hadn't caught his drift. We passed on into the bowels of the building. He proudly presented the age-old, clunking, chuntering Strowger machinery that made up the switching guts of the pre-digital network. It looked and sounded like a giant sewing machine. The walls of this sanctum were studded with dials and switches that belonged on the dashboard of a pre-war motorcar. Even then, it was incredible to think that this was the beating heart of London's telecoms network.

We moved upstairs into the open office where the operators worked. They were seated on high stools at teak desktops, chatting away at the walls as they plugged cables, flipped switches, scrabbled through directories and scribbled notes. It was a scene from countless sepia tinted photographs. I felt my heart sinking again; what was I doing in this place, in this job. But then my heart lifted as it slowly dawned on me what the underlying purpose of my visit was. For there in the corner of the room, still swathed in its clear plastic wrapping, was another glimpse of the future, huge and glistening, its glowering presence seeming to grow as I stared at it. A massive computerised directories system, which I came to learn was due for installation and launch over the subsequent months. It would over time reduce the operator labour force requirement by some sixty per cent. I know, since I did the calculations and wrote the subsequent post-investment review.

It was to be my first real taste of modernisation, of transformation, creating the business case for change and progress, and I realised then that this was how I would spend my working life at BT. I had no desire to continue reporting on what had happened last month, or last year, looking backwards and inwards. I wanted to be planning what would happen next month, and next year, looking forwards and out. But where, and how?

By a quirk of fortune, which didn't feel particularly fortunate at the outset, I was asked to oversee an inter-company trading activity, by which we recovered the cost of providing products, services and manpower in central London to other parts of the BT organisation. The upside to this tedious enterprise was the chance to catch up with my counterparts from these other units, notionally to agree the monthly trades but more especially to find out more about their part of the company and the scope for career and personal advancement. I had regular dealings with a cable television business, the international and satellite divisions, a broadcast television network subsidiary and a range of corporate and development units, so I was not going to be short of options when it came to finding my next role.

I was beginning to feel I had spent sufficient time and gleaned sufficient knowledge in my local operational role. It had been fun and I had enjoyed the company of some great people, but it was time to be moving onwards and upwards. I got wind of an opening in a product development organisation, in need of finance and investment support to launch a new range of digital services; it was a calling. So I dusted down my CV, sent it off and a week or so later I was walking over to High Holborn to meet up with their commercial manager. The recruitment process was plainly run a little more efficiently in his part of the company.

2

Routemasters

As I sit here today, at my desk in the heart of London's Fitzrovia, amid the hum of traffic and the hulking mass of office buildings, a warming sun dominating an otherwise pale blue March sky, I can readily call to mind a similarly beautiful spring morning twenty six years ago when I approached the second in my series of interviews at the hands of BT's trained inquisitors.

It was to take place in Procter House, an uninspired and tired looking box in glass and grey polymer, dating from the 1960s, cantilevered over Procter Street at its junction with High Holborn. A local urban myth would assert the building was only held in place by its own weight, and could therefore never be refurbished since any reduction, however temporary, in its central mass would lead to the entire edifice exploding upwards. A hilarious prospect, which would only have enhanced the look of the place. It was hideous.

I checked in at reception and was dispatched to the second floor where I was met at the lift door by a shortish, bookish type in brown tweeds, puffing through a gingery beard on a classical pipe. He held out his hand and spoke from the side of his mouth around the pipe's stem. "Mike." We shook hands, then he stepped hurriedly passed a foul smelling men's toilets, muttering something about "disgusting drainage arrangements", and gestured me to follow him into an office. It was a relief to be out of that corridor. There behind the obligatory interview desk sat a prim looking woman and a fey looking man. He introduced himself as Tim, from personnel, and her as Margaret, the head of finance, who would lead the meeting.

The previous weekend, with this interview in mind, I had gone out to buy a new suit, and brought home a single-breasted lightweight wool suit in a grey Prince of Wales check, replete with bright red highlight. The look suggested a compelling blend of dependable, word-is-my-bond Britishness with more than a hint of dashing, Madison Avenue dynamism. Ideal surely, for the world of telecoms product development. I had also co-opted the latest 1980s, foppish hair style and upgraded my briefcase from black leather to stainless steel.

It was with some alarm that I noticed that Margaret was wearing a suit in an almost identical check. She noticed too, pointing it out with a warm smile and graciously suggested that mine was actually the more stylish. If nothing else it broke the ice. It transpired she was a chartered accountant, with ten years' experience of "big six" accounting firms. She then remarked upon my CV reference to a short stint spent with an obscure accounting firm; she hadn't heard of them. "There's no reason you should have," I said. "They're one of the small six."

This serve-and-volley repartee was lightening the atmosphere considerably and we rattled through the subsequent formalities like a group of English strangers on holiday who become the greatest of friends for two weeks. The interview came to a close in no time, and I left the room to the sound of flushing emanating from the men's toilets. "It's free and ready if you need it." quipped Mike after me.

I was contacted a few days later and offered the role, to look after investment appraisal for the new digital services business. I let Alan know, and his only concern seemed to be the date and location of my leaving do. These tended to be lavish affairs, particularly when people left the company, but since I was remaining in BT and only moving ten minutes down the road, I settled for a few drinks in a local pub. It was more of a leaving don't.

I joined my new department a few weeks later. Mike, a veteran BT man with a rapier wit, was the commercial manager, while Margaret was notionally head of finance, but acted as the brains of Mike's entire department. She was my boss. The commercial unit was there to support the product management unit and a marketing function, and I would meet them all in due course. In the meantime I shook hands with my finance colleague Bill. While I was to be responsible for business cases and commercial projects, pricing and contract bids, Bill, when he wasn't drawing on his rollups or nursing his hangovers from nights on the stout, was there to cover accounting and reporting, budgets, billing and financial controls. But despite the breadth and scope of responsibilities assigned to each of us, it soon became clear we would both be severely underemployed for some time to come.

In the mid 1980s, in the first flush of its privatised existence and determined to put the boot into its fledgling competitors, BT was in a hurry to invest in a range of new digital services, aimed at both the residential and business markets. Technological advances were accelerating and it was busily building a national digital network which would enable faster, more complex communications services.

These would include three flagship services which our product line was responsible for bringing to the UK market: virtual private networks (VPN), which would enable commercial and public sector organisations to behave like owners of BT's digital network circuits and use them as they wished; Centrex, which subsumed into BT's network the switching and intelligence capabilities of privately owned, in-house exchanges and switches; and the integrated services digital network (ISDN), offering both voice and data services, aimed at small businesses and consumers and effectively an early forerunner of today's high bandwidth network access product we know and love as broadband.

While these services would sit alongside each other within the core of BT's new network, each would require its own, discrete software provisioning, programming and integration activity. Despite the massive technological development taking place within the backbone network itself, these product specific activities would need to take place at multiple sites around the country, which would take a lot of time and involve a lot of people. This all meant spending a vast amount of money, so there needed to be sound commercial justification for the investment. Mike's department was there to provide that justification.

The three products were each at a different stage in their development, which meant differing types of work and levels of involvement for both Bill and myself. The least developed was VPN, which had just gone in to the BT laboratories to be customised for the UK corporate market. This would take months and would in the meantime involve us spending lots of money on a major programming activity. This was a job for Bill. As for the ISDN product, this was in the labs too, but said to be nearer completion. There would be some work for me when it came to the trial stage and the subsequent launch but this still looked to be several months down the road. In the meantime, Bill would have this on his plate too.

The most imminent product was Centrex, which was already out of the Labs and currently being trialed and made ready for a full market launch. It was being managed by a sharp witted, smart suited technocrat named Tony. What he needed was an up to date, detailed business case to quantify and justify the investment requirement to make the product available nationally. I was to support Mike on this; the fun and games would now begin.

In many ways, this was shaping up to be a great place to work, as though we were on the cusp of something significant and memorable. The old ran up against the new on a daily basis. This applied equally to the people, the thinking and the behaviour and made for a dynamic and entertaining environment. There was a constant tension and wariness between the two camps as to external strategy and internal policy which in turn made for in-depth and searching debate. At the same time, there was a real sense of camaraderie across the entire unit, fuelled by the knowledge we were breaking new ground, making the future.

There was little formalised talk of team and personal objectives, since we all knew what needed to be done and who would do what. We were all tucked up, side by side, in a few small offices in one building and the process would flow from room to room. You knew what you were expected to do and when you were expected to do it; it wouldn't need to be spelt out. This generated and reinforced a respect for who and what you were and what you did. This was an immensely grown up and civilised way of working, one which I have rarely encountered since.

It certainly contrasts wildly with more contemporary methods of man management, through spoon fed targets and micro-management of weekly, even daily goals. This is from another, infantilised world, where a uniform lack of trust undermines, however unwittingly, the excitement and peradventure of attempts at something new or at breaking the mould. Everything is brought low, and made to feel like just another grinding day at the office.

★

The process of investment appraisal I was to lead was and remains a straightforward, functional activity involving cash flow forecasting and the application of financial parameters and hurdles to levels of expected returns. The goal at the operational level is to correctly forecast levels of revenues and costs which together largely determine the projections for the cash flows. Once I had hold of the forecasts for product sales, the necessary operating expenses and the costs of the network investments, I would laboriously key these into our investment appraisal programme (ironically labeled 'Rapid'), which would apply BT's financial strictures on working capital and investment criteria to generate the expected overall returns. The approach was all very structured and organized; a sausage machine, I just needed something meaty to push through it, and I would be assisted in this by members of the marketing and product management teams.

I was introduced to my marketing colleague, Peter. Sporting an anachronistic bow tie and moustache combination, Peter talked me through his professional background in traffic management and specific expertise in queuing theory. How this qualified him to undertake market analysis in telecoms was not immediately clear to me, however he could be relied upon punctually to produce highly detailed forecasts of product take-up based on any mix of tariffs and geographic rollout plans his minions would throw at him.

He had handcrafted a forecasting and pricing model to manage this entire activity, a prodigious feat of software engineering for that time by all accounts, not least his own. Nobody else ever actually got to see this thing in action and for all we knew it may never have existed. Yet somehow he would produce, for scenario after scenario, reams of numbers that appeared to make sense. Our gain was traffic management's loss.

For the cost information, I was directed to Ian, an affable, wonkish chap who cheerfully laid out for me on one sheet of foolscap the basic configuration of the network we needed to cost up. The number of access points, the volume of concentrators, the stacks of switches and the manpower required at the databuild centres. He then took me through the supplier's rate card and matched the costs to the items on his diagram. His calm, measured tone suggested an absolute mastery of the subject, and I told him so. "Nice of you to say so, but not quite accurate. I got Tony to draw it all up for me yesterday."

"But you're the product manager on this," I countered. "Surely you know how it works?"

"God no," he said. "It's just a lot of magic boxes as far as I can see." He was as new to all this as I was. To enhance my knowledge, and his too, he dragged us both off to a switching site in the City of London, where we were shown the kit that was still in use on the trial. It looked like a walk-in freezer. "Does it do anything?" we asked of the on-site techie, expecting visible entertainment.

"Not really. It hums sometimes." So much for magic boxes.

★

There were growing tensions between members of the management team and others over the optimal strategy for deploying our Centrex product. Additionally, from outside of our immediate circle, a debate had been re-ignited over which supplier to select, the outcome of which could take us right back to square one, and back into the Labs. This was new to me then, but was a blueprint for the way in which all strategic investment programmes I would encounter in BT for the following decade would progress. Equipment manufacturers would naturally crave a supply contract with a national operator like BT. They would employ "point men" to continually dripfeed information into the company, offering marginal improvements to their commercial offerings when it became clear they were falling behind in the race to sign a major deal. It meant that on any project, we analysts faced a continually shifting financial and investment landscape, and it required years of experience to understand where you stood in it at any one time.

This, combined with the absence of powerful leadership and rapid and insightful commercial decision making, was becoming a source of immense frustration. We didn't lack for the right individuals, of whom there were plenty. Rather, we were hindered by a cultural overhang from decades of management by committee, of blurred responsibility and accountability, which meant that no one person or organisational entity was properly empowered to commit the company to significant contractual and financial undertakings. Of course, nobody actually saw things that way at the time. At worst, it was seen as just the way things got done around here, a small but necessary price to pay for the benefits of the wider, dominant culture of inclusiveness and consensus, which was seen as a good thing. But from my perspective as a relative newcomer, it felt debilitating and morale sapping: why couldn't they just leave us to get on with it?

There then followed what I learned was a classic demonstration of how competing interest groups within the business would attempt to resolve vexing internal conflicts. They took themselves off to the US for a couple of weeks. This was justified as "we really need to see" the options available at work and "we really need to understand" how the decisions over these options were arrived at. So Mike, Margaret, Tony and several others from the ethereal hierarchies packed their bags and disappeared for a fortnight, while Bill and I packed ourselves off to the Princess Louise pub.

The Louise was a throwback to the drinking dens of Victorian London, where parties would gather in a row of partitioned spaces along the bar, to share a private and intimate occasion. More pertinently from our perspective, it maintained the more progressive opening hours of the West End. While not yet able to remain open during afternoons, ensuring the working masses were back at their places of work in reasonable time, it did enjoy extended evening hours, unlike those frequented by our corporate colleagues based in the square mile of the City, where most hostelries were still required to close by nine o'clock. This condescending form of social control was eventually washed away by wider liberalisation measures enacted a couple of years later, which we duly honoured by spending the entire day drinking; all victories have to be celebrated.

Two weeks later our superiors were back and, miraculously, everything was now on track: there was an agreed plan for rollout, suppliers and the product feature set, a schedule of costs and a pricing plan. We just needed Peter to work his econometric alchemy and all would be ready to go, and amazingly before the week was out, we finally had the entire package complete.

Mike had mentioned that as part of a side deal with one of the Bell telephone companies, a US partner during the supplier negotiations, they had offered him a few days' free consultancy which would involve one of their "senior product guys" flying in to London and spending time with us on the business case. Mike had taken them up on this and was now parking the responsibility for exploiting it squarely on my shoulders. I should run our plan in detail past this guy, get his input and use his company's experience and knowledge, and then we would get on with the job of obtaining the necessary approvals from the BT Corporate hierarchies.

And so it was that "Chuck" arrived the following Monday. A

rather sweet, chubby and unimposing chap, he had brought over his wife in business class, and here they were being put up in a five star hotel on Piccadilly; his company had arranged it all. It was their first visit to England and his wife couldn't wait to see Ann Hathaway's cottage. They were going to the theatre too. Wide eyed and humble, and forever shaking his head in disbelief, he plainly couldn't believe his luck.

We set to, and made some small talk over the numbers. I had to keep it fairly bland, because the moment I got to any level of detail the poor guy started to sweat and shift uneasily in his seat. He was plainly out of his depth. I had expected a bit more from a "senior product guy", but let it go. We completed our review in a couple of hours and went to lunch. I really couldn't think what to do with him for the rest of the day and cravenly made up an impromptu excuse about needing to attend an urgent meeting in the corporate office in the City. He was happy to have a few free hours back and I suggested he went shopping around the West End.

On Tuesday, I handed him off first thing to our own product people, who found him likeable, attentive and ultimately quite unknowledgeable, before collecting him at lunchtime and again letting him loose on London's cultural cityscape. As he was leaving, I suggested he accompanied his wife to Stratford-upon-Avon on the Wednesday and so we made tentative plans for Thursday, when I initially managed to elude him for a good few hours. He spent the morning discussing Shakespeare's legacy with Mike.

We affirmed what a productive week it had been all round, then repaired across the road to the Princess Louise. By two thirty we had filled him with a sufficiently broad selection of quaint English beers to render him comatose, then bundled him into a cab, bound for Piccadilly and thence to the airport. I never came across Chuck again, but I hope and believe he is still as blissfully happy as he was that week. And evidently, Bell had a problem with underemployment that made our own look trivial.

★

Mike, Bill and I would regularly take lunch in the functional in-house restaurant. On one occasion, huddled together on the shabby armchairs and taking coffee, we were joined by Bonnie, our head of marketing. A brittle, nervy wisp of wit and wisdom, and clearly once as cute as a kitten, she was bobbing along on the sea of a solitary, loveless life. Ingesting the smoke from her cigarette, she set about describing how she had spent the previous evening: playing music at full blast, while sitting astride one of her speakers. Mahler had never felt so good, apparently, as the sonic vibrations crept along and around her thighs, each as sleek and slender as a cat's elbow. In due course, the concerto and the head of marketing had each come to a satisfactory climax. I cleared my throat, while Bill hurriedly cleared the table. Mike was so transfixed, his pipe had gone out. "I didn't know whether to suck or blow," he later lamented. How she loved to toy with us.

She was invited one evening to a black tie dinner at the Connaught Rooms, allegedly representing us at an awards event, though I couldn't begin to imagine what we were up for. She shimmied across our office floor in a flowing black velvet dress, in need of assistance in securing the buttons of her matching elbow-length gloves, and we raced to assist her. A career smoker, she was puffing on her regulation fag, wedged as it was that evening into a long black, cigarette holder. Fastening the buttons proved problematical, and it was taking four of us an age to complete the task, whilst she puffed away and closely supervised the operation. Tears streamed down our faces as the smoke poured forth from her in ever greater quantities. With a peremptory "Shit!" she realized her fag had burnt down into the plastic holder, which had caught fire and was rapidly filling the office with its acrid fumes. She made purposely for the door and the ladies loos, finally allowing us to clear out our lungs; even the smokers were struggling. Still, it would all be worth it when we got the gong. Bonnie returned next morning, sheepish and empty handed; it transpired she had only been required to hand out an award, not receive one. But she had received many compliments on her outfit, so it hadn't all been in vain.

It was interesting to observe how aspects of office life here compared with those I had witnessed in my previous role, none more so than in the question of office accommodation. Whereas in the district offices, department heads had been allocated their own rooms, Procter House had a dearth of separate offices to permit the same conceit. The equivalent management grades here would therefore have to compromise.

This involved them retreating to the ends of the general offices, and isolating themselves from the rest of the staff through the strategic positioning of a five foot high screen. This would serve little or no practical purpose since, for example, their every confidential discussion would be broadcast across the office, just in a disembodied format. You saw them arrive, you saw them leave. I suppose we were spared the sight of them picking their nose. But it was the thought that counted, their status as our betters confirmed. By the time I attained their elevated grade, all singleton offices had been abolished, and I would search in vain for a five foot high screen.

★

We were to receive another debilitating blow as we sought to finalise approval of our product plan. It had somehow found its way into the hands of a meddler from a product strategy unit; they did seem to proliferate, meddlers and strategy units. Unfortunately for us, he was a very senior meddler who had worked on earlier plans for the digital services business. A copy of our paper, now bearing his furiously scribbled comments, was faxed across to Mike's office and made for dismal reading. It tore into our plan on all levels and from all angles. The strategy was inept, the supplier unreliable, the marketing "inchoate" and, my favourite this, the finances were "at variance with the facts." It was an extraordinary, pathological diatribe, copied to a list of various names I had seen plated on doors around corporate headquarters. This was not good.

It emerged that the person responsible had held a deep and lingering personal grudge against Mike for some time and for reasons that were not being made clear. They had had their run-ins in the past and this was but the latest. It meant that we would have to provide long and very detailed rebuttals of each point of contention, reiterating the rationale for everything we advocated. We would need to spend several weeks if not months rebuilding credibility and trust across the development organisation. It was a devastating blow. Mike should surely have seen this coming and confidence in him visibly and rapidly waned.

It was enough for both Tony and Margaret, whose respective resignations were announced within days of each other. Margaret ostensibly left to take up a course at the London Business School, while the reasons for Tony's departure were less clear, the memo simply citing "other opportunities". I believed it was due simply to his absolute despair at our collective and corporate inability to make any meaningful progress with his project, after nearly two years of effort on his part.

These two had always borne a look in their eyes of clear-sighted purpose and we would soon begin to miss their dedication and drive. They were the sort of people who today put their details onto LinkedIn in the surefire knowledge they are not wasting their time. As Mike wistfully put it: "What hope do we have if we can't hold on to the likes of Margaret and Tony?" I took this as my own cue to start casting around for my next role.

Working for Margaret had been my first experience of having a female boss, a fact perhaps more notable for its perceived significance than for its true importance, to either myself or Bill. She was a normal, likeable and professional person, chatty and friendly, clear and polite about what she wanted, without ever being curt or abrupt. After a short while, her gender was about as consequential for us as the colour of her hair. Of course it was a small but eloquent step for a woman to have adopted a senior role in one of the functional areas historically circumscribed for men. But she made it seem quite run of the mill and natural; she just got on with it, and so therefore did we.

I would hear a number of men remark inimically upon their own female bosses, often with sly allusions to alleged fault lines in their psychological aptitude, rather than with observations on the specific individual concerned. To me, this belied a mentality which believed that all women would fall foul of the standards set by their male predecessors; a mindset which arguably signified their own insecurities and fear of change.

Throughout the summer of 1988, the sun burned furiously through our office windows. The heat was intolerable. Opening the windows, which in those days was still an option, simply ushered in waves of more heat and the unrelenting stench and noise of nose-to-tail traffic. Down on the street below, in the suntrap created by our extraordinarily designed building, Routemaster buses would regularly "brew up", overheating while stuck in the congestion. They would stand there abandoned for hours, marooned in the middle of the street. They were a potent metaphor for our own isolation and frustrated struggle to make any meaningful progress.

What had hitherto seemed such a civilised and adult minded place to work now felt naive and rudderless. After a wasted period of slow and negligible advances, and in light of recent and upcoming departures, there was to be a management shakeup. Mike was finally drawing stumps on his BT career. I could no longer pretend to be fully employed on my projects and suggested that Bill took on my commercial activities in addition to his other scant responsibilities. I had read of and successfully followed up on a vacancy for an investment analyst in BT's expanding cable and satellite TV subsidiary.

With the date set for my departure, I organised the necessary leaving do. I was advised there would be a small collection, and did I have in mind a gift they might purchase for me? From nowhere, the idea of a Panama hat sprang to mind. Days later, as we stood in the sunshine outside the Louise, I opened the gift box, removed the hat and put it on. "Very nice" quipped Mike. "Don't hang it higher than you can reach." That was to become my motto for life.

I was to learn a couple of years later that each of the digital network services – Centrex, VPN and ISDN – was finally being launched, and on a vast and national scale to boot. I was pleased it had all eventually turned out well. To the external market it would doubtless appear a relatively trouble-free evolution, if perhaps a little late in the day. Internally, the bodies had long been buried, the dust had settled, and all was now quiet and well with the world.

3

A Ropey Prospect

I was invited to an interview at another of BT's less salubrious locations, Euston Tower, a thirty three storey monolith at the northern tip of Tottenham Court Road, famed at the time for housing London's leading commercial radio station. Of lesser renown, the twenty sixth and twenty seventh floors were home to BT Vision, the company's then cable and satellite television business. The building, since its construction (or perhaps I should say arrival, since it appeared to have simply dropped, fully formed, straight out of the sky) had been a part of the public sector's property estate, and inside it bore the pallor of dust, the odour of cheap plasterboard and the general shabbiness that was redolent of various offices I had encountered during my temporary period with the Civil Service a few years earlier.

The BT floors were accessed via an elevator service which would prove to be a source of regular grief and on at least one memorable occasion, outright terror, when a lift managed to arrive at the twenty sixth storey having overshot the level of the floor by several feet. The doors nevertheless opened and the handful of poor souls within had to negotiate a hazardous exit while avoiding toppling backwards down the lift shaft. This incident still haunts me to this day, while the lifts themselves feature dizzyingly in occasional bizarre dreams of mine.

If you did manage to make it to the top of the building, and in one piece, you would be rewarded with some of the most spectacular views of central London. Autumnal sunsets especially would provide a sumptuous treat as they illuminated west facing elevations across the City and the West End, a sight which would bring meetings to a halt and entire offices to a standstill. This was to prove the most visually stunning aspect of BT Vision.

My interview was with Katherine, the sparky and ambitious head of finance, and Pete, a maturing ex-hippy who looked after the cable television (CATV) network investments. I was quizzed on my technical capabilities, which was a welcome novelty, as well as my knowledge of CATV, which was not. Fortunately I had uncovered sufficient facts and figures during the course of my preparatory research to sound plausible and so bluffed my way into my first brush with the media.

Seeing opportunities to expand beyond its tightly regulated core telephony business, BT had quietly been following in the years since privatisation a strategy referred to as "letting a thousand flowers bloom". This had taken the company into a number of new areas: mobile telephony, through a joint venture called Cellnet; handset production, via the acquisition of a Canadian manufacturer, Mitel; IT and systems integration services, run by a unit called BT Systems; and the putative cable and satellite television businesses, under the umbrella banner of BT Vision. By the autumn of 1988, none of these new business areas had yet achieved significant scale or maturity and the focus of each would remain on investment and growth for at least a further two to three years, when the recession of the early 1990s would lead to a review of strategy and a degree of retrenchment towards BT's core network services.

The Vision operation itself was rather labouring under its title. This was not a forerunner of the national "on demand" digital television service of the same name which launched in 2007. Regulation at the time prevented the company from using its core telephony networks to broadcast television signals. It was however permitted to compete for cable franchises and had over several years built up a collection of rather sorry, downbeat subsidiary operations which were responsible for building the cable networks in towns and cities where BT had won the local licence. These were randomly dotted around the country, and included Aberdeen, Swindon, Coventry and Westminster. There were also some smaller "new town" systems in the likes of Washington Runcorn and Milton Keynes where BT had originally experimented with an elementary form of the service in the early 1980s.

On a more refreshing note, Vision was also responsible for managing and expanding a portfolio of investments in satellite television channels – for distribution through the cable networks – and for developing a direct-to-home (DTH) satellite television proposition. While Pete and the rest of Katherine's team had their hands full trying to make a success of the motley CATV businesses, I was given the relatively glamourous role of supporting the programming team, who were charged with leading the growing array of satellite television projects. This was going to be fun.

By that point, Vision had been involved in the development and launch of three channels: The Children's Channel; the Premiere Film Channel; and a retro television channel called Bravo. Of particular interest to me were the several new channels that were then still under consideration, since it would fall to me to produce the business case and investment plans for these as and when they came to fruition.

The cases would prove both complex and challenging to produce, since no two would be alike. The business models for generating revenues and the underpinning cost structures were unique to the particular partnership involved or to the type of programming being produced. This would require a rapid assimilation of expertise in the drivers of revenues, from advertising, royalties and subscription management. It would also demand that I understood the detailed elements of the cost base of television production and post-production, media management systems, and the magisterial complexity and immodesty of charges levied for broadcast distribution rights. It was all a far cry from the economics of telephone kiosks.

I would be aided and abetted in this enterprise by the guiding hands of the programming team, a select bunch of media savants who nonetheless each wore a somewhat guarded expression, as though they were nervous of being discovered splurging BT's cash on back-catalogues of Noddy and The Man from UNCLE, or the blisteringly expensive rights to transmit ET. Fortunately for both BT and myself, they knew the business inside out, which was a deal more than could be said, at the outset, of their boss David, a wide eyed, bearded member of the BT old school who couldn't quite believe his luck at, nor fully take in, what he had walked into.

A very decent sort nonetheless, his role was to represent BT on the boards of the various companies set up to run the satellite channels, and to manage the relationships with our investment partners. These partners were mainly cable broadcasters from the US, who wished to build a UK and European footprint for their pre-existing cable channels. They were aware of BT's growing presence in the market and saw in us an innovative, bold and ambitious communications company, which also happened to have very deep pockets full of cash. We were their first and obvious port of call.

And so it would prove with the arrival in the UK of one such company, Viacom. A producer of a range of cable programming, it was renowned for one channel in particular that had been making great headway, not to mention headlines, for several years across the US. They now wished to replicate that success in Europe, with BT as their partner. Amazingly, they wanted us to join them in launching MTV. I would need no help in writing this business case; it would surely write itself.

It is stunning now to recall the speed with which this project progressed from an initial outline plan, through detailed business cases to an approved funding plan, via operational readiness, and finally to launch; it was all completed in a matter of months. Sad to report, one of the chief reasons for this was that BT was an investor first and a technical and commercial partner second. We weren't involved in any executive or key operational decisions; we weren't running the show. The Americans were, and that made all the difference. It may read like a cliché, but their businesslike focus, ruthless approach and sheer ability to get things done was light years ahead of where BT was at the time. Even our funding payments were late.

Two of my finance colleagues were Irishmen who shared their illustrious countrymen's outlook, perspective and sense of humour, which would make my working life at Vision memorably entertaining. Diarmuid, Barry and I had been allocated our own office on the twenty seventh floor, alongside those of the Vision board members. How chuffed we were to rub shoulders with them and to share access to the executive teabags, toilets and televisions. For one of the benefits of working in the television sector was the gratuitous proliferation of television sets around the offices, particularly so 'upstairs'. These huge black boxes were an arresting sight perched precariously on the tops of filing cabinets and hanging from corridor walls. While I felt a degree of self-consciousness, I was more than happy to join in the collective delusion that we were a happening part of the UK media industry.

There were several regular strands of programming that came

to shape our day. Early morning programmes involved attractive young women performing aerobic displays in skimpy leotards, while mid-morning coffee was taken in the company of an old Indian mystic, gazing into his crystal ball. Late afternoons revolved around the infinite pleasures of a daily no-budget talent show which featured some of the most depressingly untalented people from around the country. It was all dazzlingly bad, utterly compelling and quite hilarious. Multichannel television may have come of age now, but it has no doubt lost some of its priceless magic in the process.

Our most momentous viewing took place one late afternoon during the Italian World Cup in 1990, when Ireland faced Romania for a place in the quarterfinals. Barry, Diarmuid and I, along with our accountant Patrick, screamed in anguish and ecstasy as a defining penalty shootout progressed, almost blasting the windows out when David O'Leary converted the final spotkick to ensure Ireland's eventual qualification. While it is commonplace now for televisions to appear in offices for the duration of major sporting competitions, it was quite different back then and I think we four felt a privileged connection with the events in Genoa that day. Especially as we should have been in a planning meeting at the time.

★

Post MTV, programming and satellite television activity slowed down. Everybody was now awaiting a government tender to bid for a national DTH licence; investors, including BT, were reluctant to commit too much too early without knowing what shape the industry would take or how the ground rules would operate. MTV was up and running, hitting its targets and was already deemed a success. There was thus little for me to do, so

I asked Katherine if help was needed on the CATV side of things. Needless to say, there was.

As a complete cable novice, I decided I needed a crash course in CATV and engineered a couple of days "training" in the offices of our Westminster operation, based on Baker Street. Once there, I was shown around the inevitable collection of shiny boxes with their obligatory flashing lights, by the local general manager. A genial type who was clearly underemployed too and happy for the chance to talk, he explained to me how a cable television operation was set up and then run.

In summary, the business in each franchise area would undertake two main investment projects. Firstly, you built the central office, or the "headend". This was the physical hub of the local network, which consisted of various assets: the satellite dishes, which took the programming downlink feeds; video coding, decoding and distribution equipment, which would broadcast the programming; and subscriber management computing systems, which maintained customer records and accounts. Secondly, you rolled out the physical cable network, which would carry the television signals to the end users.

I had seen at first hand across London the turmoil caused by cable network construction, and could just imagine the annoyance and frustration of the locals at having to contend daily with major traffic disruption for the period of the rollout, which took several years. As the cabling project went past the homes and businesses of the franchise area, so a local sales and marketing effort would commence, aimed at getting people to take up the service, and as many channels as possible. Given the burning resentments that residents doubtless felt towards their local cable operator, I imagined it was a pretty hard sell.

In addition, the selection of channels available at the end of the 1980s was nothing compared with the cascade of programming you come across today on the Sky programme guide, for instance. A "video on demand" service was being trialed, but again the programming selection was weak given the reluctance of film studios and TV production houses to make content available at reasonable, usable prices. (It would take BT almost twenty years to finally launch a version of this service, under the more recent guise of the BT Vision brand. I guess that is some kind of record.)

In all, it looked a pretty ropey prospect to me and I returned to Euston Tower feeling glum. CATV was an example of the classic telecoms investment model, but with bells on. You faced a massive fixed cost to build a network and all the supporting systems. Then you had to buy in expensive programming in the hope you could sell it on at a margin. Even with a line rental charge factored in, you would still need an unimaginably large number of transactions to get your money back and turn a profit. It looked hopelessly bankrupt. I couldn't see how this would ever make money.

The business was indeed struggling to make significant headway in each of our franchise areas. We clearly needed some commercial and motivational inspiration to give the business a lift. One week, we were marshaled to the outskirts of Oxford for a couple of days to be brainwashed in the culture of total quality management, a modish fad among management thinkers and the first in a series of modish fads that throughout the 1990s BT would throw itself helplessly upon. Based on methods and behaviours learned from the Japanese manufacturing boom of the late 1970s and early 1980s, TQM was all about placing your customer at the heart of a company's thought and operational processes.

The workshop was led by a member of an apparently newly formed Quality unit which had materialised quite undetected over the previous couple of months. She used the word customer an awful lot. To such an extent in fact, that after a while it appeared that the sole purpose of the entire two days was for us to hear the word used so often that we would eventually fall under her spell and start to repeat the mantra ourselves. A facilitator had been brought in to try to keep the show on the road but was adding little to the proceedings. His sole meaningful contribution was to wind up Patrick over some petty but pertinent issue as we were about to leave, which resulted in Pat squaring up to him with clenched fists. I kept my head down and walked briskly to the car park. I had never attended a more fatuous event. Were we all starting to go crazy?

We returned to London to learn that the managing director of Vision was being displaced, and the following day we all filed dutifully into the main office to meet his replacement and hear his plans for taking the business forward. Coming from an obscure corporate ivory tower, and looking as though he would be more at home polishing his nails in his club in St James's, he did not inspire confidence. To stiffen the backbone of the management team and to provide operational clout, he announced the appointment of his right hand man, a chap called Malcolm. Further changes were also afoot, but we couldn't have guessed at the extent of them.

A bumptious Brummie and long time BT man, Malcolm had been making a reasonable fist of turning around our franchise up in Coventry. He was good value, with an infectious enthusiasm which rubbed off on everyone around him. He had bags of ideas and certainly some of them would make an impact. In truth though, the die was already cast and to his credit I am sure Malcolm fully realised it. But he had been handed the keys to the engine and told to try and get it on track. He had no option but to press on and develop his own version of a multiple systems operator (MSO) strategy that would hopefully make the best of a bad job.

A passing acquaintance with the realities of running a multiple cable franchise operation would have told us that the key to success was not walking around like zombies muttering TQM inanities, but by running a fully integrated commercial entity, with a single set of systems, products, and sales and operational processes that sat across a collection of geographically contiguous franchises. That we didn't actually have the latter meant we had started out with both arms tied behind our backs. The original planners behind the BT cable strategy had overlooked this rather fundamental point. It looked and felt, well, amateurish wasn't too strong a word for it.

★

The government finally announced an upcoming beauty parade to find a consortium to launch the national DTH satellite television business. There had been much discussion about this at Vision, and it had been on the agenda at numerous meetings with our partners. In our quieter moments, we would sketch out the dream team of partners and channels which together would comprise our winning application. A strategy paper was now drafted and circulated to our superiors at corporate headquarters, to assess their appetite for engaging with our partners formally and putting together a bid.

In parallel, a second strategy paper was circulated regarding an unexpected opportunity to bid for a CATV licence in, of all places, Hong Kong. The opportunity had come from BT's local sales team, ostensibly based out there to manage the company's international links with the colony and local Asian markets. They were now being asked to bid for the CATV licence as part of a wider negotiation with local regulators. This second paper caused a great deal of excitement; a bid document was hurriedly prepared and approval was sought to submit it.

So there we were, in the bizarre situation of preparing tender documents to undertake two extraordinarily high profile, cash consuming investment projects on opposite sides of the planet, when we were losing considerable amounts of money in our home market and struggling to turn it into a sustainable, let alone half-successful business.

This unreal turn of events would serve one useful purpose, in that it would finally glean from the company the true measure of its disappointment in the progress of our cable business, and flush out its intentions, which were now to knock it into shape and then sell it at the earliest opportunity. To maximize interest, this would commence with the sale of the programming investments and continue with the cable franchises once they were more presentable financially; hence Malcolm's window dressing initiatives. There would be no Hong Kong or DTH bids. Sanity would be seen to prevail. With the economy visibly slowing, the company was drawing in its horns. Vision was first on the block.

The disposal process was run by BT's head of corporate finance and Vision's finance director. I was co-opted onto the team to provide detailed operational knowledge and financial analysis. The stakes would be offered in the first instance to the other shareholders, at a price that reflected the cash injections to date plus a premium for the growth opportunity each presented. The bulk of my work would end up only taking a few days since it merely amounted to identifying a handful of debatable growth scenarios and providing the financials which reflected each of them. Negotiations would then centre on which scenario was the most believable.

We met up in the evenings to review the analysis and to

discuss other options and refinements which I would work through the following day. Over the course of a busy week we hammered out the scenarios, the detailed financials and the consequent valuations.

It so happened that same week I was to fall ill with a testy bout of flu. I would go to bed each night feeling drained and dreadful, but then wake up the following morning feeling sufficiently okay to return to the office to continue on the project. As the days wore on I would feel progressively worse, not helped by the fact I wasn't eating very much. Finally, on the Thursday night I was travelling home on the Underground when I passed out, falling face first onto the floor of the train. It was after nine o'clock so the carriage was thankfully mostly empty, and I was left to pick myself up and endure the disapproving looks of my fellow passengers, who plainly thought I was pissed out of my head.

With the sale of the programming investments concluded, attention turned to the cable companies. Malcolm's operational review was understandably taking a good deal of time to work through, and there was no conceivable way they were saleable in their current condition; any sale was realistically twelve to eighteen months away. I was happy to work on a couple of development initiatives and had thrown in my own suggestions, but this was now largely an operational problem and beyond my sphere of competence, so I stepped aside. As part of a wider reorganization of the company, the Vision business was to be merged with another unit, responsible for visual communications products. There were a lot of numbers to be crunched as part of this merger and I offered to help out here while I thought through my own options.

Despondent at the latest developments, Pete left to work as a freelance consultant within the CATV sector. I helped him out in the evenings on a couple of projects and came to appreciate the attractions of a more independent working mode and lifestyle, as well as the inherent instability of a life on short term contracts. Then I saw an ad in the Financial Times for investment analysts to work on television and media projects. I followed this up and was subsequently interviewed in a Mayfair flat by a shifty looking individual who had some very interesting commercial plans and some even more interesting sources of potential funding if only he could convince these investors to come on board. Finally, on a recommendation from Pete, I met up with an ex-BT Vision financial controller now installed at a cable company in north London, which was apparently undergoing an internal restructuring, an imminent merger with a couple of other local operators and an urgent refinancing. It seemed that all around was a sea of uncertainty and undercapitalisation. I decided to hunker down for a while. The near term prospects for the economy were wintry at best and BT felt as solid a place as any to see out a storm.

There were, as ever, lighter moments which provided temporary respite from the gathering gloom. In order to promote the new video and visual services portfolio, and to avoid spending any money while doing so, we spent a day being photographed using these products. We pouted and smiled, while staring earnestly at our screens and keyboards. At one point, the photographer complained of a strange imbalancing effect through his lens and held up proceedings as he and his technician reviewed their slides. It transpired that I was the problem. My newly acquired media tie, a maelstrom of colours in paisley swirls, was apparently creating a powerful distortion on the finished shots. The camera simply couldn't cope with it. As my good looks could not be entirely dispensed with, I was politely asked to button my jacket and face slightly away from the line of direct focus.

With pay TV still in its earliest days, and its take-up limited to a relative handful of drinking dens and the homes of a brave and resourceful few, the office was the only place I could rely upon for access to the occasional television spectacular broadcast over satellite channels. One such occurrence was the heavyweight boxing match-up between reigning world champion "Iron" Mike Tyson and Britain's amiable contender, Frank Bruno. It was billed as the "fight of the decade" and scheduled for transmission at two o'clock one Sunday morning. A friend and I were determined to go to my office to watch it. I made some enquiries, which confirmed that as a twenty four hour operational building, Euston Tower would indeed be open on the night in question.

It was well after midnight when we fetched up at the door; I flashed my pass and we were swept in unquestioned, our bags of liquor unsullied. We stepped from the lifts and into the FD's office. We drank in the views and from our flasks of Armagnac. We settled in front of the screen, and lit our cigars. The fight was over almost as soon as it started, lasting barely five rounds, but for those twenty-odd minutes we felt like magnates in our ringside seats. Ash and brandy flew to the floor as we jumped to our feet, cheering a Bruno left-right combo which almost sent Tyson to the canvas; "Get in there, Frank!" We roared him on but ultimately to no avail, the referee bringing things to a safe and speedy conclusion once the poor sap's annihilation was assured. Still, it had been quite a night, with the lasting damage to the boss's carpet a minor inconvenience. He would surely have understood: the power of television.

By the time the DTH licence was finally awarded, BT had withdrawn entirely from cable and satellite television, it was a mere blast from the past. It was won by a consortium of incumbent broadcasters called British Satellite Broadcasting, which would be remembered solely for their infamous "squarial" satellite receiver; you still come across these in junk shops today. A self-aggrandising and overbearing organisation, with a sanctimonious ethos, and which had prematurely set itself up in what it deemed a suitably grand headquarters just south of the River Thames, it was quickly to prove a commercial catastrophe. It was eventually subsumed by its main rival, which had taken an entrepreneurially independent path to growth, piecing together its own satellite-based distribution capability incrementally and at ruthlessly commercial rates, and taking an aggressively populist approach to programming. Notwithstanding its cheap talent shows, Sky had been a breath of fresh air.

In retrospect, BT's venture into cable and satellite television appears half-baked and shambolic, and in truth it was. As ill-conceived as it was mis-managed, it betrayed an undeniable corporate arrogance. Spoiled for cash, the company believed it simply had to point its people in new directions and have them turn up in the mornings to administer automatic success. As an organisation, it lacked the razor sharp commercial acumen that it had never itself required nor developed, but which epitomised the new wave of media operators. Hapless and clueless by comparison, we never stood a chance.

4

A Lingering Malaise

Upswings in a company's fortunes, and growth in the economy, are generally characterized by pace, change and instability, while recessionary eras tend to be associated with hunkering down and lying low, hoping not to rock the boat. My own experience of the economic contraction of the early 1990s went against the grain, as I worked my way through multiple roles, several bosses and at least six desks. I endured a similar experience a decade later following the dot.com crash, and again when the 2008 financial crisis was at its peak. While being in the economic doldrums suggests a deadening of corporate activity, it can be a topsy-turvy place for the individual.

As if knowingly to exacerbate these effects upon myself, I now intended to take a deliberate step into what I hoped would be a more rounded commercial experience and leave behind the pure numeracy of finance. Having done my share of reporting of outcomes and project investments, I had a vision of stepping back along the business management process, through planning and eventually to strategy development. It would take the best part of a decade but I would eventually achieve it.

Following the sale of the television programming interests, David, the head of department, had disappeared from Euston Tower to help run a reorganisation project. Several of these had been bubbling away in the corporate background for a while but thankfully had failed to make any impact of substance on me personally or on my working life.

For many others though, they had been an absolute menace. A huge shake-up had occurred in the core UK organisation earlier that year, when a project by the grandiose name of Sovereign had done away with geographically defined units (such as BT West End District, my former stomping ground) and replaced them with groupwide functional lines of responsibility (such as finance, marketing and customer service). This was presented as an effective means of de-duplication and providing people with clearer career progression paths, which was undoubtedly true. But on the downside, it would leave tens of thousands of people reporting to a new boss who did not inhabit the same office, indeed quite probably not even the same county.

This remains the case today, and is now overcome to some extent through the tyranny of conference calling. Twenty years ago however, it meant endless driving up and down the highways and byways of Britain for those poor souls for whom face-time with their line manager was the primary objective in a strategy to avoid being targeted in the next round of manpower cuts.

A further, more positive outcome of this shake-up was the ring-fencing of a set of activities which were outside the scope of regulation and which would require continuing investment and a focus on growth. David had successfully argued for these to be placed in a separate, new unit, which would be called, leadenly, Special Businesses Division (SBD). This in effect was a collection of those business areas the company had sought to nurture post-privatisation, although now bereft of the CATV misadventure. The remainder, in mobile networks, Yellow Pages, IT systems integration and, now, video communications had survived the economic and organizational upheavals intact and would be encouraged to grow in a more hands-off and entrepreneurial environment.

Having helped out on the merger activity within Vision itself and fancying a further taste of the newer businesses, I approached David about a role in the new SBD central planning team that he had designed for himself. We had worked well together on the MTV and disposal projects and I had earned sufficient of his trust for him to offer me a role. No interview, no CV to brush up: this was a far better way of getting around.

In all it was a team of ten, with three of us specifically looking after the planning. David and a chap called Les would handle the relationships with the various businesses while I would cover commercial analysis and proposals for new business investments. I had first met Les some years before, and I recalled the meeting vividly since half of the people in the meeting room had been smoking pipes, including Les. He had maintained the habit and while I really didn't mind the smell around the office, after inhaling the smoke for a while I would begin to get a little light-headed. On occasions, he would produce such prodigious volumes of the stuff that I would be forced to go for a walk around the block to clear the giddiness.

This was to be my first job in BT Centre (BTC), a newly constructed corporate headquarters building opposite St Paul's Cathedral in the City of London. When Les wasn't puffing away on his pipe, I had a magnificent view from my desk that looked over Paternoster Square down to the Cathedral itself. When he was puffing away on it, and the fug had enclosed me completely, I would disappear on fact finding missions around the enormous office complexes that comprised BTC. There were some two thousand people based there, like a strangely childless village.

As the most junior member of the team, I was initially leant upon to help out a new, temporary colleague who had been taken on to create an executive management system. She would build the engine while I would assist in getting the data flowing into it. This would at least give me the opportunity to build relationships with people across the various different parts of the division while persuading them to provide the information, something I perversely enjoyed doing as it allowed me out of the smoggy office and I could find out first hand what was going on within the businesses. I asked them to provide us with the last two years of financial data and some supporting performance statistics. Straightforward enough, or so I vainly thought.

However there was a fundamental disconnect at play. We in the centre had recently been switched over to Microsoft Windows, while the business areas as orphans from the old core organization, and quite unbeknownst to me, remained on older packages such as Lotus. The first files arrived on disk, and of course we couldn't read them. I had discussed formats with them all, but over paper copies; a *naïf* when it came to computing applications, it had simply not occurred to me to specify the precise software package. I duly asked them to resubmit in Excel, and I was duly laughed out of court. So I followed the only course open to me and went and found an old desktop PC still running Lotus. I loaded and printed the files and then spent the best part of two weeks rekeying the data into Excel. I regarded this of course as an insane waste of my time, my education, and the cost of my salary. It was particularly galling when the version of Windows I was using would unaccountably crash and wipe out the data I had spent a full day loading, a problem I was apparently sharing with millions of others around the world at that time.

A new finance director was recruited to manage all the commercial aspects of the division. Maybe he arrived a few weeks earlier than anticipated; maybe he upset someone on the way in; I am not sure. But for a while he was unable to obtain an office in BT Centre, nor in one of the handful of satellite offices to be found at that time in the streets around St Paul's. Having scratched a living around the fringes of the restaurant and café for a couple of weeks, his predicament was partially alleviated with the allocation of a tiny office located to the rear of the building, on a narrow winding lane near to Smithfield's meat market. It was housed in an early Victorian "two-up, two-down" terraced property. The brickwork was crumbling and stained; a *faux* gaslight stood on the pavement outside. The scene just lacked a snaggly-toothed crone lurking in the doorway.

The ground floor was given over to an archives office that was run by a whiskery old buffer who could have stepped straight out of a Dickens novel. The first floor, which the FD would claim as his own, consisted of a small but cosy book-lined study, with a boxroom off to the side converted into an ensuite loo. When more than two of us went to see him, at least one would have to perch uneasily on the edge of his desk, squat on the toilet or, preferably, remain standing outside on the landing. It was comical. Les would tease him relentlessly with jokes about quills – "we'll leave Merlin to his ledgers" – and would walk out of meetings early "afore the fog descends".

The FD eventually moved into BTC, just as the financial performance of the division turned down and our accountability for it was turned up, at which point we all came to miss our wood-panelled escapes back to Olde London Town.

As we were a small unit and charged with managing all levels of communications into and out of the division, it was decided that we should invest in a little presentational training. The ten of us headed for the English countryside and booked into a nice hotel for a week, where we were joined by an American team who had flown in from Manhattan especially to perk up our communication skills. Led by a sprightly chap in his fifties named Jack, these fellows would work on two specific areas which together would hone our ability to grip and maintain the attention of an audience; the "value to the listener" of what we were communicating, and the physicality of our performance. By stressing the former upfront and then elaborately exaggerating the latter as we continued, this created a blend of theatricality to stand alongside that of the great hypnotists and mime artistes. A well executed turn would meet with a "nicely done" from Jack. Years later, I happened to be watching a documentary about the auction house, Christie's of New York and was immediately struck by their presentational style with clients. The burning eye contact, rounded hand gestures and zealous messaging were unmistakably the result of Jack's handiwork. I checked out his website and sure enough, there they were on his client listing. I was soon to put these techniques to a productive and profitable use of my own.

I was getting more than a little frustrated. The data loading task was out of the way and the analytical work I was now doing was fine, but it didn't add up to a proper job. I had some interesting projects to see through but they were piecemeal, and the work reactive. I wanted more involvement in direction setting, plans and deployment. On one particular occasion I was asked to review an investment proposal concerning a mobile opportunity in Spain. This would be my first brush with our nascent international business and despite the fact it was only a couple of million pounds for a three per cent stake in a start-up, I had a vivid sense of both excitement and destiny. Four years later I would return to mobile investments on a far grander scale and it would become the best job I ever had in the company. For now though, it was a diverting half-day's worth of levity.

I tried to muscle in on managing the higher level relationships with the businesses, as had been promised to me, but David and Les were jealously guarding this as their domain. I was underemployed again and wanted to stretch myself further. More pressingly, I had bought a house in Camden Town and needed more money to pay for it; I needed to get myself promoted. So I scoured the internal job supplements and came across a suitably graded vacancy in a planning department within the behemoth of the Business Communications Division, which looked after the company's corporate clients. Interviewed by my prospective boss, I applied each of Jack's presentational tics to the limit, and left the session on an adrenaline high. I was in. Nicely done.

★

I started 1992 in my new department, and was now re-graded as a 'U'. I had begun my career as an 'A' and over the course of seven years had edged my way up to be an 'F'. With this latest move it now seemed they were soon going to run out of letters for me. That said, the lettering system was then reversed, so you could now work your way up the organisation and down the alphabet at the same time (until you got as far as P, where it unaccountably stopped). It was all very confusing.

So, I was now eligible for a company car, medical insurance and a free phone line at home. It was a shock recently to receive my first phone bill since 1992, for one hundred and fifty pounds. I rang and asked if this was for the entire twenty one year period, but was told it was for the last quarter only. I had been out of the country for two months as well; no wonder the company still makes profits.

I reported to my new office, Dowgate Hill House, a small headquarter outpost round the corner from Cannon Street station. Here, the layout was a throwback to the 1970s, a warren of singleton and two-man offices where the staff would squirrel themselves away all day, only meeting up at lunchtime in the tiny canteen on the ground floor. The toilet cubicles were hermetically sealed too, so you couldn't even socialise when you were in there, although on reflection this was probably just as well.

I began life there, as I seemed to everywhere, in a business analysis and reporting team. A team of six, a motley collection of old sweats and new bloods, we would receive detailed reports each month from the twelve or so operating units that made up the division, and from these we compiled a set of summary reports for the divisional executive board. In all, this would take about a week. It wasn't at all clear what we were supposed to be doing for the rest of the month. It was perhaps appropriate that the team was managed by a chap who shared the name of a renowned retailer, since he himself was clearly never knowingly under-staffed.

I set about keeping myself busy and trying to earn my recently sharply enhanced remuneration package. One of my colleagues would produce a weighty tome each month, ironically entitled the At a Glance report. This actually made more for a leisurely afternoon's reading than a quick glimpse, since it did contain a lot of information, and a good deal of it was actually quite useful; key performance indicators and the like. So, returning to my essential mission in BT, and with due regard to the future of the forests, I decided to computerize the production of this report. Remembering this time to do my research on the software package of preference of the board members – Windows, to a man – in no time we had a software driven data report to accompany the summary narratives. The latter would gradually be phased out and the monthly reporting was reduced from a small tome to just one disk. The trees remained intact and I had earned that quarter's car allowance. For the first time in a long time, this felt like progress.

CALLS OF DUTY

★

During the course of 1992, the size of the BT workforce contracted by almost forty thousand people, due in part to the sale of Mitel (the Canadian manufacturing subsidiary) while almost half the reduction was enabled by a wildly generous voluntary severance package, christened Release. In response to continuing market and regulatory pressures on revenues and profits, the company was accelerating its manpower reduction programme, this time making the scheme available to everyone in the company and not simply in specific areas that were targeted for restructuring. Depending on your length of service, you could receive up to three years' salary as a payoff plus the promise of a full and undiluted pension once you achieved the grand old age of fifty. There was a veritable *tsunami* of interest. One particular Friday in June of that year marked the departure from BT of some seventeen thousand staff. It was mooted that over half the pubs in the country were hosting a BT leaving party that evening. For me though, the sums just didn't add up, and far from it. Release? I was trapped.

For those of us hardy souls who were staying on, and with so much management time and energy being expended on getting the leavers out of the door, there was strangely little going on to concern or detain us. We churned out our reports as and when required but we seemed to be drifting for lack of a course, waiting for something to happen to us that might bring us into contact with the real world, requiring some action from us. The entire planning department, now thirty or so of us in all, would meet periodically in the dust and gloom of yet another shabby old office block, in Gresham Street in the City, to discuss the state of the world. The banter, humour and rumour mongering couldn't disguise a gathering sense of purposelessness, as a lingering malaise drew over us like a damp, heavy blanket. It was a form of corporate depression. The company didn't seem to know what day it was, or to care. What did they want of us? It was all very odd.

Nature abhors a vacuum of course. To distract from this corporate slothfulness, to create the illusion of masterly activity and keep us all driven and occupied, two new inane fads were launched. The European Quality Assurance (EQA) programme was unveiled as a corporate self-improvement discipline whereby our management processes would be subject to rigorous analysis and optimization, and deliver efficiencies across the organization. A critical underpinning to the worlds of health and safety, hazard management and environmental controls, it had been adapted for application in wider circles, including, bizarrely, our own. To achieve accreditation status, we were each issued with a "job file" and told to fill it with a series of documents which would place us each in a series of work processes and procedures. For form's sake, and with little else to occupy us, we dutifully complied with this drivel.

To this day I have no idea what the purpose of it was. Of course it made sense for our operational teams in the field, the people up telegraph poles and down manholes, to have a clear set of boundaries and step by step processes mapped out, if only for the sake of their physical well-being. But for those of us in commercial offices, to write up our monthly, weekly and daily interactions on multi-coloured slides was like being back in nursery school. We were supposed to be burying bureaucracy, not rekindling it. At root, the problem here was somebody's meddling desire for action, any action; an expression of a lingering culture of self-justification.

A second strand to this management-by-fad approach was the Leadership Programme. Marshaled again to the English countryside, this time it was about taking the initiative and corralling the troops to deliver together. A group of us were thereby "led" into making a short talking heads video in the style of Alas Smith and Jones. The company was going nowhere and there we were, sitting in the English spring sunshine for an afternoon, rattling our brains for comic punchlines. It was all becoming a bit of a joke.

★

Following a minor shakeup across the planning department, I found myself in a forecasting team. My deftness with an Excel spreadsheet had been noted and I was put to work on a business modeling project. Gripped with enthusiasm, I spent three months building a forecasting monster which covered the entire product portfolio, price structure and sources of demand, only then to be told to put it on ice, since it had now been decided that we should in fact use the model that BT Corporate had recently had designed and built at vast expense by some external consultants. I began to question my purpose.

The company was clearly now struggling in the wider market from recession, competition and regulation. To combat growing fears of structural downgrades in its financial performance, and to create a further sense of us actually doing something, the group managing director announced the launch of a top-to-bottom corporate renewal exercise. This was intended, as they always are, to provide from scratch a new, market leading direction for the company, with new products, services and ways of working to the fore. Sadly that would not prove to be the case at all. For months, dozens of the brightest and best would be holed up in BT Centre, along with their assigned pairs from the larcenous body shop that had hoodwinked BT into this delusional nonsense. There they crunched numbers and worked their way through the lexicon of business analysis models and every textbook artifice, with scarcely a moment's consideration for the views and opinions of the wider and wiser communities around the Group. It was a classical example of how not to go about managing change.

Months later, we were summoned in our thousands to a roadshow at Wembley Arena to hear the GMD's encomium to the project and to the transformative outputs that were pouring forth from it. It was presented to a sea of blank faces, and to a stunned silence. His eyes swiveled in bewilderment as the deathly quiet took hold, and with the blood draining from his disbelieving face, he slumped back on to his stool and took in the unspoken message from the floor, of the mystery, remoteness and utter fruitlessness of the enterprise he had set so much store by. Nobody had a clue what he was talking about. I struggle now to recall the name of this vapid initiative, which probably says all there was to know about it.

In a surreal turn of events, I came home late one night to find the director of this insipid project, tired and emotional and slumped on the front step of the house next door. When I later asked my neighbour what this had all been about, she implied the poor sod's love life was working out almost as well as his professional one.

With ever more time on my hands, and at BT's expense, I took up an MBA course at Henley Management College. For nearly two years, I would disappear there for a few days each month, go for walks alongside the Thames as it idled its way through the grounds, sit by the fire in idyllic pubs dotted along the river banks, and read learned articles on corporate development strategy. I managed a respectable pass and although I can't say it exactly transformed me, it did help in seeing the wood from the trees, and where to focus the analytical spotlight.

Above all, it taught me how to say no and not to have any more of my time wasted.

It was a running theme that wherever I worked, I would always manage to find one or two like-minded souls with whom I shared a sense of humour; it is doubtless one of the reasons I managed to remain with the company for so long. This time was no exception, as I, being a quarter Welsh, found myself sharing an office with two fully fledged fellows from the valleys. Alan was a laidback salesman with a foul vocabulary and raucous laugh; Rob, an earnest product geek for whom the word and world of multimedia were of biblical significance. Rob had an engineering genius working for him in the next office who was building a software driven videophone system for desktop PCs, a groundbreaking technology which, on demonstration, actually worked. "Christ," exclaimed Rob, "I wasn't expecting that."

"Shit," sighed Al, "now I'll have to start selling the fucking thing." It was all very underwhelming for a *eureka* moment. It would never find its way to market, though. In the background, discussions were taking place concerning a corporate development intended to present us with an alternative dazzling array of new services to sell, and new ways to sell them.

A recent senior appointment had introduced a novel international perspective to proceedings. Noting this new guy's experience in acquiring companies, and merging and disposing of subsidiary businesses, I had ruefully shared my view that his arrival would presage an eventful period of change and opportunity, though I could not have imagined quite how much. Within a few months, we learned of the company's purchase of a twenty five per cent shareholding in MCI, a relative newcomer to the American long distance and international telecoms market, which would give BT a stake in the biggest market on the planet. In addition, we would be forming a joint venture (JV) with them to address the growing market for global communications. The news that we would be climbing into bed with an American partner was greeted with excitement by some and portent by others; there would be fresh ideas and new opportunities, while many of our own projects and plans would now be abandoned. The PC-based videophone product was shelved. A pity really, since I had hoped to appear in the brochure for it.

Planning for the JV would begin straight away in our offices. It was to be led by a band of BT marketeers for whom this was but the latest stage for acting out their idealized visions of the next generation of communications services. They envisaged a "walled garden" approach, building specific services for specific industry sectors. Despite their best endeavours, these had never really taken off in the UK market; they were often too complex and always too expensive. Perhaps it was time for a new approach. The MCI guys loved it, however. It cast their own bold ambitions in a bright light; there was no client sector that would remain untouched. And so the seeds were sown for a long and protracted struggle to get the venture ever to make any money. I would become closer to Concert, as the venture was christened, in my next role, but for now I watched in morbid fascination as a protracted exercise in complexity, over-ambition and commercial shortsightedness played out before me.

I tried to concentrate on more mundane planning matters. There was finally some light appearing at the end of the tunnel. This rather sorry, aimless three year period of corporate thumb twiddling would eventually come to an end as the long mooted green shoots of recovery would finally begin to make themselves felt during the second half of 1993-94. And my interest had been piqued. Despite my own reservations over its market strategy, the very fact of the Concert JV initiative spoke of some new and enticing future, a first step down the road to global...what? I would need to see this for myself.

Part Two

A Global Folly

1994 – 2003

5

A Blank Sheet

There are few milestones that occur in the life of an organisation which, in hindsight, can be said to be of truly lasting significance, to represent a turning point and directly account for the shape, nature and mindset of the entity we see before us today. For BT, one such event occurred during April 1994, with the creation of the first divisional unit charged with the specific objective of growing the company's reach and scale of operations outside of the UK. It may be said that on that date, BT took its first committed and meaningful step towards becoming a global business.

In asserting this, I am leaving aside the company's previous foray into international management, its temporary ownership of Mitel, which represented a diversification play rather than an expansion of its core business into new markets, and never credibly took hold of the company's strategic destiny. Beyond that, there had only ever been a tangential global dimension to the organisation, an inevitable consequence of the provision of international telephony services, which meant that for years BT had maintained commercial, contractual relationships with its peers in countries across the developed and developing worlds. These relationships were managed under the so-called "correspondent" regime, whereby the revenues and costs of transborder calls were shared equitably between the telcos at either end of the line. It was essentially an exclusive rich man's club, which had enjoyed extortionately high margins throughout its monopolistic past, and which was only now being targeted by new market entrants. The company had also had a small share in another cosy, lucrative set-up, the satellite and sub-maritime cable consortia which provided the transmission circuits carrying the international traffic. These too were seeing new competitors emerging, in the sky, on the ground and under the sea. The scene was thus being set for a showdown.

The management of the correspondent business within BT had been managed by a select team of a couple of hundred people, scattered around the planet in the manner of a diplomatic service representing a small independent country. They would generally inhabit a small office in a smart quarter of the local capital, living the life of quasi-consuls, concerning themselves with building and maintaining relationships and blissfully administering the status quo. But as the grubby commercial world progressively wound its tentacles around their vitals, so these representatives had been forced to take on more business-like responsibilities. These former branch offices were becoming mini-businesses in their own right. Several of them around Europe, in particular, were now established as subsidiary companies and branded, for instance, as BT France and BT Spain. Following deregulation of cross-border services by the European Commission, they were now recruiting local sales and technical personnel to boost the level of international traffic going back and forth between their local markets and other countries within the European Community (EC).

Now a further development was in sight, the liberalisation of domestic telecoms markets in all fifteen EC states, a process planned for completion by 1 January 1998. This offered BT, other incumbents such as France Telecom and Deutsche Telekom, and new entrants from further afield and from other industries altogether, the opportunity to take part in the next wave of the telecoms advance. They would be able to set up and operate in EC markets as direct providers of local services, for instance in digital mobile telephony, corporate telephony and data services, and in the emergent field of multimedia.

A strategy for addressing these market developments had been constructed within BT. This envisaged the Concert JV, owned jointly with MCI of the US, moving in on the rapidly growing market in international traffic as a new entrant itself, while BT, through its subsidiaries and local affiliates, would target the major European markets. These would be targeted in tandem with local partners, who would provide market expertise, assets and a share of the funding. In this way, BT would build a portfolio of country-specific joint venture companies charged with delivering rapid growth as the deregulation and liberalisation agenda were put into effect. In the US, MCI had been following a similar strategy as local markets there were opened up to competition. This was the model for expansion that BT now sought to emulate.

To bring a clear focus onto the opportunities and threats posed by these transformative developments, the Business Communications Division of BT was to be split in two. The Global Communications Division (BT Global) was established to address directly the market potential overseas and internationally, while the National Communications Division would seek to minimise the risks to our UK business. This had knock on effects for us in the BCD planning team and we were consulted as to our preferred destination; I had no hesitation in plumping for the BT Global option. And so it was that three of us, myself together with Andrew, a colleague from my previous forecasting team, and an enthusiastic finance chap called Mike, would form the BT Global business planning team, reporting direct to the finance director. I mentioned having seen light at the end of the tunnel and it was now positively phosphorescent. A bright new day had dawned.

The BT Global organisation itself was taking shape. There were four geographically based units, one each for the UK, Europe, the US and Asia. The former dwarfed the latter three, housing as it did the top one hundred or so of BT's UK-based corporate accounts, each with a significant international dimension to them and thus highly profitable from BT's perspective. These would provide the necessary cash flow that would be pumped into the growing businesses overseas, starting with Europe. Global also contained the international correspondent business, management responsibility for BT's share of the Concert JV and the maturing IT systems integration business that was finally gaining market traction, notably in the UK financial sector. In all, it was made up of by far the most interesting parts of the entire company at that time, and it unquestionably made for the most stimulating period of my career up until then.

★

Andrew was our team leader; a middle-ageing, corporate survival expert with an international background, he had been handpicked by the FD to act as the presentational face of our team to the Global board. My colleague Mike was a cheery type, a bustling personality full of vim and vigour, in stark contrast to my more languid, measured, analytical disposition. He was a golfing and cricketing fanatic, with a strange metabolism in that the more sport he played, the more weight he appeared to put on.

As deftly as I could, I asked him why this should be the case. "I hadn't noticed; probably genetic." Thus was my latest possible line of personal coalescence coolly dismissed by him. We subsequently struck up an effective enough working partnership, largely by keeping out of each other's way. We split the geographic business units between us and forged our own relationships with the planning characters to be found therein. From time to time we would come together, under Andrew's aegis, to discuss matters that applied across the division as a whole, but other than that we kept ourselves to ourselves.

This arbitrary separation continued into the process of planning itself, where I concentrated on the words while Mike took on the numbers. This was a rather simplistic view since I could not describe a planning activity without reference to the financials, and Mike could not appreciate a financial plan without reference to the underlying strategy.

But Andrew had acutely recognised he had two contrasting egos to manage, each needing its own areas to lead on and take responsibility for. This also meant that Mike spent a lot of time with the detail driven finance director, a relationship I was more than happy for him to monopolise. I preferred to hang out with the strategy and international development teams, plotting how we would turn the map pink and debating tax efficient shareholding structures. A further step away from my experiences of BT to date, I found it all strangely riveting.

We got together to think through our own plan of action. Plainly this was a brand new enterprise starting from scratch, there were high expectations, and there were just the three of us. We needed to focus, prioritise and be ruthless with our time. So, drawing on the lessons from my MBA, we began by listing all those things we would not be doing. From this, we positioned ourselves, through a mix of design and default, as a band of high end corporate planners and analysts; we would speak to the board members and their direct teams only, we would set targets, organise and run review sessions with the managing director, and then present the plans to BT Corporate. And in the absence, for once, of anyone to stop us, we just got on with it. It felt rather good.

We now found ourselves staring at a second blank sheet of paper. We had inherited a high level strategy, the international development teams were busying themselves trying to do deals with partners, while the operational teams were trying to win and deliver new business. We had a set of targets and budgets for the current year and a vague aspiration to double the size of the global business within five years. It all looked and sounded pretty ballsy, but when you scratched the surface there wasn't a great deal that told you how we would do it, nor about who would do what and when.

While we weren't at all the types who wanted to see a day by day project plan or a line by line operating budget, it nonetheless seemed to us there was a lot of detail missing. Where was the medium term view of turnover objectives and profit targets, over three to five years, and the list of major programmes and projects that would deliver them? Where were the investment plan and the funding approval, and all of it presented in concise, clear language? Then it dawned on us: ah, yes, BT Global needed a business plan; that's what we were there to provide. And so we plotted how we would fill in the blank sheet of paper, and devised our plan for a plan.

We would build it from the bottom up. Between us, we had had sufficient experience of top-down, grand planning to realise that it only worked at best for high level, directional strategy. We wanted to build a credible corporate business plan based on the knowledge and expertise to be found around the global organisation. To get away with this sort of approach, we would need to design a tightly drawn series of critical activities and run them in a light touch way. This would hopefully keep us out from under the feet of the in-country management, but sufficiently well briefed and informed that we could do our job properly.

We would make very clear what it was we were asking for, why it was of value and explain precisely how we were going to utilise it. This is never an easy trick to pull off, but by taking the time and trouble to sit down with people, to paint the bigger picture for them and to make it clear how their contribution fits in, and how they themselves can and will benefit from their participation in the activity, then it is perfectly possible to gain their commitment and support. You just let them know what's in it for them; "value to the listener" and all that.

We devoted the first few months to building our relationship with these business units, getting together with the planning directors individually to understand the details of their current businesses, their aspirations and strategies for growth and development, and the support and investment they would need from BT Global and the rest of BT in order to achieve them. Outside of the UK, the country operations were all still relatively small at this time (under fifty million pounds in turnover in most cases) and they had hitherto been managed in relative isolation and on shoestring budgets.

The launch of Global had coincided with the start of a recruitment drive to introduce more commercially minded, indigenous management teams with a track record in launching start-ups and growing market share. This had been the clearest sign yet of the company's commitment to its globalisation strategy. The follow-on round of investments in networks, products and marketing, which we would be planning, would be the next one.

We ran a planning conference which brought all the planning directors together from all over Europe into a small, dingy room in the bowels of Dowgate Hill House. In the general buzz and enthusiasm for the event, nobody noticed the creeping damp on the walls nor complained about the indecorous sandwich lunch. This was in part, I suspect, because they were a mix of start-up veterans, used to a more frugal existence and only too pleased to be in London for a few days, and a smattering of BT veterans, used to living high on the hog in their stylish enclaves abroad, and quite happy to enjoy the rarity of time back in the old country, surrounded by homely and familiarly unfussy architecture and foodstuffs. It felt like we were establishing our own little private members' club in there; we should have put a plate on the door, it felt that exclusive.

There was now a growing level of seriousness and for once a genuine sense of purpose to my work, qualities which had been largely missing from my first decade in BT. I believe this came from the tangible and more onerous responsibility of creating something new, something of real substance which wasn't there already, and it being highly visible across the company. A life of making incremental improvements, of grinding out more from what you already have, was simply not in my nature, nor in my range of skills, and nor frankly to my personal taste. Operational management, in its execution and administration, was another game entirely, as serious and purposeful as ours, but for people with a differently shaped head to my own.

Mine was sculpted, so I had realised, for the forward looking aspect of strategic planning, that sense of creating the future, and the outward facing perspective, of setting off on an adventure into the not quite unknown, taking measured risks and plotting the company's way forward. Never a morning person, I was now rising early and with a lightness of heart and sureness of resolve which was evident in my outward demeanour, attitude and behaviour. I seemed to have become a quite different person.

★

Far from the moonshine of non-core pursuits such as cable television, where the drivers of success were scarcely telco-related but way further along the value chain, BT Global was pursuing a far more logical path of corporate evolution. There was a deep underpinning in the relevant technical proficiency required to bring it to fruition, built on a similarly deep-seated appreciation of the commercial success factors applicable in our target markets, which the local management teams and partners provided. We were laying the foundations for a surge in growth, which for several years would reflect a steady but substantial increase in our presence across much of Europe, and in pockets of Asia and the US. I was at last truly and intimately involved in creating something that I can look back on today with a semblance of pride.

We had very little in the way of contact with other BT divisions during this time. As a highly UK-centric organisation, what took place beyond the British Isles was largely beyond their comprehension and concern and thus entirely within our own control, and this helped enormously in gaining approvals for plans and in generally getting things done. Operating within a financial envelope, we were entrusted with the good name and interests of the company and its shareholders wherever we chose to fly the BT flag and sought to invest their funds. This was another highly motivating factor which kept us running at full pelt, a sense of freedom and empowerment, and with a few pennies in our pocket too. It was a once in a lifetime opportunity, but to keep the show on the road, some corrective interventions would soon be required, starting with the Concert JV.

We had invited two of our MCI-secondee colleagues from the venture to our planning conference, and they had duly arrived and predictably booked themselves into suitably grand accommodation in the West End of London. This was always the way with senior telecom types, particularly those from across the pond; it was an attitudinal remnant of the old order, of the bureaucratic elite; the arrogance of the unaccountable. Unfortunately, it was a symptom of the evolving culture of this new venture too. It was getting a little too big for its baby booties, and they had ideas on making it far bigger still.

Where the original strategists from BT had made innovation and service the central themes running through the plans for the venture, their MCI cousins, who were now in the strategist's chair, brought with them a classical New World vision of scale. It was certainly bold. Maybe we were just guilty of British condescension and reserve, but we thought the plans naïve and overoptimistic, and sought to inject more realism, as we saw it; more modesty. We were afraid of failure, you see, and didn't relish risk; that, in so many words, was the MCI view of our quibbles. We brought in BT people from Europe and the UK business to confirm our objections in a final attempt to downgrade the forecasts, but to no avail. The heroic Concert business plan would stand; publish and be damned. It was presented to the board of BT and approved, and now all they had to do was achieve it. We wished them luck; the best of British, in fact.

As we moved into the second year of our global endeavours, we rejigged our team, and I took on the numbers from Mike, who was moving on. I was content to be back in the financial hub after four years as a "commie" and had but one lurking unease; dealing with Concert. I had seen the blood, sweat and tears Mike had shed as he sought for weeks to reconcile and align all the individual country plans following the fallout from the recent Concert planning debacle. I had absolutely no desire to be snagged on that particular hook myself. But with the wheels already starting to come off the venture's financial performance, this was to prove a wish too far.

Just a few months in to the following financial year it was becoming crystal clear we would need to reforecast the Concert plan and bring it back down to a more orderly and credible set of projections. I was ordered to get on a plane to Washington and explain to the venture planners what needed to be done. I booked my flight and hotel – my first business trip overseas, the first of many dozens that would follow – and notified them of my intended arrival the following week. I also sent them a few template schedules we would be working on together when I arrived. I looked forward to seeing them.

I have only the sketchiest memories of the flights in and out, and the taxi rides to and from the hotel I recall merely because they were almost a hundred miles long. But the prevailing recollection of my voyage to Virginia is of whiling away the most farcical week of my working life.

I spent my first hours each morning trying to physically track down the people I was supposed to be seeing. They were never at their desks and never to become available, "tied up" in "unexpected" unspecified meetings or "urgently off-site". The CEO and CFO were travelling abroad, so I had nobody I could readily appeal to for assistance or to bring the local scrimshankers (for that is what they were) to book. I would be handed scribbled notes and messages by their go-between colleagues, apologising for any inconvenience caused; maybe I could make a start on the schedules myself? I completed them and handed them over to the go-betweens in the hope they would find their way back to the relevant people. Curiously enough they did, only to return covered in scribbled edits and more notes on what else I could do for them. Unbelievably, this went on for four days. I became convinced they were in a cupboard somewhere, hiding from me, too nervous to show up and collaborate in any material changes to their employer's business plan.

It's a fact that American middle managers live in perpetual fear of their bosses, of missing their targets, of losing their jobs. But to take it to such comical lengths? I returned to London with my own version of a revised plan for Concert, which was noted for the risks it highlighted against the original plan, rather than approved as the new definitive one. I felt some disappointment at that, but maybe that was being too harsh on myself; maybe I was just trying a bit too hard.

Perhaps I was too bound up in the gathering sense of purpose we felt for the work and the way we went about it; perhaps it was becoming too personal, I was getting too involved. It's an interesting process to explore. Some of it comes from within, from a growing sense of self worth, personal responsibility, and care for and involvement in outcomes, all helped along where appropriate by incentives and reward. But there is a clear sense in which this is also driven by external factors, by accountability, expectation and by observed behaviour. This latter is commonly, and perhaps too casually labelled as leadership, when there is something more fundamental at play; the senior apes in the cave, being watched, copied, aped indeed, by junior members of the troop. I was perhaps apeing somebody myself, and I wouldn't stand for failure.

I recalled our arrival at a planning review, scheduled on the Global board members' floor at BTC – all bridges and glass, plants and views – nervously hanging around, awaiting the MD, when he emerged from his quarters, all five foot four of him, his executive assistant to one side, the board secretary to the other, striding towards us like a mafia *capo* flanked by his *consigliere*. It was all stage-managed, and while gently comical it was in fact wholly effective. We all went along with the charade, adopting our roles, playing our part. As he purveyed his views in a low-key mid-Atlantic drawl, we earnestly scribbled every word, noting every "leverage" and "equity", signs of a new language within general BT management, which we would lap up and knowingly rehearse ourselves in meetings and conversations. This was the new grammar of growth, the syntax of success and we schooled ourselves in it at the knee of a dealmaker, enslaved by his mastery of the universe, his drive to succeed. The guy whose arrival I had forecast would presage major change; I had been apeing him.

★

In recognition of the importance of the work we were engaged upon, we were now rewarded with that greatest of accolades, a suite of desks in BT Centre. In the years since my most recent residency at that regal abode, access to its hallowed portals had been tightened considerably, with only the grand priory of corporate souls entrusted with the heraldic seal of an entry pass. Now we found ourselves sharing a roof with the BT Group executive committee and its minions, able to be called upon at the drop of a hat to explain to them face to face the intricacies of our strategies and our likely calls upon their pots of newly minted readies. We would soon be joined by our international development, project finance and reporting colleagues to create a BT Global hub of our own at BTC with a hotline to the chairman himself if need be. If we thought it was getting serious before, this would confirm it.

There were several collateral benefits to being based at corporate headquarters. Should you drive to work, then the attainment of a parking space in the basement was a perquisite of such scale and distinction that people were known to volunteer it on their tax returns. I myself joined and endured a twelve month waiting list for a spot in which to park my Vespa. The recent introduction of a gymnasium, whilst itself of modest proportions, was nevertheless in the very vanguard of corporate health facilities. I joined and made sadly irregular use of these, thus serving to confirm, in the eyes of my future wife, my psychological fitness merely to aspire rather than to truly achieve; there was no answer to that. The staff restaurant was of epic proportions, while the same could then be said of the servings. We would regularly convene there to discuss strategy over platters of Italian, Indian or Asian specialities, their savoury aromas blending seamlessly and evocatively with the international flavour of our conversation. Yes, there was much to be said for the place. For above all, it imparted an enhanced sense of centrality and import to our daily lives. It was our turn to be in the sun; just beneath the glass atrium, in fact, high up on the left.

It was during this period that we got our first taste of two specific technological developments that were to be as revolutionary in their impact on the workplace as the introduction of the PC had been some ten years before: email and the world wide web. As we changed out our ageing desktop machines for the first generation of laptops, itself an enormously liberating step, so we were exposed to the latest suite of applications, which included a mail package and a browser. Email initially had an almost subversive quality, enabling you to swap confidential messages under the wire and engage undetected in surreptitious gossip. Only very gradually did it replace more formalised paper-based methods of communications and evolve into the all-embracing medium it is today. Similarly with the web, which in its earliest form was essentially no more than a source of mild and humdrum entertainment, a library of mawkish home pages maintained by enthusiasts and hobbyists of every conceivable strain of esoteric sub-culture and earnest private pursuit. As with the original PCs of a decade before, these applications were regarded more as toys, diverting games that simply made for a lighter and looser environment; as with the SMS texting feature on emergent digital mobile phones, their power and ultimate transformative effect upon our daily lives was not immediately apparent in the slightest.

I was becoming particularly adept at directing our colleagues across the Global division in how to plan for their specific businesses, and in how to comply with our requirements as a growing business as part of the wider BT organisation. It was an art rather than a science, since there were no golden rules or tablets of stone. The frameworks reflected where we all were in relation to each other, within BT Global and across the rest of the company. The submissions reflected the levels of trust extended to us since these determined the levels of detail necessary to alleviate any misgivings over strategy and operational management. It was apparently known as contingent planning, and I was sure I was becoming a practising expert at it. I became fully convinced of this the second time we came to put a BT Global plan together.

I drafted a four page document detailing the strategic background, key assumptions to be made when planning, the cash investment available and the required returns, plus the submission and review processes we would be following. Before issuing it I sent it to the global chief of operations (COO) who was in charge of strategy, international development and finance, for his approval. It came back the following day: apparently, I had omitted a comma from the final paragraph which, when restored, averted the risk of a rather clumsy sentence. It may simply have been his way of telling me to go away and get on with it.

We shared our accommodations with our colleagues in the international development unit. These were people who spent five days a week getting on and off planes, buzzing around the continent, seeking out and negotiating deals and partnerships, attempting to piece together the jigsaw of BT's pan-European business. Sometimes they would disappear for a month at a time, maybe longer, before returning to the fold, waving a signed document in their hand, to be greeted as wandering heroes. Slowly but surely the map was turning pink, as we finalised joint venture agreements in each of the major geographies and set about launching local start-up enterprises comprising our own small bands of adventurists and those of the partner companies. These latter were a mix of television companies, supermarket chains, banks, utilities, entrepreneurs and railway operators, to name but a few, all of them with a thirst for growth and a taste for telecoms.

I had listened to the pub stories concerning the travelling, the negotiations and the expense accounts with a mixture of profound disbelief, detached concern and no little envy. I had been spinning around the planning loop for two years now and while I had absolutely loved being at the hub of the thinking and direction setting, I felt myself increasingly on the fringes of the main action, which was now taking place week in, week out on the other side of the English Channel. I could sense this was to be the next port of call on my journey. It was just a case of locating the right ship that was heading there, acquiring a ticket and then climbing aboard.

One quiet Friday afternoon in early 1996, I was at my desk waiting for an overdue planning submission to arrive by fax. This was not unusual since many of our overseas offices had not yet got onto the main email network, and planning submissions are always late. The machine beside me finally coughed into life and started to whirr. I assumed it was my fax coming through and turned to watch the glistening paper emerge. It was actually addressed to my latest finance colleague to labour under the name of Roger, and marked "for authorisation".

Idly glancing at the body of the text I made out the words "finance contractor" and "Italy". Something vaguely primeval stirred within me, and led me to read the fax in full. In short, it was from the head of our international mobile unit, requesting clearance to recruit an external consultant to provide BT's financial input to an imminent joint venture project in Italy which would bid for a national mobile licence. Sensing destiny, I took hold of the fax, folded it carefully into my jacket pocket and headed home. I spent the weekend plotting my next move, updating my CV and drafting the email I would send first thing the following Monday to the head of international mobile.

6

The Sweetest Spot

My unconventional means of approaching the international mobile unit was noted as a sign of both ingenuity and enthusiasm, and within days I was invited for an interview. More importantly from my perspective, I now had a free run at the job. I should caveat that, since I was actually subjected to no less than three interviews, with five representatives of the team, before the head of the unit, Donald, finally offered me the role. A member of London's prestigious blackballing Carlton Club, he clearly applied a rigorous membership procedure here too.

Having secured my move into international mobile, I felt a duty to bid farewell to my UK colleagues. I had a sense of going away for some time, unspecified but for years rather than weeks or months, and of making a break with the past. London life suddenly felt richer and more intense than ever before; maybe I was already feeling a little homesick. My leaving do turned up the sentiment, as it involved renting a cricket pitch for an evening at London's Regent's Park, and inviting thirty of my closest colleagues to a match after work, followed by a picnic by the lake. The warm evening sun shone over our sporting endeavours and followed us down to a local pub where I said my goodbyes. I felt I was leaving more than just a job behind; it seemed my entire life was about to change.

The mobile team consisted of twelve people from a mix of backgrounds, essentially marketing, technical and financial, and the focus was solely on acquiring mobile licences across Europe which would enable BT to build, operate and market cellular networks. It had started life within the BT Mobile unit, a reseller of network capacity operated by our UK subsidiary Cellnet. The team had originally come to my attention several years previously, when they had proposed a small investment in a potential new operator in Spain. That had been successful; the company had grown and so had BT's share of it. Since then, they had also taken a stake in mobile start-ups in both Germany and France.

The BT Global board had recently approved a plan to address the other main European mobile markets as licences became available, the next batch falling due in Italy, Switzerland and Holland. These were all second generation, or 2G licences, which marked the initial digitalisation of mobile services. They were intended to act as a spur to overall market growth and to provide competition to incumbent operators and other earlier market entrants. They tended to be issued via beauty parades, with competing consortia proposing to build out new networks as quickly as possible and offering a wide range of new and economical services. They pre-dated the third generation, 3G licences which would be auctioned across Europe at the turn of the century at vastly inflated prices as an element of the telecoms-media-technology (TMT) boom.

The team was based in Jefferson House, a smallish 1980s office block named for the chairman of the company who had piloted it through the privatisation. I supposed it was the thought that counted. Situated just off the Tottenham Court Road, I thus continued on my odyssey through the company's London office estate.

On my first morning, I walked in to find a new colleague of mine standing on a rotating chair, taping a map of Italy to the office wall, alongside those of Switzerland, Holland and India.

"Hello, I'm the new boy," I said, "Is this double Geography?" "Just planning my holidays," he quipped, before swivelling out of control and crashing heavily onto his desk. "My name's Kail," he grunted. "I won't shake your hand, I think I've broken my wrist." Patched up, he talked me through the initial market analysis he was doing on the upcoming European opportunities. He was going on a whistle stop tour the following week, to Amsterdam, Zurich and Milan to present his findings. "You should come too. It'll be fun, and you might learn something."

"Something about mobile would be a help," I replied, reaching for the phone to arrange my tickets.

Our first trip, the following Monday, was actually to Utrecht in the middle of Holland, to visit the Dutch partner, a local railway company. I was shadowing Kail – after an early flight and a long train ride, we arrived at midday, then spent two hours in a meeting before taking the train back to Amsterdam and flying back to London. I got home at nine o'clock in the evening, exhausted. We had a similar experience on the Wednesday, when, somewhat surreally, we travelled to the Swiss countryside to review the local market plan with some Danes, and then again on the Friday when we made the round trip to Milan. "So, what have you learned?" asked Kail on the return flight that evening.

"That this is going to be a rather tiring experience," I yawned.

"You've not seen anything yet," he retorted, "Just wait till the projects get going." He was right.

The trip to Milan was notable in one additional aspect, although the significance would not make itself felt for a couple of years. We were accompanied by a team from Cellnet. While Kail and I slummed it in the airport terminal café with our boarding passes for economy class, the Cellnet quartet had taken their places in the airline lounge, anticipating a seat in the executive cabin. As the flight was called they emerged briskly through the lounge doors and strode purposefully toward us. I didn't know it then but as I shook hands with the person in charge of their team, I was meeting for the first time the woman who two years later would become my wife. As it was, we simply exchanged pleasantaries and small talk about our respective employers' travel budgets. From little acorns do mighty oaks grow.

Our day in Milan had been spent in the company of the partners in BT's Italian fixed line business. They were keen to bid for the mobile licence due to be issued that autumn. Kail and they had each produced a set of market numbers which we compared and discussed. They had a more bullish view, forecasting that over the ten year period to 2005, mobile penetration would peak at around sixty per cent of the population. The BT view, formulated by Kail, was that this was too aggressive, that it would likely top out at around forty per cent. It is strange to think today, with penetration across Europe generally in excess of one hundred per cent (due to multiple subscriptions) that by compromising at fifty per cent we felt we were taking an excessively risky view. But we settled on it, based on various updated economic and behavioural assumptions, and drafted a strategy paper and project budget for internal approval. This was duly obtained – notwithstanding the fifty per cent take-up being noted as "questionable" – and a few weeks later we were back on Alitalia heading for the project launch.

The project was to be based in a development to the East of the city, known as Milano Due. Built and owned by Fininvest, the holding company controlled by Silvio Berlusconi, it was the base for a number of companies from across his business empire. The most prominent of these was Mediaset, a commercial television group which operated a number of national channels. They were BT's key strategic partner in Italy and they made two floors of office space available to us for the duration of the project. The sprawling development had the air of a university campus, with separate sectors given over to residential buildings, office blocks, a gym, a couple of supermarkets and several bars, cafes and restaurants. There were gardens, lakes and a network of cycle paths. If you worked for one of the Fininvest companies, you need never leave the compound; you had everything on your doorstep. They certainly knew how to look after their own. There was even a primary school.

They had also organised our overnight accommodation. We were to be holed up in town in a rather grand hotel next door to the Duomo, called, intriguingly, Grand Hotel Duomo. This was fabulously central and handy for all aspects of after-work life, but unfortunately it was also some ten miles from our offices. Milanese rush hour traffic is as dense as a dish of the local risotto, which meant we faced daily a minimum of an hour's drive by taxi to get to work. The stress engendered by this was best addressed, on arrival at Milano Due, by a brisk walk to the lakeside café followed by a frothy coffee and a *crema*, a delicious sweet pastry. Any sense of guilt at taking time out to soothe one's nerve-ends was soon assuaged, as the café rapidly became the meetinghouse for the project as a whole. Most mornings a group of us would assemble there from eight thirty to plan the day's activities. We were definitely beginning to feel at home here.

It was late summer when we had first arrived. I had taken the risk of wearing a black linen suit but the Lombardy climate would not let me down. I was conscious immediately of the standard of dress of the northern Italians: everyone was done up to the nines. They not only coordinated their own clothing, they seemed to complement everyone else's too. It was like a permanent and ubiquitous fashion shoot.

On top of that, they all looked like film stars; tanned and slim, wrapped in their ever present sunglasses. We Brits would have to up our game to make a decent show of ourselves, and you felt a certain pressure to do so. They had a way of making you feel slightly awkward, even inadequate, such was their level of style and panache. It was a mask, sure, but it could be effective. You might feel at home, but you would never forget it was their's; and that they wrote the rules.

They even smiled more than we did. I couldn't fathom precisely what it was they were so happy about: maybe it was the fact they had money and secure jobs, good genes, a sense of style, magnificent culture, great skiing, the lakes, fabulous weather, sumptuous food and delicious wine. Whatever it was, they seemed pretty pleased with themselves. I later learned it was a national trait, another mask, used to overcome frustration with bureaucracy, political gridlock and economic stagnation. They had plenty to fall back on, but they needed it too.

★

A typical mobile bid team would consist initially of a handful of people, maybe less than a dozen in all, representing the main functional areas of market analysis, network planning, finance and project management. The precise number of participants would be driven by the number of partners in the project, the scale of the project and the size of the investment required. As the project progressed so the numbers involved would grow rapidly, reflecting the growing interest of the partner companies in the project and also the approaching deadline for the bid when the detailed work on the submission itself would demand more bodies be thrown at it.

Our consortium was an ever changing kaleidoscope of potential investors and suppliers, centred on a core set of shareholding partners: BT, Mediaset, Banca Nazionale del Lavoro (BNL) and the Norwegian mobile incumbent Telenor. BT was primarily the technology partner, drawing on our ten year involvement in Cellnet, a mobile venture whose market image would never quite set your pulse racing, but was nonetheless technically proficient. Mediaset were the local market experts in this group, while BNL would arrange the syndicated financing. Telenor were effectively being sized up as our potential pan-European mobile partners.

Given the perceived attractiveness of the licence, the number of partners already on board and the huge scale of investment that would be required to build a national operator in a country the size of Italy, there were dozens of people on site in Milan from day one. A team of marketing consultants were flown in from Madrid. A local team of management consultants were bussed in to act as the eyes and ears of Fininvest. BT provided an entire network planning team from Cellnet. And each and every investor, actual or potential, dispatched a finance representative to contribute in some way or other to the business plan. Within a couple of months, there were in excess of a hundred people on site every day.

Fortunately, I arrived on the scene early enough to grab my own desk, and set up in a smallish corner office with Graham, a chirpy project management chap. He had just completed a similar project in Germany where our bid had been successful and he was keen to apply the same principles and methods here in Italy. He had, however, reckoned without the Milanese psychology, which went something along the lines of "you are now in Italy, you do as we say here". It was a subtle twist on "when in Rome…" since we were in the North of the country where they were a tad more direct in their style.

I too was learning that as we were in their country, and

despite BT being the largest shareholder in the project, we would need to adapt our approach and mindset to accommodate local practices and priorities. In my case, on the financial and business planning side, this effectively amounted to "we don't want to spend any money" and "we don't want anyone to know what we are doing". Parsimony, *omerta*: lines were being drawn in the sand.

The international mobile team in BT had developed a standard financial planning tool which was flexibly designed to be readily bespoked for each country's project. It ran to over a thousand lines of code but despite this it was actually not overly complex. It was built on basic arithmetical formulae and was thus readily accessible to anyone with a passing knowledge of Excel. This meant time need not be consumed working out how the model operated, and could be more usefully spent debating the wider business and the specific assumptions to be used. It gave the project a running start. It also meant, crucially, that BT would end up controlling the planning process, the inputs and outputs. Thus went the theory, at any rate.

So we needed data to populate the tool. The marketing consultants ran a macroeconomic model and this would provide the demand side numbers, based on the take-up rate or market penetration, the market shares of the respective operators and the likely revenues per user. In order for the consultants to set the gears of their forecasting engine correctly, they organised a series of workshops, the first of which would be devoted to market positioning, and the thorny question of branding. This is of course an area to which everybody feels they have something to contribute, on which everyone has an opinion.

It was no surprise then when fifty or so people from the consortium companies, the various consultancies and the Fininvest associate businesses crammed into a meeting room designed to hold considerably fewer than half that number. I managed to last about an hour before making a tactical withdrawal, in the interest of preserving my health and my sanity. In that time I think we had touched on, or indeed set out to emulate, every local brand from Giorgio Armani to Ermenegildo Zegna, and that was just the shirts. The Italians played up to their reputation for having an obsession with style. A new mobile phone was passed around the office, eliciting stereotypical responses from the nations represented round the room. The Norwegians knocked it on against the table to assess its hardiness, we Brits were concerned over its likely price, while the Italians simply held it to their ear, smiled and asked winningly, "Darling, how do I look?"

The later workshops were a little more orderly and we began to get a clearer sense of the potential market we were addressing, their tastes and buying habits, the price points that would trigger their behaviours, and the means by which we would communicate with them and sell to them. Numbers were now starting to come through for various market scenarios and the planning was beginning to take shape. Sharing the numbers with the technical team would then drive the supply side figures: network dimensioning, numbers and locations of mobile stations, and the required switching capacity. I adapted the BT financial model to absorb the demand and supply data sets electronically and we pretty soon had a neat, slick process for evaluating the financial impact of whichever market scenario we wished to review. I had again managed to position myself at the centre of something that was starting to feel rather good.

To complete the planning toolbox, and to appease our Italian partners for whom investing any money bore risks akin to spaceflight, we brought in a banking advisor who constructed a syndicated funding module so smart, it virtually extinguished the need for any substantial shareholder cash injections at all. With these tools at our command, we would set out to produce a compelling business plan. And it soon became clear that whichever way you looked at it, this bid was for a licence not only to run a mobile network, but also to print money; over a billion pounds worth in certain scenarios. On the project, business planning was becoming very popular. Indeed, back in BT, mobile was becoming flavour of the month. And for all of us, in one way or another, Italy in particular was starting to look hugely attractive.

★

Increasingly, and no doubt in light of the valuation we were putting on the business, unseen forces were conspiring in such a way as to give the Italian partners almost complete control over the project, precluding anyone else from shaping it in any meaningful way. Small cabals of local partner representatives held clandestine meetings and carved up much of the commercial and financial planning activity amongst themselves. This was irritating, but on the plus side it did mean that a bit of the pressure was taken off the rest of us. While there was still plenty of work that needed to be done, and much of the critical modelling activity would remain in my hands, we were being excluded from the main decision making processes and forced to concentrate on providing purely functional support as and when required.

This meant the profile of work became uneven, and so with a bit of time on our hands Graham and I decided to make the most of it, taking lengthy walks around the campus gardens, luxuriant *capuccini* by the lake, and leisurely lunches in the numerous smart staff restaurants. Our host at many of these was Mr Ghezzi, a Sicilian fixer no more qualified to participate in a mobile project than I was to run a Catanian trattoria, but he was our vital link man into the increasingly introverted Italian investor group. He also had a way with the catering ladies that ensured a small bottle of Tuscan red *gratis* with our daily *varieta di pasta*. He was a most useful ally.

We were being increasingly exhorted by our UK-based sponsors to exert more control, to champion BT strategies and interests, and to ensure we were building, as far as possible, another fully fledged outpost of the BT empire. Such naivety was borne of a touch of the old arrogance, of course, but more often than not, out of sheer ignorance of the local cultural environment. It also overlooked the presence and personality of one Elserino Piol.

Mr Piol was the designated project CEO. A telecoms and IT veteran with over thirty years senior experience at Olivetti and elsewhere, he knew everyone and everything there was to know about his business in his own country. With an ego the size of Sardinia, he set about corralling the bid process in our favour. He would spend hours each day roaring into his phone at Roman bureaucrats, leaking stories to conniving journalists, and plotting with potential investors on side deals, all in an effort to create the maximum visibility and credibility for our consortium and a momentum behind our bid which would swing in our favour when the crunch time came around. The unintended consequence of this approach was a series of delays and revisions to the tender process, which were signalled by further volcanic eruptions emanating from beyond his office door.

I was pleased to have had my exposure to this forbidding and ferocious character minimised; it also gave me some respite from the thick, pungent smoke emitted by the dark, tapered Italian cigars he habitually smoked. For reasons unexplained, he was missing a couple of fingers, and if he ever felt the need to disquiet you, he would take hold of the cigar with the remains of his left hand and dangle it precariously between his thumb and wedding ring finger.

Then one morning I took a call from BT's senior project representative which suggested he was unavailable for that afternoon's board meeting, so could I ensure a discussion would take place regarding fixed and mobile product convergence? Steeling myself, I entered Piol's sanctum and clawed my way through the smoke to his desk. "Mr Piol," I ventured, "Er, Mr Parmar is unable to attend the board meeting today. He asked me to advise you he is not happy that the convergence strategy is not being discussed." He levelled his cheroot and eyed me across it. "Mr Cianna,' he growled, "Thank you for telling me this. Now please tell Mr Parmar…to go fuck hisself!" Assuring him of my forthcoming compliance in the matter, I took my leave.

As BT, we had at this time a vision of mobile as an overlay to the fixed network; we spoke of "convergence" between the two services, and their eventual "integration". These were conceptual rather than specific proposals, which to this day have never demonstrably come to fruition. Smart mobile phones dominate the telephony market today, while the fixed network is increasingly seen as the platform for broadband. In the UK, they may share BT's backbone network that relays traffic across the country (the four UK mobile operators are among BT's biggest customers) but for users the two products and services remain indelibly separate. Where it has come about, fixed-mobile convergence has been enabled and monopolised by the interplay between ranges of devices in people's hands, on their desks and in their homes.

This was an alternative vision espoused by Piol himself. Commercial to his fingertips – those that remained – and a battle scarred investor, he was convinced of the vertical view of the business world, of horses for courses. Wary of fuzzy overlaps, he believed in specialist companies meeting specialist needs; so, simplistically, fixed companies did fixed telecoms, mobile companies did mobile. Repeatedly petitioned by BT's senior executives to adopt their unproven one-stop-shop model, and to work in tandem with BT's Italian fixed line start-up business, he dismissed them with a blend of soaring rhetoric and savaging tirades. "Your grandchildren will ask you why your telephone wires ever exeested!" It was quite a performance and it left them bereft and bemused. They knew they were stuck with him as Mediaset's man, and they had no idea how to handle him. They had never been spoken to in these terms before. It all made for great theatre, and I had a front row seat.

★

This was becoming a rather special time for me. I was quite sure most people in the company would happily have swapped what they were doing for my job. It was interesting, fun, challenging, and quite beyond the norm. These positives were compounded by the relationship I had with my colleagues, both within the tightly knit mobile unit itself and our extended team on the project in Italy. The fact that many of us still to this day meet up every year for a Christmas meal speaks volumes for the strength of the bonds we formed at that time. Borne of a chemistry, it reflects the shared experiences and the bloody-mindedness we forged collectively. We were a cussed minority: championing a business and a technology which the company as a whole was still struggling to get its mind around. We were in the mobile sweet spot, and the sweetest spot of all would be in Italy, or so we hoped.

We were invited to attend a BT Global conference on

international development, hosted by the COO, which was due to take place on the Franco-Swiss border. This was aimed at all those BT people currently engaged on development projects around Europe and a few beyond. There were around a hundred of us all told, and for three days we took over the entirety of a beautiful hotel situated on the shores of Lake Annecy. The views were spectacular, the blues of the water and sky merging in the mid-distance, fenced by snow capped Alpine peaks which glistened under the pouring sunshine. We tried; we really tried to talk shop. But the lure of the lakeside bars and restaurants, the slopes and the clubs made it necessarily challenging and, ultimately, fruitless. It was meant as a thank you, and we took it in good faith.

We were living a good life and making the most of the opportunities afforded us. My time in Milan became as much a social whirl as a business commitment. Dinners were regularly organised to bring together the teams from both the fixed and mobile ventures, the various partner companies, or simply the functional teams around our own office. In absence of these events, Graham and I worked our way through the local hostelries and would wax lyrical on the virtues of the latest magical trattoria we had stumbled upon.

The project was becoming a magnet for all manner of BT people, no matter how peripheral or superfluous their involvement in our international development activities. I lost count of the number of "observers", specialists, corporate executives, budgetary controllers and other time wasters who would fly in for a gander and assert their self-importance. There was no disguising the envy in the eyes of many of these fellow travellers. They would arrive and depart in glorious sunshine and gaze in wonder at the handsome, smiling local population. They seemed to think we were there for a holiday; so to play this up we poignantly shared with them our running joke regarding the Milan weather forecast: it would be mostly warm and sunny, followed by light cloud and occasional rain in December.

Each and every one of them felt they had a salience to the business plan and would require a run through it. Sadly, given the mind numbing bureaucracy of our internal approval processes, this was scarcely an exaggeration. I bemoaned this to Piol. "Don' worry," he growled through his cigar smoke, "We goin' to win." For once, his certitude seemed strangely uplifting, and I drew strength and belief from it.

The relentless political circus that surrounded the bid process was generating more and more delay. The original date for the release of the request for tender (RFT) had slipped from the autumn of 1996 into the following year and had been due in the spring. We were now into the early summer months of 1997 and there was no immediate prospect of things starting to move. I had been travelling to Italy most weeks for almost a year and we were no nearer to submitting a bid than we had been twelve months previously. In an effort to proactively avoid the sort of drift that had plagued much of my career, I asked Donald for an additional project to look after until the Italian situation was resolved.

★

A mere thirty miles north of Milan lies the Italian border with Switzerland, and I was duly consigned to bestride this exotic frontier and support BT's projects in both countries. The contrasts between the countries and cultures stood as stark as the Alps that reached up between them, and these were mirrored in both the government process and the project itself.

The Swiss initiative was in its very early days, and housed in a small office development on the remotest fringes of Zurich. It was due to get underway formally in September with the issuance of a draft RFT document, to be followed two months later by the final version. The submission was due to be made in mid-December with the licence due to be awarded in the middle of January 1998. And on the allotted day in September, at the allotted hour, a copy of the draft RFT was placed into the hands of our regulatory lead. Someone said it was working like clockwork.

It was to be a straightforward beauty parade between two competing consortia. At stake was the second 2G licence; the first was already in the hands of Swisscom, the local incumbent telco. As in Italy, the market was as yet undeveloped, with barely fifteen per cent of the population owning a mobile phone. Again, BT was the technology partner, this time supported by Union Bank of Switzerland (UBS) and Tele Denmark (TDC), another Scandinavian suitor looking to become BT's strategic mobile partner across mainland Europe.

The Danes had put up a team to look after the broadly defined commercial areas of marketing and finance, so here my role was less operational and more consultative, which would allow for more time to be spent on the internal BT approval shenanigans once we arrived at the crunch period in December. The working style of the Danes made for a welcome change from that of the Italians. In place of the secretive, furtive defensiveness I had grown accustomed to, I now encountered an open, communicative and straightforward attitude which made for far greater levels of trust and responsiveness on both sides. It may have been helped along by the presence in a back office of several crates of bottled beer which was freely available to the project team. Either way, there were few barriers in the way of us making decent and rapid progress.

The snow began to fall in October, and as far as I could tell it continued to fall continuously for the following three months. This and the biting cold meant that the centre of the city was thinly populated at best, the merest signs of life being vast, shiny black Daimlers which silently crunched their way over the snow-laden cobbles. On the face of it, this left Zurich as a rather dull, even forbidding place. Our hotel was set in a narrow lane just off the main square, opposite a small and unimposing church. Nobody had thought to warn us that it contained the loudest bells in Christendom. Sleep was patchy at best, but at least that would keep us from drinking too much beer in the office.

We quickly completed the business plan for the venture and did the rounds of executive briefing in Copenhagen and London. Again, there was a marked contrast in styles. After the first set of presentations, which took place at the ornate TDC corporate headquarters building, we were escorted to the basement where the local management had laid on a feast in what looked at first like a film set. It wasn't; the flames rising from the torches hanging on the wall were genuine, the thirty foot long oak table was authentic and the giant wine flagons were brimming with it. We were treated like feudal barons. The following week the Danes came to London, where the BT Global COO's secretary had organised a cheapskate meeting room, sandwiches and tea. I mentioned a contrast in style; in truth, we had none at all.

In order to carry out my twin centre mission to best effect, I made fortnightly trips back to Milan from either Zurich or Copenhagen, wherever I happened to find myself. The Milan-Copenhagen run was clearly not a favourite of the travelling classes; I made several flights on this route and on at least two occasions I was the sole passenger on board. I monopolised the time of all four air stewards, who were amazed when I turned up on my own again a couple of weeks later. It's an eerie thing, sitting alone in a vast cabin, looking out through the window at the moonlight illuminating the Alps. I felt like Dan Dare.

A flight from Zurich to Milan felt like an over-indulgence; they are only a couple of hundred miles apart. So I booked a ticket for the much-vaunted *Pendolino* express train service, which left Zurich Central Station at seven o'clock in the morning. Unprepared for the extraordinary rolling and pitching sensations as it took bends at upwards of a hundred and fifty miles per hour, I had to abandon the journey half way due to extreme nausea. I then opted for a glass-ceilinged tourist train, which took the rest of the route at a more stately pace. I eventually arrived at the Milano Due office three hours late for a planned meeting. This being Italy, the meeting hadn't yet started and after a restorative lunch and glass of red in the company of Mr Ghezzi I was set up nicely for a good argument over the latest version of the business plan. But I did make a mental note to fly from Zurich in future.

With a final flurry of activity the work on the Swiss submission was completed early and painlessly. We went to press without a hiccup and the bid document was handed in on time. This was a benchmark in professionalism, partnership and teamwork. It left me wondering how things would pan out when the equivalent moment arrived in Italy.

I began to prepare some analysis that I felt would ease the Italy project's path through the BT investment approvals process. The quicker that was over and done with, the more time I would be able to devote to the main objective of completing the bid submission itself.

The valuation of the Swiss project had been none too shabby, while that of Italy would be significant too. The standard metric for presenting these valuations was on a US dollar basis, expressed as the value per head of population: or "dollars per pop". My two projects were set to generate around eighty dollars per pop in Switzerland and thirty in Italy. I knew in my gut that questions would be asked: why so? Mobile's mobile, isn't it? I knew the values were correct; I would just have to be prepared to demonstrate it.

It wouldn't be as simple as saying "Oh, Italy has more people in it." It was a mite more complex than that. The clues were to be found in the detailed mire of statistics buried in our forecasting models, while the factors determining these were to be found in the contrasting social, cultural and economic features of the two countries. I spent a day combing through the code and preparing the reconciliation, based on parameters of behaviour, wealth and competitive intensity. This had never been articulated at BT before, and was a minor work of genius. I presented it to the BT Global COO, who labelled it the best bit of analysis he had ever seen, and promptly took it off to present it himself at that afternoon's BT board meeting. I saw my chance and scarpered back to Milan *pronto*; I had more than done my bit to get BT's commitment to invest two hundred and fifty million pounds. Assuming of course, that we actually won the bid.

★

Back in Italy full time, and realising we would be around for a while yet, I signed up for a course of Italian lessons. It is in fact one of the easiest languages to learn and, having studied French, Spanish and Latin when at school, I made reasonably rapid progress. I recall a disagreement with my tutor, in Italian, over the then forthcoming single currency and of Italy's mistake, in my opinion, in their intention to join it. She was astonished by my attitude. She was typical of most Italians in believing it was absolutely the right thing for them to do, the fulfilment of a historic destiny. The irony of my newfound facility in her language, and my complete lack of cultural affinity, was striking. It hit me there and then that we Brits were so clearly at odds with the philosophy of our hosts, this might jeopardise our chances of winning the bid.

It had been noted within BT that a rival, German led consortium might be favourite to win the licence, given the political positioning of Italy in relation to its proposed entry to the imminent monetary union. This had created a bunker mentality within the project. We had a clearly superior distribution network in place in the Fininvest group's supermarket business, we had technical excellence from Telenor, we had financial clout with the banks, and political connections of our own; we would give them a run for their money. But I was worried now.

My mood was not improved when word came through from Switzerland that we had lost the bid there. It had been clearly won by the opposing consortium, which included Orange from the UK. This was a disappointment for those who had worked on the project, and a setback for BT's plans in the country, but in the broader strategic context it was not disastrous. However, it did put additional pressure on us to win in Italy.

Eventually the regulatory bodies got their act together and published the RFT. They had been vigourously petitioned by the existing operators Telecom Italia Mobile (TIM) and Omnitel, who had bought themselves almost two years in which to further entrench their duopoly; they were clearly formidable operators in all senses. Whoever ended up winning the bid would clearly have a fight on their hands dealing with these two.

Various twenty-somethings in short skirts and boxy suits began to populate the Milano Due offices. PRs and designers from the Mediaset television empire were being introduced to provide the gloss and glamour which was the wrap to our bid. It certainly lifted spirits and was a welcome shift from the drab administration of bid management we were used to. While outwardly a show of vacuous narcissism, these kids brought an energy and pizzaz to the packaging and presentation, and in particular to the branding, critical to any mobile business, which was visually stunning, and on its own would have won any tendering process. With the Italians at last shifting into gear, we all felt a surge of wind in our sails; there is nothing like the sense of imminent success to get a team working together.

Then, at the eleventh hour, another internal dispute broke out. A minor industrial shareholder reminded everyone that they in fact were responsible for the branding. A side deal negotiated months previously and seemingly forgotten by all was brought back centre stage. They presented their work, which was truly dreadful. Amid the chaos of bid preparation, and pushed for time, the earlier deal was finessed whereby we would use their styling for the bid only, but when we won the launch would be based on the stylish Mediaset template. I wasn't the only one to see negative portents in all this. We were, it seemed, our own worst enemies.

Our submission was finally completed and despatched in June 1998, and we all disappeared on holiday, expecting to hear the official response in six weeks time. Within two weeks, I had a text from Milan with the outcome – we had lost. Our financials were solid. Our network was sound. But our product portfolio was flawed. The authorities had wanted even more innovation, even more (ironic this) convergence.

Over the course of two years I had made over sixty return trips to Milan. I had spent almost two hundred nights there. I had spent fifty thousand pounds on expenses. It all now seemed a fruitless waste. I flew back for one last trip, to collect my meagre belongings, clear the offices, close out the budget and say goodbye. Where there had been a hundred-odd souls there were now just empty desks, abandoned. We had convinced ourselves, individually and collectively, that we would be back to make it all happen. I had harboured serious thoughts of spending a few years working out there. It now felt so bleak and pointless, and so sudden. I had a sense of grieving.

A few months later, BT began lobbying for a fourth mobile licence to be issued in Italy. I was reluctant to be involved. Our scenario planning had always suggested that with two dominant players already entrenched in the market and still growing, and with a third entrant picking up growth from innovation and market agility, a fourth player would have nowhere to turn to grow and establish itself. I presented this argument to BT's European boss, a brute of a man of high intelligence and low tactics. I promised him it would not work out. He didn't want to hear this and would proceed with the bid, which a revamped BT led consortium duly won, albeit in the face of zero competition.

It eventually launched in 2001 and, predictably, it struggled to perform from the outset, before an acrimonious dispute arose between the shareholders over funding for a 3G licence (the Italians wanted BT to stump up over half the cash; no surprise there) and this rapidly led to the breakup and closure of the business. On learning of this, I permitted myself a wry smile of recognition only; one shouldn't mock failure. But the sweetest spot had ended in bitterness.

7

Caveat Emptor

Returning home, we found an organisation in a heady, feverish complex of uncertainty and swagger. Rumours abounded week by week, stories of mooted takeovers, mergers, disposals, their scale and reach ever more elaborate and compelling. Suddenly, everyone was in play and anything could happen. While this would create an energising frisson and bring a sharper, more urgent commercial edge to our thinking and planning, it also meant the unnecessary expense of huge efforts exploring distracting and ultimately unrealistic scenarios: if anything was possible, nothing would get done; the paralysis of analysis was taking a grip.

My life in the air had had a rather beguiling effect on my relationship with the mother country. This had first made itself apparent during the spring of 1997, barely twelve months into my internationalised role. The UK election that May was being hailed as a seminal moment in post-war politics, a pivot in history. I found myself looking in on this event as an outsider, a detached observer; I had lost some of my sense of citizenship, my sense of belonging. This was in part a result of the emotional investment I had made in our Italian project, although this feeling of a loosening affiliation with my cultural heritage would linger for the remainder of the time I was committed day in, day out to our international business. But while I would eventually regain in full my English sensibility and intellectual attachment to the UK as my homeland, I would never fully recover any similar sentiment or impassioned interest towards BT's domestic business. Once you've enjoyed playing bridge outside in the garden, you don't ever revert to games of snap in the shed.

The strategy for our European expansion was evolving. BT had developed a set of in-country joint ventures, which had been focused initially on providing domestic and international telecoms services for local corporate clients. As the importance of mobile was becoming increasingly obvious, so these ventures were now all bidding for cellular licences. Competition for these was intense and success was by no means assured, as witnessed by our failures in Italy and Switzerland. So a backup plan was devised within the international development team, which would involve BT buying into existing mobile operators, and then acquiring additional shares as they became available until these companies too became part of the BT family.

I took myself off to a hotel near Heathrow airport, where just such a plan for Scandinavia was being put into effect. Representatives from the Swedish second operator were holed up there, having flown in at BT's request to discuss options for their company's strategic development. I had been briefed by Donald that in his view this particular proposal was not a profitable use of BT's cash and, as importantly, other elements within the BT Global organisation were looking to seize any opportunity to get onto the mobile bandwagon, our bandwagon indeed, and this needed to be urgently sat upon. I had unwittingly walked into a trap. As I arrived, the development team hosting the Swedish party were rattling through their agenda: acquisition, provision of development capital, synergies with our existing local fixed line venture, and favourable access to BT's pan-European network footprint: it all sounded perfectly sensible. Moreover, the Swedes were in complete agreement, and so we decided between us that we should proceed to make a conditional offer there and then, subject to due process. I later returned to the mobile office and was asked how the meeting had gone. I played a straight bat and outlined the advantages to BT, as I saw them, of proceeding with this deal. Crucially, I also outlined the advantages for us, as a team, of proceeding with this strategy. By advocating the deal and leading on key aspects of its execution, and being seen to be doing so, we would thereby position ourselves at the centre of the new plan, allowing us to exploit our expertise to define and lead on all similar initiatives in future. My political antennae had come of age.

While Donald had nodded sagely at the logic of my argument, and encouraged the wider team to follow suit, it later emerged that he had been quietly and effectively working on an altogether different vehicle for his own ambitions, which would soon become clear. A gnomic sort, he once confided his approach to staff development. When he spotted a likely talent, he would introduce them to a member of his *recherché* brotherhood, and then seek their opinion of the up and coming prospect. If the response was favourable, then doors would open for them. If, however, the response was "Who was that wanker?" they would be advised to look elsewhere for professional advancement. For the moment, thankfully, my reputation fell into the former category.

*

Hubris is invariably invoked in corporate life when risks have been taken to excessive lengths, once blindness to reality has set in. A minor and more common form of disassociation from the gravity of planet earth is the application of essentially witless ideas which purport to "re-imagine" a product or a business, to "reengineer" the experience or execution of it, and in so doing, re-compose the very language that surrounds and describes it. This is usually the result of concerted periods of underemployment, navel gazing, defensive posturing and self-justification, with little or no visible roots or traction in the competitive landscape.

One example of such mindless meddling was the creation of BT Mobility, a corporate unit reporting directly to the Group CEO (as the company head was now styled) which sought, innocently but naively, to bring together under one roof all the company's interests, assets and resources devoted to the most loosely described notion of "mobile". Overnight, our international mobile team of twelve had become part of a unit of over sixty people, the vast majority of whom we would never meet, never see the point of, and never miss. But in the minds of this wave of mobile opportunists, it represented an opportunity to foist a range of inane, half-cocked, pet projects on to the mobile operators in which we had an equity interest and, it was unspokenly believed, thereby convince the wider business of the unmitigated indispensability of their doughty originators.

The company had always had a blind spot to these nutters, and the chap appointed to head up BT Mobility was equally wall-eyed. And so we were bombarded with cherished wish lists of fatuous propositions and product enhancements, everything from virtual private mobile networks, fixed-mobile product integration, "fusion" phones, and some barmy notion of multiple "cloud-based" answer machines: anything that might require of a customer a masters degree in telecoms to understand what it was he was buying, together with a remarkable lack of commercial foresight. Unimpressed by this attempt by big BT to rein it in and bring it under control, the mobile business continued to grow and establish its own credentials, primarily as a classic consumer product that wraps itself to the individual who owns and uses it and is liberated by it. It most definitely did not see itself as an integrated, subservient *purlieu* to an all powerful fixed line hegemony, and BT never quite understood this. Its master and servant *schtick* would never apply here, and BT Mobility would not be long for this world.

A second dose of hubristic calumny was in store, this time in full public view and on a truly momentous scale. Amid fanfares of cosmic proportion and epic clamour, BT and MCI announced they were going to merge into one, global entity, to be named Concert. They would trade under their own names in their home markets, and under the new banner elsewhere across the globe. With a new headquarters in London's prestigious Berkeley Square in Mayfair, this self-proclaimed giant would stand as the world's first communications company for the twenty first century.

This was all news to us on the mobile team. Feverishly, we devoured the dispatches and noted the creation of Concert Mobile, which would subsume us and our counterparts from MCI. Work was to begin immediately on the build of the new organisation and its constituent parts. The future was here, then; this had been our destination all along. Never mind building it from the bottom up, creating by hand and by brain a new millennium of light and liberty, it had all been just a stroke of the pen away. We were dumbfounded. The PR puff in the press packs rehearsed the tiring old lines regarding the market for global services, which we all knew continued to disappoint and underperform. Maybe there was a compelling reason behind it, but it was hard to discern.

Within months, the proposed deal began to unravel, with the release of data revealing MCI's regressive performance in its local US markets. BT reduced the price it was offering to MCI shareholders, and was then roundly trumped by an upstart bunch of hoodlums by the name of Worldcom. They set the presses running and handed over a fortune in shares in the biggest merger in US corporate history; that these shares were subsequently devalued in one of the biggest scandals of US corporate history was someone else's problem. But BT had shown itself to be almost comically inept at playing the bigger game. It hadn't done its homework, and it was embarrassing for us all. But we still came back to work.

The question now was, where? Our building had now been deemed surplus to requirements. A strategy of consolidation and disposal of BT's London properties had been running for several years, but as I had always found myself ahead of its curve the effects of this had not visited themselves directly upon me. There were a few weeks of uncertainty as to our destination, with some wilder notions of internal exile to the ghastly wastelands of the M25 (London's orbital motorway) gaining currency; my central London corporate existence was under serious threat. Mercifully, these speculations were to prove wide of the mark, and while some were offered the option of a desk alongside the runways of Heathrow, the bulk of the team would move to Holborn.

This was a return to happy hunting grounds for me. I had spent my university years in these familiar precincts, and then my first few years in BT too. The area was improving with each passing season, the boulevards of Kingsway and High Holborn now a crucifix of bustling, midtown aspiration. I would soon assume the mantle of social leadership, as I carved a cultural niche for my colleagues among the Georgian splendour of courts and squares, and along the shadowy lanes and alleys. In no time at all, I had them playing tennis in the ancient fields of Lincolns Inn, and drinking vodka in the modern Polish bars.

I have used the analogy before, but again it felt like we were members of an exclusive private club. We had London at our feet and Europe on our doorstep. We would alternately jet off for a week together on the continent, or spend a few days back at the clubhouse tending to our local pursuits. The work itself was seamlessly woven into the fabric of our lives as to become almost invisible. There were tensions and deadlines and the usual merry-go-round of corporate diligence, but we had a philosophical sense of perspective toward these, borne of self-confidence, destiny and, dare I say, a certain power. Nobody was going to get in our way and stop us. For once, BT truly needed us. The world was going mobile, and mobile was our world.

One summer morning we abandoned our desks for an hour to observe a once in a lifetime total solar eclipse. Through gathering clouds, we could just about make out the passage of the moon across the sun. As the temperature fell, an eerie silence took hold. This primal urge to witness momentous, uncontrollable events, to confirm both our place in nature and our singularity, is rarely more tellingly realised. It also spoke eloquently of our vanity and vacuity. It was a humbling moment, and we headed straight for the pub.

*

Following the proposed merger with MCI, the market was now alerted to BT's global pretensions and its ambition to grow the mobile business. We were approached by a US based operator with a proposal to buy their non-US assets, which included several across the major economies of Europe. This wasn't cheap, but was of a scale which if undertaken would propel is into the top handful of operators across Europe. A little later, we were approached by a major German operator to become their strategic partner, which would involve the merger of our respective European footprints into one.

The details of the two deals are not important here. What is key though is that they offered the company, separately and together, and seemingly from nowhere, the chance to stake a credible claim on the future, as the major pan-European mobile operator, with a substantial presence in each of the top five European economies of the UK, Germany, France, Italy and Spain. This was a moment in the company's history that could have meant at least as much as the vaunted global merger with MCI, perhaps more, since the integrity of BT's name was still assured. But something was to hold us back. Price, probably; cold feet, to an extent; a lack of belief in the vision, possibly. Whichever it was, and there were doubters on all three fronts, it was a step too far for BT; too far, too quick. We declined each offer and resolved to pursue a more incremental, organic path to growth in Europe. This would never be fully realised, the lack of a critical mass serving to undermine both external market belief in BT's mobile credentials and internal conviction as to the company's strategic intent.

But it was neither too far nor too quick for Vodafone, who voraciously snapped up both investment portfolios in double quick time to assume the mantle of mobile leadership themselves. Which in itself was a further embarrassment. A company no older than our own mobile subsidiary Cellnet, they were demonstrating ambition on a colossal scale that put BT in the shade, and in the manner of the time we would need to respond.

Donald now returned from a strategy session with the international development team wearing a wide, self-congratulatory grin. They were going to continue on their acquisition programme in Europe and would deploy our team in support of this as and when required, much as I had surmised. However, he had additionally squeezed out of them the latitude to draw up and execute a similar plan for Asia, to be led by him personally. While of less strategic import and urgency, there were a number of interesting players emerging across the region from whom we could learn much, both technically and commercially, and who would doubtless welcome an infusion of new capital in their quest for growth and local dominance. So went his thinking, and it sounded plausible, but we would need to put it to the test.

He outlined the task before us. We would need to trawl through the literature – analyst papers, brokers' reports, news features – and draw up a shortlist of potential operators sufficiently interesting and affordable that we could consider approaching them about a deal. In parallel, he would wind up our colleagues across the region to start building the necessary relationships and exploring the options. And to keep their feathers unruffled, he would bring in the corporate finance boys, who were always a source of endless grief if you didn't let them know what you were up to, and charge them with tapping up the local bankers for any leads. We were mobilising for a general assault along the Pacific Rim.

There was a buzz of excitement generated by the imminent Asian adventure. For some, it came across more as a personal venture than a business objective, and I supposed that was only natural. Interestingly, we lost a number of people over the ensuing eighteen months or so, to rivals, suppliers and partners. Good people, who had been clear from the outset, in their own minds at least, as to what this development meant for them as individuals. They went there with that in mind and that's what they did. They were more clued up about things than first appeared, while I perhaps appeared clued up but in reality was merely surfing the latest wave of opportunity to wash over my path. Strategic at work, I remained merely opportunistic when it came to managing my own career.

We spent several weeks combing through the relevant

documents and spreadsheeting the numbers. In essence, we were after relative newcomers to the market, who were picking up market share rapidly, had a reputation for innovation, with at least industry average customer revenues, preferably little debt exposure and who were still loss-making. This would potentially provide a solid basis for growth in revenue and profit, and scope for above average returns on our investment. Operating within these constraints, we came up with a very short list of options, and even easing the criteria only brought a further handful onto the radar. Building in the feedback from the region whittled the choice down even further, so that we were only looking at a single option in each of Japan, Korea, Malaysia and Hong Kong. But it was a start, and following a second round of local meetings, two projects were launched and teams dispatched to Tokyo and Seoul. I would join the latter in due course, but first I had an appointment to keep in Hong Kong.

I had been invited to a briefing session there along with our corporate finance representative on the Korean project, Nick. We headed straight from the airport by taxi to a downtown address, where we pulled up in front of a sixty storey high glass wall. Arriving on the fifty eighth floor, a fairly deserted office suite that appeared to be hovering over the city, we were shown into a meeting room which overlooked the bay. Now this was a view. I thought I had been spoiled with aerial views of sunsets over Regent's Park, but this was the real deal, like being inside a vast glowing blue sphere. I wondered aloud how you ever actually got any work done with this wondrous tropospheric spectacle just the other side of the window. Our host had arrived, and admitted that he was usually sat some twenty floors further down the tower, facing straight into another block, so he really couldn't tell me the answer to my question either.

We reviewed the welter of financial data he had brought along in a deck of heavily branded slides. We were allowed to keep these, a set each in fact, and here were a couple of spares too, no problem, think nothing of it. Such generosity would have everything to do with the fact his bank was on a retainer with us running to more than several figures annually. The upshot was a target price per share that we should negotiate to. It would cost BT, for a quarter of the company, the thick end of two hundred million pounds. We were clear to buy new shares in the company so all the cash would remain within it. It would surely be party night in Seoul when that deal went through.

While he had us there, he felt it opportune to run another one by us, and from nowhere he produced another slide deck, this time running the rule over a local operator in Hong Kong itself. He had clearly been busy. It was the company we ourselves had identified from our own researches, and they had put themselves in play via his good offices. Another twenty five per cent stake, another two hundred million pounds. So, two for the price of one; this would keep us occupied for a few months. Leaving Nick to break this news to the folks back home, I flew on to Seoul to spend the rest of the week with our team based there.

The South Korean capital had the feel of a militarised zone, the air heavy with the insistent chopping of helicopters, the streets alive to sirens, the ubiquity of combat clothing. It was a relief to get indoors and meet the locals, our hosts. To a man, and woman, they were charming, polite and amusing. The contrast with the scenes on the streets was extraordinary. The meetings were serious and purposeful, conducted in perfect English by a cadre of graduates of American business schools. It started to go through my mind; what do they really want from us?

They made the right noises about learning from our market

experience and technical expertise, and we nodded appropriately, but as they continued with their presentations it became abundantly clear that they were actually some way ahead of us on each and every critical aspect, from network design and operational efficiency, to pricing plans and handset portfolio. It was clear we needed them more than they needed us. We managed to remain poker-faced, but it wasn't easy. It was the same when we met with the Hong Kong venture. We came away from these meetings with a revised strategic intent; that by associating ourselves with these guys, some of their gold dust would rub off on us. With their brains and our money, there would be no stopping us.

We returned to London to make the detailed case for the investments and to gain approval to proceed with the final negotiations on price. Having worked on both Korea and Hong Kong from the initial scoping exercises and through the business planning phase, I was keen to complete the circuit as the deals came to close. But this was not to be; the imminent birth of my first child meant I was now grounded.

★

A major investment opportunity in an Indian mobile group now came through. Since I was now back in London, I was tasked with checking and consolidating the financial modelling and valuation work that flooded in from our teams on the ground in India, as they completed the due diligence on the various companies within the group. There is nothing more excruciating; I was effectively marking someone else's homework.

Thankfully, there was the sudden imposition of a tight deadline, which meant all the work had to be completed within one month. The Prime Minister of the UK would shortly be travelling to India and BT wanted to be able to steal a ride on the PR fanfare that would accompany this visit by announcing our local acquisition at the same time. There then followed the busiest few weeks of my working life as we went through each layer of BT's approval bureaucracy at full pelt in order to sneak a sound bite into Mr Major's Delhi speech on UK investment into India. That we managed it was little short of miraculous, and it was with some relief and satisfaction that I lifted a copy of the London Evening Standard to see a front page photograph of the PM shaking hands with the chairman of the mobile group in question, captioned with a mention of the BT acquisition. On such mere triflings are our reputations soldered. As I cut out the photo and filed it away, I was sure my newly born son would one day be proud of me.

★

Following the success of the previous year's "thank you" conference in Annecy, we had been eagerly anticipating the next one, so it was with some measure of disappointment that we learned it would take place on the south coast of England in Bournemouth, and in mid-February to boot. Somebody was having a laugh. We traipsed off in scuzzy trains to a hotel barely a notch up from a boarding house. This was slightly odd. We were working on bigger projects, making greater investments and we were taking more risks, travelling further than ever, yet the trappings here were becoming more meagre. In place of last year's walks around the sunlit lake and the romantic old town, the options this time around were a sailboat on the churning seas or a round of golf in the pissing rain. I settled for a bracing swim in the ice-cold waves.

The sense of cognitive dissonance was compounded by

Donald's presentation on future mobile strategy, which concluded that having conquered Europe and Asia, we would soon be turning our attentions towards the Americas. As we hadn't yet actually bought anything outright and only retained a degree of influence over the running of the companies we had so far invested in, it did seem a little strange to be casting our net ever wider, and spreading ourselves ever more thinly in the process.

It was explained that the strategy was to take an initial stake, see how things panned out and then decide whether or not to buy up more; we thereby had first dibs. While sensible on first hearing, this ignored the fact that buying up later could become very expensive, since if the company did well, its share price would only increase. The strategy of not buying more substantial stakes in the first instance more than likely betrayed a continuing lack of confidence in ourselves to truly make a success of the investee companies. We would only buy up once they had proven themselves to be successful, and that in the end would, and eventually did, cost BT a lot of money.

The American mobile market was huge, fragmented, crowded and expensive. Using our strategic development methodology developed for the Asian market play, and applying them to the main US operators, we could actually only find one company that fitted the bill, and that turned out not to be a true cellular network operator at all, but an association of small companies that sold walkie-talkies. In another moment of unreality, I found myself analysing the Argentinian mobile market and the prospects of us decamping there to bid for an upcoming licence.

This was all starting to strain credibility. My belief and passion in what we had been doing as a cottage industry was being rapidly unravelled by the way BT was going about its industrialisation. I wanted to get back to making the weather. Then I read an email that offered the chance to do just that. Not with mobile but via another, potentially even more potent phenomenon of the digital age; the internet.

———

8

Interwebsters

For the best part of a decade, BT had adopted a quizzical stance towards the internet. It had been emerging around us since the early 1990s, but without issuing any clear and obvious warning signs that this might actually represent an important and lasting development in the evolution of telecoms. It all seemed to be happening on an improvised, "best endeavours" basis, rather than as the outcome of a deliberate plan and as such it had rather caught the company on the hop.

To cap this, when asked by a journalist for the company's take on the internet, the then Deputy Group CEO had grandly and roundly dismissed it as "a fad, on a par with CB radio". This implied a belief that it would remain the preserve of rather sad, nerdy types and would never break through into the wider economy and society. For a more arrogant, sniffy and misplaced analysis you would have to travel a long way. All the way to Suffolk in fact, where there is now a lecture theatre named after him at BT's technical laboratories near Ipswich. Clearly the people who hit on that had a great sense of irony.

In order finally to get its corporate head around this nagging issue, BT established a dedicated strategy unit, known as Group Internet and Multimedia (GIM). Its remit was to understand and explain what the internet was comprised of, what the opportunities and threats were, how BT itself might exploit it, and then to present and support delivery of a corporate business plan which brought all these threads together. The email outlining this organisational development arrived in our inboxes in January 1999, and I noted with some surprise and no little self-satisfaction that it would be led initially by the former BT Global COO, supported by his previous finance director. I had had a good working relationship with them both and felt sure they would welcome me as a safe pair of hands. I dropped them a quick email explaining my desire to remain at the forefront of the company's commercial developments, that this was the area for me.

Shortly afterwards, I received a response from Claire, the FD. The email recalled our experience of working well together, if rather frantically, on the Indian mobile investment projects the previous summer, and suggested we meet for lunch in the City, where she then outlined in more detail what the unit was about and what she needed to support it and take it forward in the right way. The scope of the work, I observed, from strategic analysis and planning, to execution via acquisition and corporate development, was a litany of those areas I had most enjoyed throughout my career. Above all, I enthused, it would be about making a lasting difference. She caught my enthusiasm and suitability for a role in her new team, and a month later I was back at headquarters.

Claire was responsible for all international investment papers which went to the BT board. She was tall, slim and attractive, with a wicked sense of humour. Wily and ferociously ambitious, she was also commercially acute and financially thorough. She knew instinctively where the soft areas of business cases were to be found, and was terrier-like in her determination to test the soundness of a proposal almost to destruction. It was touch and go at times, but ultimately my mobile cases had somehow withstood her forensic examination, and that had stood me in lasting good stead with her.

She had then supported me in my attempts to be upgraded. I forget the precise letter of the alphabet with which I was consequently branded, but I do recall she was diligent and fair in this as with other personal matters, a trait I have observed in many women in senior positions. While they like to join in gossip, and can be catty and cutting, when it comes to managing their teams they tend to be solicitous and empathetic, even protective. I had no qualms about working for Claire. Given her warmth and sense of mischief, her fearlessness and ability to ruffle a few feathers, I was looking forward to it.

★

A paper on the subject of the internet had been drafted and circulated to BT's executive committee. It insightfully described its likely evolution as the latest manifestation of the traditional market square, which would feature a largely unchanged mix of buyers, sellers, products and services, and the same means of exchange, only transacted through the digital medium. It was the digital market place for the digital age. This was broadly accepted as at least part of the story, but as it was as yet undeveloped, it was not clear what this digital market place would actually look like, what it would run on, how it would be run and who would run it. These were the key questions which would frame our analysis and the plans we should then build.

Before turning to the crystal ball myself, I addressed my first task, which was to bring together for the first time an exhaustive review of BT's involvement in internet-related activities: the extent of our "internet protocol" (IP) network business, which permitted different clients' computing networks to communicate with each another; revenues from IP-based corporate solutions, which designed and managed companies' internal systems; and the scope of our internet service provider (ISP) business, both in the UK and overseas, which provided internet access to consumers and businesses.

Following a detailed trawl through numerous divisional and product reports, and after endless follow-up phone calls, I finally arrived at an annual IP revenue figure of two hundred million pounds. Given the company was generating around twenty billion pounds in annual revenues at the time, these therefore represented a princely one per cent of total Group sales. It seemed we were indeed a minnow when it came to the internet.

There were some notable exclusions from this figure, in particular those revenues which related to traffic crossing the UK backbone network, which was in IP format but not billed for separately as such, and revenue from dial-up internet traffic, which was included within the voice call numbers and impossible at that time to segregate and quantify discretely. While important in their own right, the fact these were treated with secondary levels of transparency and importance betrayed their hitherto lack of significance and consequence for proactive management attention. So from a purely reported, managed revenue perspective, the one per cent figure was correct. The only way was up.

The members of the GIM team were a mixed bunch who fell into three broad camps. There were the cranky academic types who had been banging on about the phenomenon of the internet and the strategic growth opportunity it presented for some years, and who could blow you away with charts and graphs, but were hampered by their lack of derring-do from spending too much time in their ivory towers. Then there were some vaguely commercial types, for whom the digital market place was a means of transforming agents and products within the wider economy, and who were endlessly involved in workshops and debates about the next wave of the digital economy. Finally, there were those of a more practical bent, who were looking to unpick the internet to see what it consisted of, identify who was providing these components, how they were providing them and the value they were getting out of it.

I gravitated towards this latter group. They spoke the language of strategic finance, of mergers and acquisitions (M&A), the grammar of growth that I had been exposed to in previous roles, where business was condensed into concepts of assets, capabilities, synergies and value creation. While it was diverting to read about the coming of the digital networked economy and to hear about the its potential societal impact, the reason we came to work was to recommend the next steps BT should take to become a major player in IP and how it would make money from doing so. It was the latter group whom I would work with to develop BT's internet strategy and business plan.

Shortly after my arrival, a course was organised for those who felt they required a technical appreciation of the internet and how it sat alongside and compared with existing, traditional telecoms models. Ten of us were welcomed into a sunny meeting room overlooking the building site of the new Paternoster Square. I took in the familiar architectural sites of the surrounding streets, and from my perspective on them realised this was the precise location of my desk of some eight years previously. Excitedly, and unguardedly, I announced this to my colleagues. It hit me then that eight years before, at least half of them had probably still been at school. They smiled benignly, as I thought of Les smoking his pipe at his desk. How would they have reacted to that, I wondered?

Our tutor greeted us and from the moment he opened his mouth and began to speak, I felt my heart sink. "Now I'm an old-fashioned sort of chap…" He was clearly a dyed-in-the-wool apologist for BT's engineering heritage. While content to allow that the IP standard four layer signalling model contrasted favourably with the traditional standard seven layer model (on grounds of cost, speed and flexibility) he was completely against the idea of a fully IP telecoms system: "They'll never replace the old network." While I might have been wary then of an evangelist for IP trying to convince me of its ineluctable dominance and ultimate superiority, I had also seen and read enough to know that there were clear and unmistakable signs of rapid progress in that direction (most notably in the US, where it was starting to run riot). That BT was apparently employing people to try and train us to disbelieve the evidence of our own eyes seemed potty. He was polite and pleasant enough to share a pint with in the pub afterwards, but I couldn't fathom why I had spent a day in his company. Maybe we should have been tutoring him. There was still a long way to go; the notion of the internet as "a fad equivalent to CB radio" had clearly not been shaken off.

★

The media were by now starting to pick up on the increasing financial and economic significance of the internet, as a number of high profile launches, initial public share offers (IPOs) and acquisitions of dot.com businesses were raising the high water mark of the growing TMT boom. In parallel, cultural aspects were also receiving ever greater coverage, with increasing numbers of abstruse commercial and representational websites garnering plaudits and enjoying at least a transitory moment in the sun.

A review appeared in the magazine of London's Sunday Times, purporting to list the top ten most influential people worldwide involved in developing the internet. So, for instance, at number eight, they included the musician David Bowie, who was exploring internet technology as a means of creating and promoting new forms of art. The places above him were occupied by a series of apparent giants of venture capital and new wave technology including, remarkably, at number seven, a mate of mine from Cellnet called Brian, who had been working on a mobile version of the worldwide web. An egotist notwithstanding, this public elevation to the pantheon of TMT visionaries and iconoclasts would provide him with a platform for imperious grandstanding that would not have disgraced Caesar himself. We stood by for a flurry of investment proposals to emanate from his office.

This was the era when it was said of dot.com business ideas that, as with books, everyone had one in them. My own proposed slice of the action was based on a mobile quiz, where customers would subscribe to a web-based service which periodically sent multiple choice general knowledge questions to your mobile phone via SMS, with prizes for the fastest correct response or an accumulation of correct answers. I sent it over to my wireless web colleagues for their perusal and comment, and a few weeks later they actually launched a version of it. While they swore it was all their own work, I was now convinced that somewhere, my own seat on the global syndicate of online savants was being prepared. It still is.

It was in the futile quest to "monetise" your website and make your e-commerce business model sustainable, that the seeds of so many dot.com downfalls were sown. Without a regularised flow of revenues, of actual and repeat customer sales, most internet start-ups would go to the wall once their seed corn investment capital was "burnt". You might have had a dot.com business idea inside you, but in all but a few cases, that's probably where it should have remained. It was our job to ensure that BT's own internet ventures would be sustainable, could be monetised.

That was what would exercise us most in developing our strategy. It had to be so good that people would pay for it.

The team proceeded with its analytical unravelling of the internet, and in stitching it back together progressively revealed a series of interlinked and interdependent business areas. These were reworked and refined until there remained a portfolio of five theoretically sustainable business models, each clearly defined, with no overlaps and with sufficiently narrow gaps between them. This meant revenues could be maximised and other operators prevented from entering the market. The five models identified by GIM as the building blocks of the internet of the future, were:

communications infrastructure and technology, which would provide the switches, routers, signalling and capacity management to enable the efficient transmission of vast amounts of IP traffic around the network;

data centres and web hosting services, which would provide vast data warehouses and platforms for storing and distributing content and applications;

broadband access and backhaul services, which would provide users with the capability to get their hands on the content and applications through the networks, and transmit them over the networks at breakneck speed;

ISPs and portals, which would provide commercial access to the internet, and aggregate content and applications in marketable formats;

devices, which would provide users with flexible and integrated means of using content and applications.

Within this strategic landscape, the main focus for BT's own strategy would be the middle three layers, those of hosting, broadband and ISPs, the most obviously suitable areas for an incumbent operator to major on. In addition, we would use BT's research Labs to look at optimising content transmission across the network, but we would not manufacture any network equipment ourselves. While we might look to sponsor development of end-user devices where they were complementary to the portals, we would not manufacture these ourselves either.

Two significant development projects ensued, one looking at a consumer broadband and ISP business, the other looking at an IP networking and hosting business aimed at corporates and ISPs themselves. Each of these would culminate in strategic business plans, with the objective of taking BT to a market leading position for broadband in the UK, similarly for hosting throughout Europe and the US and for IP networking globally.

After months of intensive detailed planning, these all came together in a presentation to the BT board entitled Man the Barricades, an analogy that was perhaps wearing the revolutionary theme a little too self-consciously (since we were still running behind our counterparts in the US and parts of Europe) but which nonetheless made clear that some form of permanent break with the past was clearly in the air. There were follow-up presentations called for, notably on broadband, where there was a growing belief that the entire UK network would need to be rebuilt to cope with the anticipated explosion in data, but the overall direction of the plan was approved. It was time at last to get on with it. We pulled on our balaclavas, packed the Molotov cocktails, and headed for the Bastille.

There were a lot of references now to the so-called internet "space" – an aphoristic Americanism eagerly adopted by insecure telecom types seeking to ingratiate themselves into the trendier realm of the "net". Its initial usage sought to imply some metaphysical dimension, transcendent to the material world and representative of the aspirational, radical sweep of the true believers' vision. A black hole for the existing order of everything, for a while it seemed its onward march might shred and consume all in its path. The internet space; the final frontier of telecoms. As our understanding of the workings of the internet grew, and its various mundane components became more visible, so the word was suffixed onto these elements, thereby asserting their own mystical properties. By turns, it was the "hosting space", the "portal space", the "ISP space". An increasingly absurd affectation, I envisaged it bouncing around BT's legacy business: meetings enlivened by talk of the "kiosk space", the "manhole space".

Hot on the heels of the strategy paper's approval, the BT internet awareness programme went into overdrive, with a conference organised in Barcelona. The top one hundred and fifty company executives were invited to the Expo Centre on the harbour front, where they were regaled with speeches and presentations from the GIM team and from various leaders of the business units around the company who had some degree of exposure to IP and the internet itself. It was an exercise in levelling up. The highlight was to be an address from the chairman, and it is fair to say he didn't disappoint.

On stage and in front of vast digital screens bearing images of the two cathedrals to be found in that wondrous city, he suggested that the tussle for dominance of the Barcelona skyline between these two architectural triumphs, the classical *Santa Eulalia* and the modernist *Sagrada Familia*, was in itself a useful metaphor for the tussle for dominance of the future of communications, between the traditional telecoms model and the upstart internet. Lest we should be in any doubt as to where his sympathies lay, he expounded upon the timeless virtues of *Santa Eulalia*, her solidity and classical beauty, and how she would be around for centuries to come, before laying into the *Segrada Familia* as faddist, unformed and inexplicable. He plainly hadn't read the strategy paper. It was a clever trope, grippingly if misguidedly portrayed, and revealed just how hopelessly out of touch the old boy was becoming.

The wireless web boys were also in town. They had somehow got hold of the mobile numbers for all the attendees, and over the weekend before the conference began they had texted them all with details of flights, hotels and attractions. Those with WAP phones had also received pictures and maps. It was a smart demonstration of the power of the coming mobile web. They had arrived with a paper detailing their next wave of development, and after a quick discussion in a side room with the Group CEO, they had their growth funding promised there and then. There was something of the pioneering days of the internet about what they were doing, the spirit of best endeavours, and they had a galvanising effect on me. It didn't need to be perfectly planned, it just needed to work. Not exactly what the chairman would want to hear, though.

Back in London, we now felt a masterful confidence in our appreciating knowledge of the internet and particularly in our ability to spot winning breakthroughs in technology, its applications, and business models. To that end, some of the team had set up dollar investment accounts through which they would back their hunches with their own cash. It became all the rage to have a ticker running across your computer screen, detailing the prevailing share prices of your portfolio of punts.

I gave this a wide berth since I had little spare cash – the costs of west London child care were by now giving my bank account a monthly pummelling – and what little there was went on maintaining my rainbow of web-culture shirts. This didn't stop me wondering of course, and I set up a fantasy portfolio of virtual investments in a panoply of favoured prospects. This allowed me the best of both worlds: to play at being a market sage, while risking nothing. I came across one particular stock, for a mobile web Silicon Valley start-up. Over the course of several months, the share price rose from under ten dollars to exceed one hundred and fifty dollars. I made millions from that one. Why, it was almost as lucrative as running a pre-school nursery in Fulham.

★

I now attached myself fully to the web hosting implementation project, where a strategy for growth driven by acquisition and investment had been approved. We carried out a targeting activity similar to those carried out previously on mobile operators, and produced a shortlist of half a dozen or so contenders, then began to put out feelers into the market. All of the companies we reviewed were based in the US, which remained very much the nerve centre of the internet. We received a positive response from one particular company, not actually our preferred option as it was Nasdaq-listed, where acquisition could prove to be bureaucratically exhausting, but it was prepared to be bought outright. It had operations in the US and the UK, built brand new state of the art data centres, and had been running for nearly five years. They would be in London imminently, and would be happy to meet with BT.

This would prove to be one of the oddest meetings I would attend in my time at the company. Due to timings and prior commitments, the only people available to attend on our side were myself and Alan, the head of the hosting strategy. We headed for Canary Wharf where the Americans were camped out with their bankers. Alan and I were shown into a meeting room, where shortly afterwards we were joined by the CEO of the company and his father, the chairman, who was smoking a cigar and wearing a stetson, which he continued to sport throughout the entirety of the meeting.

Alan kicked off hastily with some strategy perspectives and the discussion proceeded smoothly onto their planned rollout into Europe. Out of the blue, Alan then apologised and said he had to get home quickly to attend to a domestic emergency. It wasn't immediately clear how he knew so, since his mobile had not rung. So I was left alone, to lead a meeting with a couple of slightly dumbfounded Texans, one in a stetson, planning to sell their Nasdaq-listed hosting business. I had to think quickly, and brought the conversation briskly onto one topic I was sure of, finance, which helped to get us back on track, and me my composure. I explained our investment process and said we would formalise contact in due course once our strategy for this specific proposed transaction had been agreed and the subsequent steps had been signed off. The CEO did most of the talking for their part, referring at one point to how "Pop" would take care of the de-listing activities. We closed the session and, pleased with my rescue act, I left with a slight spring in my step.

Three weeks later I was picked up at home by the Virgin Atlantic chauffeur service, driven to Heathrow and whisked through the Bond movie sequence of priority check-in. Once in the lounge I sought out the Champagne bar. A second glass in my hand, I rang an old friend to describe my latest persona, that of internet entrepreneur off to the sunny US to reel in a billion dollar investment project. I caught him at a bad time: in south west Ireland, where it was pouring with rain, out of work having sold out of his business too cheaply, and flat on his back in agony with a suspected slipped disk. Our contrasting fortunes were a source of ironic humour and shared laughter, and I supposed that was his way of wishing me luck, which understandably, given the circumstances, he couldn't quite bring himself to say.

The New York trip was a two week stint on due diligence and architecting the shape of the deal, activities split between the midtown data centre owned by the hosting company and the offices of our bankers over on Sixth Avenue, another dizzying fiftieth floor enclave. From the strategic perspective, confirmed by the financial analysis, it was clear the deal would only make sense as the first move in an accelerated play in the global hosting business. We would need to pay the current market value plus a premium for the existing company, so the only way to justify the investment would be to roll it into a significantly ramped up organic rollout, built off the newly acquired assets. On top of the estimated three hundred million dollars needed to complete this initial transaction, we planned to invest a further two hundred million dollars over the following three years. This would create within five years a business worth a billion dollars in annual revenues, which at a respectable cash margin would generate sufficient returns over time to recover the total five hundred million investment and create sufficient incremental value to BT to make it look compelling. After a while, the numbers, these endless hundreds of millions, began to lose their meaning. It all looked effortlessly achievable.

The management of the hosting company, who at that time owned the majority of the shares, would be locked in for the three year investment period, and earn their lucrative way out by hitting the growth targets. They had a track record of delivering rapid growth, and were up for the deal; mind you, given the size of the numbers involved, there was no earthly reason why they shouldn't have been.

Back in London though, the prospect of the deal was not shaping up quite so well. The MD of BT Global had revealed his serious misgivings over how he was supposed to integrate and manage a team who would come to dominate his business, and make millions of dollars each in the process. An experienced hand at acquisitions and boardroom politics – the guy whose behaviours and language I had subliminally sought to emulate, to ape, several years before – I imagined him now playing out and weighing up the likely outcome.

The balance of power around his boardroom table would tip inexorably into the lap of the management of the hosting business, while even he himself ran the risk of being marginalised. His options were limited, by the fact the CEO of the hosting business refused to report to anyone but him. And when he did, it would effectively leave the MD and half his existing team redundant, since hosting and the wider data centre business it presaged was to be the cornerstone of the new global strategy. Not good.

A more generous, less conspiratorial interpretation of events would place him at the centre of a web of market intelligence, hard wired into the thinking of major US investors, who were beginning to question the basis of the TMT valuations boom. This would necessarily require a more conservative approach. Doubtless concerned at the logic of whichever argument had seized him, the MD ordered an urgent internal review, to look into a do-it-yourself option: BT building its own hosting business along the lines of the approved strategic plans, rather than basing it around an acquisition.

In the heat and dust of a July evening in New York City, the gaudy amber glow of neon signage set against the deepening violet skies which arc over its looming towers creates on the streets the intimacy of an underground club where, fortunately for us, we had a fortnight's membership pass. For Nick, our project director, this was familiar territory, and he led us through this benign cosmogenic Hades like Charon, the mythical navigator. And as we glided seamlessly through glamorous cocktail bars, dramatic steak houses and cosy speakeasies, I had no way of knowing then, as I brushed the sky, that I was at the zenith of a parabolic career.

The internal review called by the Global MD went through several iterations to get to the right answer, a billion dollar revenue business requiring just three hundred million dollars of investment capital, and run by BT's own network of international companies. Maybe it was self-defence, to protect himself and the existing board members. Maybe it was classical self-delusion, a belief that we had all along been geniuses at building and running data centres and really could now take on and dominate the sector globally, all by ourselves. Maybe it was great market insight, a sense or belief that bust was around the corner. Maybe it was a bit of all three, I couldn't say: but whatever it was, it meant the acquisition was off.

The news was fed through to Nick who affected polite sounds of agreement and approval, "wisdom of the decision" and so on. An old hand, and with no little political nous, he had clearly been through this many times before; another day, another dollar saved, and home we came. The decision was roundly vindicated in the short term when, shocked by the bursting of the dot.com bubble, the market tanked shortly afterwards, driving down the value of hosting stocks by seventy five per cent. BT began to build out its own data centre business, but never came near to achieving the aims as originally set out, while more fundamental factors would ultimately determine the scale, scope and strategy of BT's global business.

★

I was to work briefly on a smaller, tactical acquisition project later in the year, when we looked at buying a software company and using its suite of products to launch BT's application hosting business, an early version of what is modishly described today as "the cloud", in what was an early manifestation of the self-build data centre plan. Working in the dead zone between Christmas and the New Year, I arrived at the City offices of the firm's bank to access the data room and run through the main financial documents stored therein. It was a surreal experience; there was nobody there but the doorman. I walked home later through the dark City streets, again not a soul; London after a neutron bomb attack. I had a sense of absolute professional solitude, of being maybe the only person who believed in what I was doing. It was ironic then, at a GIM team event early in the New Year, that I was to receive two awards from BT's group internet director, in recognition of my perspicacity in support of the strategy work and my resolute dedication to the acquisition projects. I came away thinking I was on the cusp of something, that all before had been leading to a centripetal, defining event. But the reality of it was, it would all be gently downhill thereafter, since I had one more minor but telling misjudgement of my own to make the following year; but that is for a later chapter.

Claire, as CFO, had been charged with bringing new finance talent into the company, as well as bringing on particularly bright and commercially astute talent from within the existing pool. Between us, we had recruited ten sparky young things, with five of them reporting into myself as finance planners and analysts. We had gelled very well as a unit, so well that I invited Claire and her entire team to my house for Christmas drinks, something I had never dreamed of doing previously.

They were the embryonic internet generation, on average some fifteen years younger than myself, and I actually felt rather fatherly towards them: a feeling that was only enhanced by the birth of my second child. They had arrived in BT charged with enthusiasm, and it was our task to channel it and guide them towards productive and enjoyable ends, keeping a watchful, almost parental eye on their progress.

There is only so much one can do to try and keep intelligent people occupied, interested and motivated when they can plainly see political forces and games being arranged so as to prevent you from making sensible plans and material progress. Our solution to this was to get them involved as far as possible in those games; get them working with the forces of inertia and self-interest to try and plot a way forward together. Some responded favourably to it, got properly stuck in and, battle hardened, have subsequently gone on to become senior executives in their own right. For others this was a challenge too far, and confirmed that BT was not the place to further their careers. You have to let them fly.

★

The priority for us was to get the GIM business plan objectives put into full effect across the company, with the main strategic thrusts of hosting, global IP networking, ISPs and broadband at the centre of the development of the company's growth both in the UK and overseas. In order for the plans to have an optimal impact on the shape of the business as a whole, recommendations were put together on a restructuring of the company's organisation. These included the creation of new organisational units to focus on each of these three areas. Needless to say the existing units fought an effective rearguard action and, in the way of these things, forced a compromise, but at least the plan itself was embedded into the restructured company's own set of priorities.

BT Global, now rebranded as Ignite, would lead on the

hosting and IP networking business; a new division, Openworld, would manage the ISP business globally; and a newly created UK consumer unit would place broadband at the centre of its growth strategy. It was a spatchcocked outcome, and would soon require further rationalisation. But at least the company had gone some way towards overcoming its fear of the unknown, and embracing the new realities. Amidst great fanfare, the new shape of BT was launched upon the world.

A press conference was called at which the company's senior executives turned up without a tie between them. BT was indeed a company that was changing with the times. The appearance of the company's top brass in smart casual attire was an extraordinary revelation. Having spent their entire careers buttoned up into classical modes of formal menswear, they now sought to present themselves as fashion conscious fops. It was quite an exhibition: they took to the stage in a procession of black shirts and jeans, natty sports jackets, cool suits and fancy footwear. They looked like an ageing rock band reunited for one last tour.

It would be a rocky year on the road, for BT was approaching serious financial troubles. A big storm was brewing, and the company's entire executive committee, together with the hitherto relentlessly upward trajectory of my career, would be among the victims of its ferocity.

9

An Open and Shut Basket Case

On the day of the announcement of the restructuring, I was offered a role in the new BT Openworld organisation, the showcase for all of BT's ISP businesses. Claire had been appointed as its Chief Finance Officer (CFO) and offered me the role of managing the M&A finances, which I had no hesitation in taking on. I had no great experience of the ISP business per se, but wanted first and foremost to strengthen my M&A knowledge and further develop the range of my commercial expertise.

I was wary of the ISP business as a whole; the business models at play were experimental at best, and the tension between content and access as to which was driving value was as yet unresolved within the company. Access, which in future would be handled by the broadband product, was now in the hands of BT's consumer division, which left the more questionable sources of value, the portals containing content and applications, to be developed within BT Openworld, with the UK consumer and overseas units the primary channels to market the services we would develop.

The business was comprised of a ragbag of BT's largest ISPs, based in the UK, Belgium, Netherlands, Italy and Singapore. It also included Looksmart, an Australia-based search engine in which we had taken a fifty per cent share, and Genie, as the mobile internet venture had been newly branded.

An ISP existed, as its name implied, to provide internet services; this was suitably and sufficiently vague to allow any interpretation to gain traction. While it might market the access product itself, such as broadband, its core business was the provision of a range of services through its main website, or portal. These would include a standard set of applications, such as email, instant messaging and chat rooms, and a suite of content services, anything from basic textual news and weather reports, to video and music download services.

In the absence hitherto of a comprehensive and structured groupwide strategy for the internet as a whole, embracing the ISP business, many of BT's in-country ventures, not simply the UK but also around Europe and Asia, had created their own ISPs. Each of these had independently developed a portal presence on the web, had struck deals with content and application providers, and would boastfully proclaim its "eyeballs" and "page views", the metrics which governed success or failure.

Each had independently developed its own server farm, the computing hub at the core of the ISP operation, and a local inventory of technology suppliers. Each had independently contracted with internet gateways, who provided connectivity with the wider internet. And of course each of them felt they represented a source of expertise, be it in technology, content rights acquisition, portal design or marketing the overall service; they all saw themselves in the vanguard of multimedia.

With the broadband access products in the hands of BT's local market facing units, the vision for BT Openworld was that of developer and operator of a multi-access portal (MAP), the brainchild of the division's newly installed CEO who had previously overseen all the groupwide strategy work and for whom, in his first senior operational role, this was a personal mission. Today MAPs exist as the default design across the internet, with websites accessed seamlessly, globally, via both fixed and mobile networks and devices, but at the turn of the century it was an ambitious and audacious objective: a portal available anytime, anyplace, anywhere.

It felt like a leap of faith. To bring together an international set of disparate businesses onto a global set of common technologies and platforms, and provide a core set of content channels and applications, was a hugely challenging goal; even to get your mind around it was a stretch. While much of the initial scoping work for this type of project had already taken place, led by the GIM team, it would still take the combined efforts of the best brains across the BT Openworld unit several months to get to a detailed implementation plan.

This would effectively involve unpicking much of the existing commercial and technical infrastructure and rebuilding it in a new and integrated guise. While it was a triumph of intellectual prowess and visionary leadership, sadly that was all it would remain, as circumstances would shortly intervene to prevent its full realisation. But you couldn't fault the ambition, the culmination of which would have then put it on a par with Yahoo! and even the emergent Google.

We remained based at BT Centre. With the restructuring of the Group, some members of my previous team had moved on to other parts of the company. I was now given a budget for five people and set about filling the vacancies. I was amazed at how quickly word had spread of my appointment and I was inundated with CVs and recommendations before I had even had a chance to advertise the roles. While broadband, hosting and IP networking were as central to BT's internet strategy as the ISP business, it was this latter element, the core of the BT Openworld unit, its *raison d'etre*, which constituted the familiar face of the internet and personified its lure and that of the ephemeral phenomenon of multimedia. Everyone wanted a piece of this, it seemed, and I rapidly had the team up to full strength.

Our role as a department was to provide direct project support to initiatives identified and led by a business development team which reported directly to the CEO and was thereby guaranteed a flow of interesting work. This team was headed up by Nick, whom I had worked with in New York on the abortive hosting acquisition. We quickly knitted our respective teams together, and diarised a set of social events to ensure we remained a united force. We neither of us had spent a great deal of time managing people, so we just followed our instincts and copied best practices from previous bosses we had worked for. Monthly evenings in City pubs and quarterly dinners in the West End seemed to do the trick. The fact BT was picking up the tab may also have helped.

Despite the widespread disruption across the TMT sector and the steady implosion of the dot.com dream, we were continuously approached by start-ups and would-be partners to review their business models and investment proposals, with a view to BT taking a financial stake in them. We spent the majority of our time turning opportunities away: for instance, a well known high street music retailer which wanted to set up a web-based shop, but selling CDs; they didn't appear to have heard of downloads, which even in 2000 were beginning to take off. We really didn't fancy getting involved in a business sending CDs through the post. Eventually, a couple of projects did command our attention, and we shifted up a gear.

★

First up was a dot.com that insisted it wasn't. wCities was a travel guide to the top one hundred cities around the world. It was run by a small team of designers and programmers, based in a basement warren of small offices situated behind Hyde Park

Corner in central London. The MD of this setup had devised a clever model for the business whereby the text, photography and reviews were all produced by people local to the cities in question, and published onto the main website, in exchange for the ability to credit the piece to their own name. In this way, the company had rapidly and at minimal expense built a catalogue of major city portraits stretching across Europe, the Americas and Asia.

They now planned to embark on a second tier of a further two hundred cities, and this development, together with an enhanced marketing budget, would require an injection of new investment capital. The content generated would be used to provide major portals such as Google and Yahoo! with a "white-label" travel channel, onto which they could paste their own branding and web navigation tools. This was of particular interest to us as a potential source of unique content for our mobile web portal, Genie, and as a potential synergy with a ground-breaking location-based advertising and promotional service which it was then researching. The team at wCities were competent, commercially minded, and ahead of the curve.

The business case was justified by the additional payments that the major portals would make in respect of the service as the city coverage expanded, defined as a share of the revenues they themselves would generate from advertising on their travel channels. To what extent this was not a dot.com was lost on me. I could see they themselves were not depending directly on advertising revenues, but since they were simply getting a slice of Google's or Yahoo!'s own advertising revenues, it surely amounted to very much the same thing. I chose not to labour the point, and irrespective of the sophistry at play, we recommended the investment on the basis of usage of the content at favourable rates for our own existing portals.

A word on internet valuations. Whilst we were diligent in our application of cash flow based valuation methodologies, these remained largely abstracted from reality in the sense that the future revenue and margin streams, and hence the cash flow forecasts themselves, were a step into the unknown. One could make assumptions, and check these based on common sense and experience, but the truth was that the comparators employed were themselves often not yet proven. You not only assumed take-up of your product, but you also assumed that the product you were forecasting would remain a realistic alternative to the comparator you were using as a benchmark. This was a source of substantial risk. Having completed one business case, you would then justify subsequent cases for investment by reference to the original case, thereby heaping risk on risk. This became known as "drinking your own bath water". It wasn't very difficult to see all this as a pack of cards, but when it did come crashing down, there may still be a couple of aces worth holding, it was just that nobody could predict what they might be. It was all a colossal gamble.

It was against this backdrop that I was invited up to the Labs to give a lecture covering the process and content for producing a business case, to a hundred or so students enrolled on a BT-sponsored masters degree course in telecoms. It was exquisite timing, since at the time the values of most of the projects I had ever been involved in were barrelling south. I prepared and presented my materials assiduously: a solemn explanation of the economic ins and outs, a magisterial discourse on identifying and mitigating risks, and a masterclass in the techniques of persuasion. As I stepped from the lectern, I caught the course administrator's eye. "How do you think it went?" I asked him.

"Really couldn't say. I didn't understand a word of it. But you've got great stage presence." It was the best back-handed compliment I have ever received.

In the case of wCities, the investment was for a ten per cent stake initially, which gave us no management rights but at least allowed us a couple of seats and a voice in the boardroom, alongside the rest of the crew who were also flying blind. The company managed to sign a few minor portal deals over the following year or two, but while these were seen as at least providing a foot in the door, in reality that door was slowly closing on niche specialist providers. Bigger, traditional travel companies with deep pockets were turning to the web, along with newcomers with a wider commercial proposition that included ticketing and accommodation. The market space wCities had identified slowly disappeared. It was in some ways a salutary investment from a learning perspective (the proposition was simply too narrow) and as with most dot.coms, it eventually proved a financial write-off. My career on the lecture circuit was also in ruins.

★

It became the fashion amongst metropolitan millennial trendsetters to nurture mysterious looking swags and patches of facial hair. Worn ironically, these sought to place the wearer at the epicentre of dot.com culture, a hipster who represented all that was funky about the net, while bestowed with gravitas and savvy business sense. Never slow to seize the zeitgeist, I too grew a vertical streak of unconvincing beard. It hung beneath my lower lip like a bristly barcode, the latest token of my maverick ways. It bewitched my young sons for several months, but few others. It was when a colleague pronounced it "a less than adequate lady pleaser" that I thought better of it and shaved it off. I would have to assert my creative credentials through more practical endeavours.

BT's UK consumer business was keen on following its own version of the multimedia dream. Notwithstanding the cable television debacle of the late eighties, the perceived nirvana of piping television programmes over BT's network and into people's homes had never died a complete death. Regulatorily banned from using the copper telephone network to distribute television signals since the early days of privatisation, the sanction was due for review in 2001 and this had already started focusing minds on the wider opportunities it might entail. As a consequence, voices were now clamouring for a television portal, which would enable downloads and streaming from a digitised catalogue of programming, thereby circumventing the regulatory limitations and laying the foundations of a wider television play. This latter initiative would eventually materialise with the delivery of the new broadband network but in the meantime steps should be taken to position BT as a player in digital television.

OnDigital was an ITV-backed consortium which had recently won a licence to broadcast digital channels over the UK's terrestrial television network. As British Digital Broadcasting (BDB) it had actually been launched in partnership with Sky, before the satellite broadcaster had subsequently been forced out by the regulator on competition grounds. The rump organisation was now forced to go head to head with them. OnDigital was struggling to grow its subscriber numbers and now wished to bring in new investment capital to finance a major promotional push.

Their requirement, and the ambitions of BT, came together in a cutely crafted proposal put together by Nick's team, whereby BT would buy a significant minority stake in OnDigital and, under the shareholder agreement, the ITV companies who owned OnDigital would commit to invest in a fifty-fifty joint venture television portal with BT. The latter was as yet unformed, indeed the concept of a terrestrial television portal would actually remain a twinkle in the eye for several years; this brought the focus ever closer onto BT's proposed acquisition.

The OnDigital business plan had proved expensive to execute. In common with many new TMT ventures, it had relied on a "land grab" strategy, investing substantial cash initially in an attempt to take as big a share of the market, as quickly as possible, and only then seek to monetise it, to fund further growth and eventually make a return. In the case of OnDigital, this land grab had come in the form of free set top boxes, issued to customers who would then be persuaded to subscribe for various digital channels, to provide a revenue stream. The numbers applying for the boxes were lower then originally anticipated, while take-up of the services had also been disappointing.

Nevertheless, their forecasts for future months showed a sharp acceleration in both metrics which, they believed, justified a valuation of the whole business in excess of one and a half billion pounds. This was surely la-la land. A few iterations of the plan were carried out in partnership with BT, but our concerns kept coming back to the unexplained nature of the forces that were apparently going to turn this business around. The deal was going nowhere and frustrations were beginning to be aired on both sides.

An executive meeting was called, and attended by many of the ITV management board, names and faces I was familiar with from the media pages of the UK press. It was all sweetness and light: the shared objectives were reviewed and agreed upon, the prospect of a portal eulogised as the golden goose, but in the meantime couldn't we just get on with doing the Ondigital transaction? They were somewhat oblivious to the details of the forecasts and weren't overly concerned about them. They believed it was simply too good an opportunity for BT to turn down; too good an opportunity for us to join their club; that BT would sign up to anything if it meant we had television to our name. To an extent they were right, but there was no way Nick and I could in all conscience recommend a stake in their venture at the price being asked.

We went round the houses on it for a further couple of weeks. In a final attempt to square the circle, and accompanied by our M&A lawyer, Rob, I went to OnDigital to see their lead planner. The company was based in the exotically designed Marco Polo building, the former home of the satellite television disaster British Satellite Broadcasting, which had gone bust a decade earlier. It was scarcely an auspicious precedent. I tried one last time to get a plausible rationale for his view of the forecast, and got the same stock response – the next promotional push would drive up the subscriber numbers – only this time with a new twist: take-up would begin to accelerate once the "network effect" took hold.

This suggested that while small numbers took the product initially, as the total numbers of subscribers gradually increased, they would create within a fixed population an ever growing share with an ever greater voice, which would only cause the numbers of new subscribers to grow and the overall number of subscribers to swell exponentially. It would, in effect, "go viral".

I slumped into my seat as I listened to this delusional presumptious claptrap. It took no account of the quality of the product on offer, the impact of likely competitor actions, let alone what viewers might be willing to pay for it. It was a spreadsheet driven off a complex theoretical algorithm, and as far as we could see it bore no relation at all to the workings of the UK pay television market. To cap things off, he had reworked his numbers and the valuation had now soared in excess of two billion pounds. He left us to our deliberations.

As the door closed behind him, Rob and I turned to one another and burst into spontaneous laughter. We swapped our abject disbelieving views, agreed the deal was dead then called him back in, made our excuses and left. Following a rebranding as ITVDigital, it would eventually close a couple of years later; the mooted network effect had never materialised. There was no basis for it to go viral, although its investors did catch a nasty cold.

★

Even if we had lost our marbles and recommended BT should pursue the OnDigital investment, there is little or no chance it would ever have come to pass. For something rather horrific had been happening to the state of BT's balance sheet. Through 1999-2000, the company had continued and accelerated its belated spree on European and Asian mobile operators by, for example, increasing its stakes in its Spanish and Japanese ventures. Its obliged strategy of paying top whack in cash rather than in shares had been taking its financial toll. On top of this, BT had bid for the next generation 3G mobile licences in UK, Germany and the Netherlands, countries where it was also progressively buying out its minority partners. The licences alone would add a hefty eight billion to the cash outgoings. In no time at all, the debt on the company's books had rocketed to something approaching thirty billion pounds, with an annual interest price tag in excess of a billion pounds, payable in cash. It made our internet investment aspirations look like a start-up in a garage.

It might have looked more sensible had the investments not largely been confined to second and third-rate operators; indeed Cellnet was then running fourth in the race to gain new subscribers in the UK. In the wake of the challenge provided by Vodafone's bravado, BT was driving itself into the ground. The

Group's finance director was sacked and the chairman finally deposed, albeit cravenly driven into a sidetrack marked "president emeritus". A new chairman was installed and a plan to clear the debt hastily drawn up. All bets were now off.

The full horror of the financials for BT Openworld were now laid bare for all to see. They had quietly been pieced together by our accounting colleagues to reveal annualised losses that year of four hundred and fifty million pounds; the colour drained from our cheeks. How on earth had that come about? The division seemed to have been created simply as a waste bucket for all the most financially stricken internet enterprises the company had touched during the previous few years. The writing was clearly on the wall for this organisation, and for most of its constituent parts. Not for nothing was the unit now tagged Openwound, since there would surely be blood everywhere.

I explained the full, ghastly story to my team, coupled with the unsurprising news that the entire division was urgently being wound down and that our jobs were going. However, as this was BT, there would be no compulsory redundancies, new jobs would be found for us all – those that wanted them – and means would be available to assist those who wished to leave the company. Unsurprisingly, few of them did, the Openworld meltdown but a symptom of the wider TMT implosion. Opportunities across the wider sector had dried up markedly.

It was a remarkable outcome. A division that had been responsible for some of the worst excesses of corporate mismanagement, and that had gone to sleep at the wheel, was being wound up, and yet nobody was actually going to pay for it with their job. None of the senior management, none of the staff. It was true that the vast bulk of the business had been inherited originally from other BT organisations; they weren't wholly our mistakes. But we were still in charge of them now, as they were falling apart and crumbling between our fingers.

Yet, after some fifteen years of privatised existence, let alone twenty years of the "Thatcherisation" of the economy, we were going to get off scot free. We were saved by our gold plated employment contracts, at that time so loaded in our favour that it would have cost the company yet more millions to get rid of us all, cash it no longer had. So while investors and competitors bayed for our blood, it was deemed better to have most of us stay, and start to work our way out of it.

The organisation had lasted for all of twelve months. Nine months settling it down and then three months shutting it down, to the slimmest management layer required to oversee those residual businesses which would take a bit longer to exit or close for good. This residue was then hurriedly shuffled across into BT's UK consumer business, where it continued to wither on its acrid vine, but with the numbers now thankfully subsumed within those of the far larger, profitable core network activities. In an ironic twist, it was eventually offered a lifeline by being submerged into Yahoo!'s UK business. But my BT career had no such means of escape and would never quite recover, having faced its own darkest and sorriest hour.

10

In the Eye of the Storm

In the early months of 2001, there was the palpable stench of mortality lingering over BT, with press and analyst coverage speculating over the potential demise of one of Britain's once leading companies, and forecasting an almost unprecedented scale of destruction in shareholder value, as one by one the company's business units brought nothing but grief to its financial standing. A drastic plan had been hastily cobbled together by the incoming chairman, which aimed to bring some sense of order to the balance sheet. But it would take time to implement a series of disposals, organise a rights issue, spin out the mobile arm, and arrange the sale and leaseback of the company's property empire. BT would thus remain in the eye of the storm for several years, during which time the entire TMT sector suffered its own severe recession, a downturn in fortunes on a par at least with that of the early 1990s. And, as then, I planned to hunker down below deck and brace myself for what I guessed would be a few years of choppy seas.

So extreme were the group's financial difficulties that, in a moment of self-laceration, BT Centre itself, the flagship headquarter building, was put up for sale. I ambled around the emptying unlit floors, enveloped by voices, smells and noises from my past associations with its cluttered corners. I had an overwhelming impression of being the last to leave, of turning out the last few lights and pulling a cover over its wanton failures.

But the sale would not proceed; once the chairman had laid eyes upon the proposed replacement as his corporate headquarters, a pink tinged, down-at-heel rookery that heaped disrepute, even then, on Holborn Circus, he rapidly undertook an urgent reappraisal and reversed his earlier decision. Some semblance of sanity was being preserved.

With the imminent demise of Openworld out in the open, we all started to cast around for our next appointments. There was a notionally managed process of redeployment in place for those without the gumption to jump ship, but placing any faith in this to redeem your career prospects was not ideal. It was every man and woman for themselves.

Claire, ever the avid networker, was swiftly appointed as CFO of a nascent technology services organisation, provisionally badged as TechCo. I was keen again on a role outside of finance and, based on her own researches, she recommended I had a chat with a chap who had had some recent success in setting up a technology incubator at BT's Labs, which would form a commercial arm of the TechCo business. He was apparently looking for development expertise to help establish a number of start-up companies. This was all very in-vogue at the time, and sounded ideal for me, based on my numerous experiences with new business ventures, so I made an appointment to meet him at his offices on the outskirts of Ipswich.

I had been aware of various internal announcements regarding the establishment of the TechCo organisation, which came to be branded BT Exact. It struck me initially as an example of a division that emerged from the personal ambitions of a handful of senior executives, rather than as a measured response to a specific market development or operational requirement. There was always a group of chancers who dreamed of having their own organisational toy, in this case in the remote backwoods of leafy Suffolk. Its creation was also cleverly timed to consolidate the technical departments from the newly established BT divisions, or "lines of business" as they were now styled. Henceforth, these LoBs would buy in Exact's services on a commercial, arm's length basis, as and when required, rather than maintain these resources as fulltime overheads on their own books. So, everyone was happy.

Exact was charged with three main areas of commercial growth: providing expert technical support to BT's market facing LoBs on bids, tenders and ongoing contracts; designing new technologies and products for commercial exploitation by the LoBs; and exploiting, through licensing and start-up businesses, BT's abundant inventory of technology patents. Some fourteen thousand of these had been filed by, and granted to, BT engineers over the previous decades, and were still being added to every month. Exact's highly effective PR story led you to believe that there was literally billions of pounds worth of untapped value lurking amongst these gems, so there was a fair wind behind the incubation project right from the start.

The incubator itself, branded Brightstar, was specifically set up to create and launch start-up companies which would develop and market component technologies: products that were not central to BT's own strategy, but which BT itself and other telecom operators would purchase and consume in the production and delivery of their commercial service portfolios. Brightstar had gained some favourable PR coverage of its own, with the recent launch of two companies together with the announcement of a substantial pipeline of other prospective businesses which were due to emerge into the wider world over the coming months. It was all very good news indeed.

Now, I had had various dealings in the past with members of BT's technology brigade, the lads from the Labs. I had found most of them drenched in an otherworldliness, engrossed in an academic process of research and discovery that was quite devoid of commercial concern or constraint. A few with their wits about them had sought my assistance in producing business cases and plans during my time in the internet and multimedia world, and had demonstrated at least the beginnings of a grip on financial matters and the cause of generating value. I travelled from Liverpool Street station in hope that these were the sorts behind the incubator companies.

I arrived for my interview with the director of Brightstar, Harry, a bumptious Mancunian with a sunny disposition which, as I discovered later, belied a steely ruthlessness. He described the business as a bit of a cottage industry (another one) at the present time, but given the scope of the opportunity before them he wanted to "industrialise the process". There would be several aspects to this: sponsoring pure research activities; working with the developers to identify and target specific business needs; building up a cadre of prospective members of company management teams; and putting in place a network of partners and investors who would work with BT to finance and advise the new businesses as they grew and then fled the nest. It was all very ambitious and would likely take a few years to come fully to fruition, but it did sound interesting. I pitched some ideas around developing the companies' business planning activities, standardising commercial models and practices and so on, and we found ourselves agreeing that I should take this on as a twelve month project reporting to him and with my time split equally between the Labs and London.

★

For a *soi disant* Londoner like myself, who had always worked in the central districts of the capital, the notion of a one hundred mile commute was not altogether attractive, although in fairness the burden would be mercifully eased in no small measure through the services of a four star hotel on the bosky fringes of the town. The Labs were but a short taxi ride out into the sumptuous Suffolk countryside, based at a self-consciously designated campus style location known as Adastral Park. A campus in aspiration only at the time, it was dominated visually by a collection of faceless, Soviet-style blocks, and from the approach road the entire place resembled nothing short of a Stalinist era correction centre.

I arrived on my first Monday drained by my train and taxi journey. Through a window into the main office, I saw Harry up on his feet, mid-presentation, so I walked in on what turned out to be the weekly kick-off meeting for the entire incubator. Seeing me slide in at the back, Harry lurched from his chosen subject to beckon me to the front and introduce me as the new commercial manager. Narrowing his eyes, and in a show of what I soon came to understand as his preferred style of management – that of the Inquisition – he asked me to say a few words myself by way of introduction. As an amateur theatrical type, with a penchant for extemporising, I didn't come off too badly, but even as the meeting broke up I sensed it was going to be an interesting ride with this guy, whom I had already marked down as a wily and likely formidable operator.

I met the chief technical officer (CTO) of the incubator, Chris, a wild haired, highly charged boffin of the first order who, judging by what I learned about his domestic arrangements, appeared to inhabit a camper van parked up in a layby a few miles along the A14 highway. I imagine he would have been happy living anywhere, so oblivious to the world around him did he seem. For his work was his life, which had even then amounted to an extraordinary track record in technological innovations, including fibre optics and cellular radio. While it would be pushing it to say he was solely responsible for creating today's foremost communications infrastructures, it would be fair to note he had had more than simply a helping hand in bringing about most of them.

He introduced me to a charming chap called Nick, who described himself simply as "the CMO". Seeing my quizzical frown, he kindly explained this stood for chief marketing officer, a soubriquet I had not chanced upon to that point, and nor have I since, truth be told. Nick was the market analyst and was assisting the incubator companies with their market planning and product strategies. Where Chris was brusque and edgy, Nick was calmness itself and as smooth as the cashmere jacket that floated over the back of his chair. Blithely swinging it over his shoulder, he ushered me through his door and into the atrium of the building for a tour of the offices where the incubator was going about its business.

Buoyed by their initial success in spinning out a couple of well received technology-based companies, and with a brace of leading venture capital houses now party to the process, Brightstar had hurriedly sought to maintain momentum and had brought in several new aspiring entities following an unsurprisingly feisty internal PR campaign. They had been inundated with proposals, and between them, Harry, Nick and Chris had whittled the selection on offer down to the half dozen teams that were now housed within the incubator building.

There were two mature units which had been providing innovative support services to parts of BT for a few years, respectively managing revenue assurance and mobile workforces, and the Brightstar team believed there were prospects of these entities offering equivalent services to other telecoms operators. Then there were two brand new ventures, each developing specialist features for cellular networks: a mobile scheduling package and a location-based tracking system, which in combination, and with other as yet unknown mobile technologies, could potentially form management platforms for the logistics industry. Finally, there were two specific telecoms breakthrough technologies which I could immediately relate to, which were all about clever and efficient transmission and control of video content as it moved around the internet.

In all, it was rather a motley collection, with some potential surely, but the lack of an overarching structure and strategic focus served to explain Harry's view of it as an opportunistic cottage industry. The scale of the challenge to industrialise it was becoming clearer.

★

Harry was keen to get the changes to the model of his business under way. He wanted to see a pipeline that stretched back into the research pool and gave him a continuous flow of projects coming into the incubator. Working with Exact's head of research, we developed a gating model, whereby an initial idea, if it got through the first gate – as a potential breakthrough, patentable idea that was not core to BT – would become a Brightstar sponsored research project.

After a specific seed funding period had elapsed, the project would be reassessed at the second gate, for further development finance, to enable it to work on clarifying the precise business need it would ultimately fulfil. It would then be assessed again at the third gate, as to whether it should in fact go through the core BT development channels, or whether it would come into the incubator, or whether the market opportunity was insufficient to warrant further investment in which case it should be stopped altogether.

It was a simple but effective model and would give us at any point an assessment of the state of the pipeline and the level of funding required to bring a given set (or target number) of proposals to fruition. Meanwhile, and in parallel, I was reviewing the business plans of the existing start-ups and assisting them in firming up their financial projections. I then consolidated those plans into a three year view for the incubator portfolio of companies as a whole.

So, we now had both sides of the coin; the costs to research and develop the ideas in the first place, and then the further investment required to turn these projects into real and usable products and services before the teams involved were spun out of the incubator as fully fledged, fully capitalised companies. I also did some analysis on the numbers and types of people that would need to be involved to keep the whole show on the road.

It rapidly became clear to me that, as presently constituted, Brightstar's industrialisation and growth plan was not realistically going to happen. In its present guise and format, it was hugely dependent on significant sums of BT's cash, on Exact's limited pool of management resource, and on the finite levels of technical expertise which were actually needed to keep the main businesses of BT ticking over. Brightstar was not a core business unit itself for BT, but a non-core means of exploiting existing, new and related patented technologies. That being the case, in any environment it would really struggle to get its hands on the financial and human resources necessary to deliver its plan. It needed more radical changes to its business model. And given the tightening financial pressures BT was then operating under, it needed to do so quickly if its ambitions were not to end up on the shelf.

With Harry's blessing, I spent a morning up in London with the corporate financier who had overseen the previous two Brightstar spin-outs. I explained the dilemma, we went through various financing and partnership options, and I came away with a very clear impression of the only conceivable strategy open to us: we would need to spin out the incubator itself. Do a Brightstar on Brightstar.

★

As a major employer in the East of England, and with the emblematic presence of its laboratories in the area, BT was lauded as a major player within the regional economy and among its investment and development communities. This burnished the somewhat puffed up egos of many of the leading characters at Adastral Park who saw themselves, rather misguidedly it seemed to me, as local barons of industry. There were regular dinners, black tie affairs, where eccentric parochial notions such as the "Ipswich corridor" of enterprise and economic development were earnestly debated with big cheeses of East Anglian commerce. The inevitable accompanying PR releases covering these events were avidly cut and pasted into the local press, thereby confirming in the minds of the squires of the BT Labs their rightful place among the Fenlands' business elite.

This abiding and rather endearing big fish, small pond blind spot made my pitch to Harry and his boss, another Mancunian, all the more plausible and welcome. So convinced had they become of their "right to play", so imprisoned were they by their own PR, that the idea of spinning out the incubator as a separate business would play very neatly to their shared narcissism. I seasoned the proposal with a dash of spice, suggesting an equity partnership with a specialist technology fund, and this sealed the deal. "Great work, son," I heard from Harry, and Project Sirius was immediately established. The spin-out was under way.

I was by now a regular guest at my hotel on the green fringes of Ipswich. It was a smart, aspirationally posh establishment, its hankering for top drawer recognition borne out by the sight (and sound) of two ridiculous peacocks strutting around the gardens. Pleasingly, the rooms were clean and functionally styled, the public areas only mildly old boy stuffy, and the bar a tangible if modest step up from a spit and sawdust local boozer. It was in the restaurant, though, where the management had truly lost the plot.

The menu was a tribute to misguided provincial notions of sophistication, and the food their woeful realisation. Every dish was an over elaborate contrivance, a discomfiting melange of flavours and textures, temperatures and colours. The meat, always served slightly too cool; the vegetables, so undercooked they almost made my gums bleed. It was a clumsy misunderstanding of *cuisine*. I would order pudding, in hope of finally stuffing myself. More pretentiousness: a plate spattered in brightly coloured sugary swirls.

One evening, as I again resigned my cutlery prematurely to the edge of my plate, a work colleague in black tie sidled up to my table. "What a place, eh? Like one of your swanky London joints," he ventured.

"Something like that," I assured him. "So, another bigshot dinner. Who is it this time, Bill Gates? Branson? The Mayor of Southwold?"

"Fuck off," he smirked, and tweaking the ends of his tie he strode off towards the private dining room. I intended to heed his words, but not quite yet.

★

I had been getting a little tetchy with my small town, small company mission, and was relieved when my role was urgently transitioned onto the commercial strategy for the spin-out:

devising the proposition, business plan and investment case that we would present to our prospective partner.

Some consultants materialised out of thin air to polish it up as a sales prospectus, and armed with it they sought out potential investors. Incredibly, and to everyone's surprise they came good almost immediately, announcing that their invitation to the CEO, CTO and COO of one of the world's largest technology funds, Francisco Partners (FP) had been accepted and that they and their team would be flying in from Silicon Valley the following month to discuss a potential deal. We had four weeks to get the incubator business into shape for a sale.

This was going to be a real test on several levels: the commercial acumen of the team running the incubator, the commercial viability of the start-ups within the incubator itself, and, above all, our collective ability to come to a workable and commercially sound deal that was in BT's interests. Within days, a letter of intent arrived, setting out how FP saw our two organisations working together to create value. They clearly meant business.

I was in London on the day FP flew in and greeted David, the CEO, at BT Centre. A short and unassuming type, in slightly too tight-fitting preppy clothing, the only clues to his gigantic prosperity were a deep tan and fresh, unlined features. He had requested meetings with senior executives from BT's global IT business units, clients for some of the propositions being developed in the incubator, and I had arranged these. The conversations were more wide-rangeing than anticipated, covering BT's global plans, the levels of support received from Exact, and on-going issues over the company's wider financial position. A few hours later I handed him over to his driver and watched as the car pulled away and blended into the evening traffic. He had intrigued me.

The following morning, due diligence activities began with

a tour of the incubator and meetings with the members of the start-up companies, but the FP team seemed distracted, and insisted on a tour of the whole Park. Ever obliging, Nick took them off, leaving FP's financial analyst with me to go through the business plan numbers. After an exhaustive review, he asked for a copy of the Brightstar accounts. With these in his hand, he then casually asked for those of Exact. At this, the penny dropped. The talk of "two organisations" working together; the discussions in London about funding Exact and its relations with the rest of BT; the desire to understand the financial position of the division. These were clearly the prelude to an offer being made for the whole of Exact. The consultants had gulled FP into believing we were planning to sell off the whole of BT's technology division.

But had they really been brought in by Harry and the Exact CEO to sell off the organisation that they themselves had designed and built in the first place? Was the Brightstar sale really a smokescreen for the bigger prize; a sprat to catch a mackerel? I had to hand it to them: if that was their plan all along, they had played a blinder.

But the dream, if indeed that's what it was, would not come true. Thorough in their diligence, FP soon learned that any wider deal would not win favour with senior executives across the BT Group. Exact had been created to generate all those billions of pounds, to help plug the gap in BT's balance sheet. And the company could never part with the crown jewels of the Labs. Indeed, these jewels were viewed in some quarters as nothing short of a national treasure, their heritage to be retained in British ownership at all costs.

Over and above this, FP themselves were unhappy with the quality of the virtually non-existent contracts that governed business between Exact and BT's other lines of business, and those between the incubator start-ups and the BT units they serviced. Finally, the terms FP would insist upon in relation to funding the business as an unproven entity were eye-wateringly onerous, and by the end of the week the deals, both large and small, were off.

In some respects, this was regrettable, since there was little doubt FP would have been an incredibly competent and wealthy partner, and BT would have learned a lot from them. But it was not to be, and with the passing of this deal into history my twelve months in Ipswich were up. It had flown by, but I had had quite enough commuting and, having put feelers out into BT's various strategic planning communities, I was due to move on. I thanked Harry for the ride; it had been an eventful year and I now wanted to build on the experience.

We parted on good terms. We had worked well together: he gave me the freedom to roam beyond my initial remit, and I had cut the key to his own prospective departure. Exact eventually completed a follow-up deal to spin out the incubator the following year. Both Harry and Chris went with it, and were still there ten years later, having made a very nice living from it too from what I gathered. The now former Exact CEO was on their investment board too, alongside a retired CEO of BT Group no less. So the boys from Manchester got what they wished for in the end, with a bit of help from me.

★

My second year of managed hiatus would not be quite so enervating. I was keen to get back into BT's global business, which had been reconstituted and rebranded as BT Global Services (BT GS) following a severe and ongoing retrenchment. A call into a fellow ex-mobile stalwart who had overseen the

Swiss bid a few years earlier, and was now engaged upon the seemingly endless restructuring of BT GS, left me with the distinct impression it remained a grief stricken place and needed at least a further year's work to knock it into a sustainable shape. I needed another interim assignment to tide me over.

There were always finance roles available in BT; this was doubtless due to the largely inhospitable nature of the function, the essentially tedious nature of the core roles, and its hard earned reputation for ineffectual and often abrasive man management. I swerved a couple of opportunities to become a financial controller and made my way instead to the office of a chap called Steve, the newly appointed director of strategic development in BT's UK wholesale business. This went against every grain and instinct, since I had set my face against the UK core business years before, but I wanted to see through my previously cited and long term personal development objective and try out a business strategy role in a designated strategy department.

Set up to identify and champion new sources of revenue growth, Steve's team had a remit to think radically, and to think big. This casually overlooked the fact it was up against a juggernaut of a business, which had rolled on merrily churning out cash for years. That couldn't go on forever of course, hence the need for some pre-emptive development strategies. But while the cash continued to pile up, the division would exhibit little or no urgency or desire for change. The place had also remained untouched by the more commercialised corporate development mentality that had taken hold of the global business. It was in a time warp.

Interviewed by Steve and his assistant, I apparently came across as confident and determined, someone who would make a difference. Kind words indeed, but which reckoned without the inert mass of the legacy business and its lack of appetite for experiment, on which my own determination was crucially predicated. We were all in for a major disappointment.

Over the course of the next twelve months, I would lead a couple of analysis projects in support of the wider business planning activity, and then as part of a wider revenue challenge programme picked up a specific commercialisation project. But it was a hit and miss affair. I had no expertise in the wholesale business, so I tended to stick to more generic and detached short term analysis projects where I could demonstrate my skills to best effect, while my limited sector-specific knowledge would remain unexposed. Identifying these niches is a skill in itself, and is considered vital amongst all serious corporate survivors. I had spent time working alongside a number of them down the years, and now I would deploy what I had observed: how they sought to make themselves temporarily useful, while quietly scanning the horizons for more meaningful and appropriate openings.

My first project was to conduct an environmental scan, a grand description for an analysis of the political, economic, social and technological forces at play, commonly described as a PEST analysis. These are notoriously difficult to carry out effectively, since there is no right answer as such and no limit to how far it can go. I stuck to a ten year time horizon, got as far as ten key points in each quadrant, then drew my conclusions and recommendations from the perceived interplay between them.

I forecast, among other things, that just as the government in the 1980s withdrew from direct economic activity via privatisation, so it would in the 2010s withdraw from the direct provision of a range of public services, due to unsustainable financial pressures. And so therefore, for example, public service networks, which BT builds and maintains for most government departments, should henceforth be built with open access capability to create flexibility and avoid the need for duplicated investments.

My second project looked into the wholesale business model, another notoriously open-ended arena of enquiry and speculation. My researches revealed that a vast majority of the wholesale revenue at the time remained, as it would for some time to come, a bounty of monopolistic riches, which might potentially stifle UK innovation and undermine the country's ability to compete. Spinning out the local access network into a quite separate company would get the regulators off our back and free up a flow of new investment into fibre and broadband access. I cannot in any way claim that this ultimately gave birth to BT's Openreach "last mile" copper network business unit; in truth, it was simply a way of crowbarring various lessons I had learned on my commercial journey thereto, in to the strategic discussions surrounding the development of BT's core network business. My survivalist instincts were in fine fettle.

One of the mindless perks associated with this role was the opportunity for more aimless trips to the English countryside, in the futile pursuit of managerial enlightenment. Only in certain quarters had this remained a ritual; those few parts of the business as yet unruffled by competitors' tanks encroaching on their lawns, where there was still time and money to be sent up in smoke. I had quite forgotten how perfectly feasible it was to gull grown-ups into "enhancing the amplitude for creative thinking" by sitting in a circle on the floor and banging some African drums. I sidestepped this charade by opting for a leadership module, which involved a pleasant day's cycling with my boss and others along endless country lanes, taking it in turns to read a map. This was apparently billed as "correlative governance" and we were quite brilliant at it; it was a shame to have to go home.

My third and final project was concerned with the company's property estate. Vast tracts of this were becoming redundant, as people continued to leave the company in droves and the volume and scale of network equipment was shrinking by the year. Following the Brightstar model of exploiting the company's inventory of underemployed intellectual property, I advocated a similarly structured approach should be adopted to re-use the growing inventory of underutilised physical property. Imaginative enough perhaps, it would be doomed eventually on economic grounds.

While I enjoyed the creative process of intellectual challenges, of taking a subject I was not familiar with, subjecting it to anatomical analysis, identifying the likely path to be taken by the various variables and forces, and then making judgments as to the likely outcomes, it all felt far too removed from managing a business, from generating value, and lacking in any real responsibility or accountability. It also struck me as simply egocentric, and I wasn't particularly comfortable with that. While I enjoyed and even relished individual struggle, I was at heart a team player. Above all, it was frustrating.

"A prophet is not welcome in his own town," intoned Barry, an even more beleaguered colleague.

"I hope to be welcomed somewhere else." I retorted, and to my great relief, I finally heard from my Swiss mobile contact, who rang me with the offer of a role on a major BT-wide strategy project he was taking on. Among other things, it was intended to set out the future plan (another one) for the global business. Was I at all interested in joining up with him? I could have kissed him. The clouds were breaking again, at last.

Part Three

Back to a Better Future?

2004 – 2013

11

New Horizons

Spring of 2004 saw BT finally emerging from the tempestuous storm of the TMT recession. I had now worked my through two entire business cycles in my time at BT, and I felt I bore the scars. Thankfully, the wider economic picture was brightening rapidly, and the company's financial position had been steadied, with the chairman's newly famed shopping list of emergency actions now largely accomplished. A new Group CEO was on board and keen to get the company moving forward again. We were re-energised, ready once more for the fight, and with the vast bulk of its debt now repaid, BT Group, as we had been restyled following the rights issue, had options.

We had foregone our mobile business – spun out as O2 – and the company was now looking for new sources of growth. A series of so-called horizontal projects were devised, to work across all the lines of business to create a transformational portfolio of "new wave" products based upon information communication technology (ICT), broadband, a new enriched network for the UK, and software-based communications services globally.

The global business, BT Global Services (BT GS), which I had long regarded as my spiritual home, had been rebuilt from scratch over the previous few years and Paul, my new boss, had been at the very heart of the programme. The global joint venture Concert, having lost a shareholder in MCI, had for a while been reconstituted in partnership with AT&T of the US. A fundamentally flawed concept, and at competitive odds with BT's own Ignite business services unit, Concert II had struggled for barely eighteen months to make any discernible headway, and its earnings had progressively collapsed under enormous price pressures. A last gasp of the previous regime, it had subsequently been wound down as a separate organisation and its people and contracts reintegrated into the two parent organisations.

Within BT GS, this had led to further downsizings, as duplicate functions were removed and operational delivery of major contracts was outsourced. This had actually left BT GS looking a pretty smart bruiser of a business. There was a growing confidence about it too, both internally and in the wider market, and a sense that it was back on the right track. In particular, it was growing strongly in its new core areas of global IP networking and corporate IT services. But it still retained a significant reliance on its traditional telephony and data services. It would be an obvious home for the prospective new wave activities.

★

Of the various projects on offer, the ICT initiative was for me the most obvious source of interest, as it looked at IT, IP networking and data centre services, all of which built on my experiences of digital networking and the internet; plus it had the international angle. Over the following year, it evolved into a project to redefine the entire strategy for the next wave of growth for BT GS, onto what came to be known as networked IT services. Comprised of representatives from each line of business, it looked to refashion the product portfolio and the means of selling it, to embrace a more consultative approach, which would treat customers as clients; it would lead them on a journey that BT would design and construct for them. It was a step up.

We began an audit of the vast range of ICT and related activities across the Group. In the five years since I had carried out a similar exercise on IP, it had grown like Topsy, progressively displacing revenues from many of the older technologies. There was now a wide range of IP product developments taking place, some of which were coordinated and joined up. But there were also a substantial number that had popped up opportunistically in the most unexpected places and which needed therefore to be wrested back into the mainstream. The groupwide urge to experiment, which emanated from our previous promptings to grow into the internet space, had unleashed a haphazard and uncoordinated approach, which took in all of BT's target markets and product sets.

Bringing all the information together, let alone trying to manage it, was a formidable task in itself. Once completed, it served to identify those areas where we were strong and where only small steps had been taken. Strategically, it made sense to rationalise the portfolio, concentrate on the areas which played to our strengths, and bring it under a unified management structure. This was the task we now set ourselves.

★

A chap was drafted in from Microsoft to assume leadership and direction over this key phase of activity. Brought in by a BT board member who had for years strategically placed his own people around the company as part of his shameless career crusade, Gordon proudly proclaimed his heritage. Ten years at IBM and ten years at Microsoft. He intended to conclude his career in triumph, with ten years at BT. He pointed out how he had achieved instant, rapid success in his previous jobs, and clearly foresaw something similar with us.

Bright and innovative, he advocated a shift to software-based services; devised, designed and implemented by professional services consultants. He was initially given a polite and serious listening, if only because he was not fully understood; the step up to applications and content management was gaining traction only slowly in BT. The company remained at heart a networks business: while it was happiest providing IP and networked IT, it was also happy to leave the froth and the cream of value added services to others.

Gordon's simplistic central assumption was that everything in BT worked, and effectively, which was nice for us to hear but some way off beam. Our networks were often patched together; systems were suboptimal and uncoordinated; working processes were still highly manual and inefficient. The façade of "telecom grade" as the apotheosis of technical excellence, belied the truth which more accurately reflected the oft-derided best endeavours of the internet philosophy. This ignorance would undermine him and his plan.

The intellectual capacity of BT's management was always stupendous. It needed to be, to keep the vast ship afloat and plot its way through the sheer weight of product and network complexities, let alone the labyrinthine overlays of regulatory and commercial intricacies. Having picked at the holes in his plan, these intellectual brutes piled in and gave him a rude awakening. "Unrealistic and naïve"; an "impatient lightweight after quick wins", where a heavyweight with a longer term horizon was needed. He had been at IBM and Microsoft when they had each been in the right place at the right time, and had merely enjoyed a "monopolist's luck". They gave him both barrels.

His strategy wasn't wrong, the mistake was in envisioning a

giant step forward to the finished article, when it needed to evolve that way over time. For someone with a software background, it is relatively easy to imagine the leap to the next generation, the next release, but to leap from telecoms to software services, with an IT consultancy wrap, was too profound a shift to be either feasible or credible.

Patronised for his past achievements, and despite top executive sponsorship, his path to delivering change in BT was endlessly blocked, and he had neither the nous nor the charisma to make things happen. At root, he just wasn't one of us; his face and his brain didn't fit. Within six months, he was relieved of his burden and found a home in a corporate cubby hole, before disappearing completely a year or so later.

As the project wound towards its conclusion, there was a sense of anti-climax. We had made some progress; the model of IP networks, managed services and professional services had been established in people's minds as an aspiration and a framework for future development. But it was incremental; a half-step forward only on the road to new horizons. And a lingering suspicion remained and was reinforced; that BT was still serving its own needs and views of the world, and this would only change fundamentally as the management and professional caucus evolved: it would not be coerced or encouraged from beyond its cultural walls.

*

With the completion of the ICT project, and with the pragmatic adoption of the main recommendations a qualified formality, BT GS did what it always did when seeking to embed strategic change, and launched a reorganisation. Another major project was launched; known as Connected World, it would create a separate business unit to handle the top two hundred contracts around the world, oversee the integration of several prospective acquisitions, and incorporate all corporate and government sector business from BT's UK division. It was a massive undertaking and would take over a hundred of us almost six months to complete.

Within the new BT GS organisation, all of the overseas businesses were swept into a newly formed unit christened BT International (BTI). This constituted ten geographically designated units, one each for the top eight countries and sub-regions of Europe, plus the US and Asia Pacific. It also included a series of small but important acquisition projects, aimed at filling in a patchwork of geographic and portfolio gaps, to provide a more broadly based platform for future growth.

During the six months of restructuring, three specific projects were completed: the acquisition of the outstanding shares in Albacom, our fixed line venture in Italy; the outright purchase of Radianz, a subsidiary of Reuters which provided its financial services and news network; and the addition of Infonet, a global IP networking provider. These were psychologically important, in that together they constituted the clear intention of the Group once again to expand outside of the UK, and to continue the corporate transformation project that had begun over a decade before. There would be no turning back: BT would not revert to being simply a UK-based utility business.

The nature of the acquisitions was telling. They were overwhelmingly network plays; and for years, the core business pitch would remain that of a network that was broader, richer and deeper than its competitors'. There was no mention of software-based services, although their day would eventually come.

My main contribution to the reorganisation would be to

allocate alphanumeric codes to each of the twenty seven thousand individuals who would work in the new organisation. I am pleased to relate that I recall very little of that time, or of fulfilling that responsibility. But, by the time it was over, in the summer of 2005, we had a newly refurbished global business to present to the world. After five years of grief and hardship, embarrassment and stop-starts, it was proudly unveiled as BT's primary engine for growth.

The restructuring concluded, I was invited along to a boozy evening event laid on in a cavernous old City institution, for those of us involved in the Connected World project. Within half an hour of arriving, I had bumped into probably half a dozen people I had had at least some close contact with during my pre-mobile days in the global business. They had survived the various shakeups, shakeouts and shakedowns and were now busy staking out new roles for themselves in the new organisation.

A couple of them mentioned they were aware of planning vacancies and that I would be well suited to the roles; it was pleasing to still have some form of personal network in place despite all the changes, and I would soon follow up on their recommendations. To cap a rewarding evening, the GS CEO announced we would all receive an extra bonus for our work on the project. Soused in alcohol and shattered from twenty seven thousand encodings, I wearily raised a glass to the coming glories. We were on our way again.

★

As with the global business of ten years previously, we needed a business plan and strategic context to grow this latest collection of worldwide assets, and by leveraging my contact network, I somehow contrived to get myself appointed as head of planning for international operations, as grand a job title as I had ever managed, and found myself responsible for delivering them.

My new boss Neil was himself a colleague from the old global days. We knew each other well and once he was made aware of my availability, he had hurriedly hauled me in to help in sorting out the planning and commercial priorities for the new BTI organisation. He was based in a new office destination, from my perspective: Ambassador House, a scruffy three storey office block adjacent to a telephone exchange building in the shabbier quarters of Paddington, Central London.

Neil's cheery good nature and intellectual detachment left him somewhat oblivious to the state of the place, in particular the carpets, so hideously stained they had seemingly borne witness to ritualised animal slaughter. The lift heaved and churned as though adrift in the cross currents of the English Channel, as it creakingly bore me daily to the third floor where, amidst the leaky eaves and draughty dormers, was to be found the latest central planning hub of BT's global commercial empire.

Under Neil, a practical minded, bright-eyed brainbox, a BT planning role would veer between austere intellectual pursuits, salesmanship and petty organisational tasks which would have raised a sneer from the most junior of assistants. It would range from modelling the future direction of the business, presenting the findings and spinning the outputs, to identifying and nabbing the most appropriate meeting rooms and time slots in people's diaries in which to hold the planning reviews. It was certainly different.

It all had the sense of a decade earlier when we had originally set out on the global journey, but how small those early steps now looked in retrospect. Where previously we were looking at an initial business worth a few hundred million pounds across Europe and beyond, here we were now overseeing a business worth almost three billion pounds in revenue terms, despite all the retrenchment and disposal activity that had taken place over the previous few years. It was comprised of the remnants of various joint ventures set up a decade previously – where BT had in the interim exercised its rights to buy out the partners – plus the latest acquisitions and a smattering of reasonably successful specialist businesses.

Our aspiration now was to increase the size of this international business by fifty per cent over a three year period, which implied an average growth rate of over fifteen per cent a year. These were relatively mature assets now and so that sort of growth rate looked pretty challenging. But it was remarkable how flexible and professional the international teams proved to be, and all around Europe and Asia in particular, they rallied their troops to focus on rapid profitable growth.

The heads of the country operations were a new breed, a distinctly clear eyed, business schooled bunch in their late thirties and early forties, and compared to their chummier, "play it by ear" entrepreneurial predecessors who were involved at the start-up phase, they brought a more measured, analytical and professional approach to their plans. They accepted stretching targets and over time would use the new networked IT portfolio to develop highly customised and effective offerings in their local markets. They were properly and impressively commercial.

The vast majority of the assets that BT had been forced to dispose of in the earlier part of the decade had been mobile businesses, and so on the face of it the majority of the fixed line jigsaw around Europe was still in place. A similar picture prevailed in Asia and America, albeit on a smaller scale. However, a cursory strategic audit revealed a number of inconsistencies and financial issues remained to be solved. Over half of the country businesses were still not cash positive, and remained a significant drain on the company's investment resources.

In addition, the business mix of any one country was quite different to all the others; the level of consistency was astonishingly low. Italy was dominated by small business customers; Germany was predominantly a wholesaler of international services; Spain was a major provider of services to the public sector; France was dominated by a consultancy business.

We planned to tackle the variable country profiles by levelling up their performance in the new arena of networked IT, introducing a new portfolio of IP communications services aimed at major corporates, government departments and businesses. The portfolio itself, a unified set of software-based fixed and mobile voice and data services, had been refined as part of the ICT horizontal activity. The reluctance to adopt these services we had faced earlier was now crumbling as our overseas colleagues saw the opportunities they presented. The costs of developing and launching these was a fraction compared to those of previous generations of similar services and as these fed through into more competitive prices, we witnessed a rapid acceleration in their usage and a gradual turnaround in profitability. If only Gordon had been there to see it.

★

We developed a structured framework for managing the country businesses, with a ranking system of gold, silver and bronze depending on the size of the market, rate of growth of the economy, our market share, the mix of the local product portfolio and the availability of skilled resource. Nothing overly technical or new, but simply a rational approach that could be simply and effectively communicated. These sorts of models have a habit of merely confirming what is already in place and of stating the obvious, and in truth there were few exceptions to this rule on show here.

We left it to the countries and regions to challenge the specific outcomes, but they would prove to be surprisingly sanguine; I suspected, cynically, because they had been through similar processes countless times before and had nonetheless gone ahead with their own self-interested plans regardless of what the models were saying they ought to do.

There was a similar, quiescent response to our proposed approach to planning. We had ten contacts around the world who were the targets for our strategic planning outputs, and the sources of the resultant business plans. We told them the "what" (the product portfolio that would be available over time) and the "how much" (what they needed to achieve in revenue, market share and profits), and they would give us the "how" (the plan as regards client sales, investments, networks and manpower). It was straightforward enough in theory and, as they had been brow beaten for so long, it proved simple enough in practice to attain their compliance. Or so I mistakenly construed things.

Our approach went to the essence of people as humans: asked to reveal an insight into themselves and their lives, they will do so, but on their own terms. And the more you reduce the scope for them freely to think and to choose, the greater will be their desire to do so, within the ever reducing scope that remains open to them. By limiting our overseas teams' freedoms to think and to act (concentrating not on "what" or "how much", but only on "how") we were channelling their thoughts and energies into their operational and fulfilment strategies, areas where as a business we had been negligently weak in the past. This was a deliberate and canny ploy and paid dividends in the quality of the plans submitted. As a direct consequence of this, our business plans for BT International were, as the saying went, stretching but achievable.

While I enjoyed the intellectual, almost metaphysical aspects of a job involved with the international sphere of BT's activities, I would leap at the fleeting chances that fell my way to actually hop on a plane, even if it was usually only as far as Brussels, Paris, Munich or Amsterdam, where we maintained luxuriously spacious, if not luxuriously appointed, offices. The locals were always pleased to see us, and it soon became clear why they had been so agreeable and helpful.

They were truly fascinated with how we were managing them, how we were prioritising them, and to learn about other countries' ideas. Without fully realising it, we had found the precise tilt at which to pitch our requests and to harness their enthusiasm. I felt somewhat ashamed at my earlier, stonehearted presumptions. They weren't at all the browbeaten, self-interested types I had envisaged, but genuinely motivated and committed corporate citizens. I sensed I might be losing my touch.

They pleaded with us to spend more time with them, and we would explain the company's strictures on travelling and the increasingly penny pinching attitude when it came to spending time abroad, when the discussions could just as easily be carried out via the growing phenomenon of audio conferencing. I would go whenever I could, but it was sufficiently rare and fleeting that I never really got to know the personalities of the people I was dependent upon for information and insight. And without getting to know the people properly, I couldn't really get to know how they made their business tick. Frustratingly, I developed a partial, two dimensional understanding only of what their business could become. I was having to do my job with one arm tied behind my back.

★

A new BTI COO was appointed to run the central and support units. An ex-army man who never missed an opportunity to remind us all that he had risen to the rank of major, he was still adjusting to the world beyond his previous military confines. An extremely likeable and trustworthy chap, he ran his team in typical armed forces mode, where every project was an "operation", every objective was a "mission", and as you would expect of a former commanding officer, he proved outstandingly effective at man management, getting the best out of his troops.

He flattered Neil and me as the brains of his outfit, the "acute, analytical insight of the planners" another rhetorical relic, no doubt, of his khaki-clad existence. This was his way of gently prising us out of our planning comfort zone and engaging us in the real-time commercial problems that were landing in his lap as troubleshooter in chief of BT's international operations. It certainly made for a more colourful and interesting experience, particularly when he loosened the travelling strictures.

Able at last to spend more time with our colleagues, we resolved rather than merely reviewed contractual problems in Scandinavia, project resourcing challenges in Italy and investment priorities across Europe as a whole. This direct involvement in the practical and day to day realities of the business was at once stimulating and rewarding. It provided real insight into the practical problems facing the country operations, and gave me a renewed taste for a stint on the commercial front line once we had concluded our strategic planning round.

As part of a programme to consolidate BT's London accommodation, our building was to be taken over by another division. We were given a week's notice to pack up our things before being unceremoniously hoiked out and down to an obscure exchange building tucked away behind Trafalgar Square. It was the oddest place I ever worked and almost entirely deserted. With Neil and myself in residence, the population had doubled to four.

It was built into an enclave, surrounded on all sides by forbidding looking government buildings, with only a narrow frontage onto a single lane side street. It felt shifty, suspect even, to arrive at the door, key in the entry code and sidle in; like an assignation in a spy novel, forever in shadow. Inside, it was suspiciously well equipped, the cupboards brimming with stationery and computing supplies: a fallout shelter, perhaps, to be overrun by Whitehall officials when the balloon went up.

This was soon after the 2005 London bombings, and security had remained ramped up to an almost impossible degree. Getting in and out of the place, you ran the gauntlet of a series of manned entry and exit posts, as well as the usual gamut of sealed portals and lifts with coded doors. There were as many guards on the premises as there were staff. I have never felt as safe, nor, strangely, as vulnerable.

Mike came to reconnoitre our billet. Having renounced the desk that had been waiting for him over at the Ministry once his commission was over, he was living out the mufti dream here with us instead. He retained his military bearings, and he certainly knew the protocol for getting around unhindered: a wink here, a nod there; first name terms with the "men". I once tailgated him as he navigated his way through the assault course down to the street. A true professional, I swear I saw one of the doormen salute him.

With a combination of strong central direction, effective local operational management, and support from the specialist, troubleshooting teams, the overseas business did indeed grow by the planned rate of fifty per cent over the three year period to

2008, to outturn at around four and a half billion pounds in revenue terms. The portfolio was becoming more consistent, the networks more resilient, and the operations more efficient. This would continue right up to the autumn of that year, when BT would astonishingly reveal to the London Stock Exchange that catastrophic financial performance on some twenty unnamed major global IT contracts would result in two billion pounds worth of losses being recognised.

This would completely overwhelm the division and the excellent work we had carried out on the overseas domestic businesses. Once again, the dream of global dominion had bitten the hand that fed it, and so once again, the entire international businesses would be in the company's and the market's cross-hairs. But by then I was long gone. Having spent my regulation two years at the core of the international planning activity and witnessing a host of investment proposals come through the door, I had become unavoidably gripped by a desire to move away from the centre and into a market facing role. And the world of commercial bid activity had once again come to my aid, this time in the form of an approach from the CFO of the Asian business, to whom I had been recommended for the planning role on a multi-million dollar ICT network project in Singapore. But maybe I was getting a little careless in what I wished for.

12

Novelty Island

I was recruited on to one of the first projects to be led out of a newly established global consulting venture, based at the BT Labs. It was set up to provide technical and commercial support to major client bids for networked IT solutions, where the requirements went beyond standard and bespoke product offerings to include expertise and delivery in the design and build of so-called "next generation" networks. Clients for these services were typically national telecom operators and service providers, who were looking to emulate the kind of IP-driven transformative changes that BT itself had been undertaking for the previous five years or so.

These networks would also enable clients to design and launch the kinds of sector-based specialist service offerings that BT had itself created for the likes of the financial services, health and energy sectors. This, in turn, would create a further spin-off opportunity for consultancy services. This was an unintended but very real and potentially lucrative innovation dividend; by taking the plunge and committing itself to a substantial investment in the modernisation of its core networks early in the 2000s, to address the coming "data wave", BT was now positioning itself as the go-to telco for advice on what to do and how to do it. The Singapore network project was to prove an early exemplar for this strategy, if not in quite the way it was originally propounded.

I had for some time been itching to get back into a client facing environment, and had registered my interest in working with the burgeoning consultancy venture some months previously. While it was predominantly a technology and technical-driven consulting operation, I recognised from my past exploits overseas that these projects would require continuous on-site commercial and financial expertise to fulfil all the day to day business planning responsibilities and the culminating business case requirements, neither of which could or would conceivably be entrusted to operational and sales resource. That wasn't how these things were managed; it required mediation, which was where I came in.

My pitch was well honed by now and centred on my experiences in Europe and the US, of mobile and IP, with networks and content, alongside partners and bankers; I felt I was in a relative minority of one. This belief was not exactly up for debate as my phone rang and I took the call from the incoming Asia Pacific CFO who, having requested of HR a list of potential candidates for the role in Singapore, had been presented with, apparently, just one. It seemed I was a shoo-in, but for good measure we met up in the newly founded headquarters of BT's global empire, a wintry, wind swept glasshouse on the fringes of Watford.

Over a twenty minute coffee, as the February rains lashed the windows, we sized each other up. He was a baby faced Dutchman by the name of Germon. His direct, brusque style of communicating caught me off guard at first and it took me a minute or two to recognise and adjust to his demeanour; he was already speaking to me as my boss.

Some months later, during a week back in Europe, he would drive me from Munich down to the Alps for a team away day. Strapped into the front passenger seat of his Porsche, I felt my eyes recede into their sockets as his foot eased the pedal to the floor, propelling the car along the *autobahn* like a bullet. I watched in horrified fascination as the needle flickered over the two hundred and fifty kilometre per hour mark, convinced we were travelling forward in time. It was his way of working out his stresses, his anxieties, and it was faintly terrifying. Two days later I cadged a lift back to the city with a Serbian colleague, who drove his large powerful Mercedes in remarkably similar fashion, doubtless for remarkably similar reasons.

Back in the UK, and relieved to join the evening traffic heaving gently along the motorway into London, I pondered this latest evidence of a new generation weaving its way into the company: multinational, tough, focused, high on stress and hormonal energy. They were another symptom of wider disruptive changes that had been creeping up on me for a while now, making working life less comfortable, demanding more from me, of me.

But these changes and their implications were far from my mind as Germon completed outlining the requirements of the role and the package on offer: he took it I was interested. The roll of a thunderclap almost drowned out my affirmative response. Were the Gods trying to tell me something?

There is a benign, almost tangible magnetism exerted by far-flung tropical destinations, where planes out of London land at the cocktail hour. As I left to head back to Watford Junction station, I sensed their balmy air and strange gravitational stirrings, and indeed the next time I clapped eyes on Germon was in the bar of my hotel in Singapore.

★

The island government's stated strategic ambition was to position Singapore as the leading ICT hub in the South East Asian economic region. To achieve this, it had launched its "i2015" initiative, intended to capture the spirit of the information economy that had so transfixed BT. Many of the same arguments were propounded and many of the same examples presented as facets of this new golden age of the digital networked economy. Benefits would flow through to education, employment, healthcare and to the social, commercial and cultural spheres. And at the heart of it was a brand new optical fibre network that would knit the entire island society together via a pulsating system of value-driven communications.

While the existing but quite separate cable and cellular networks would remain critically important assets through the medium term, the longer term picture was of a seamlessly integrated utopia of instant digitalised content across all devices. It could have been written by a BT marketing consultant. Notwithstanding that, we were here in town to bid for the licences to build and run this new network.

The local landline market was at the time shared by two players, Singapore Telecom (SingTel), the incumbent operator, and Starhub, which had developed beyond its original guise as a cable television operator. Each of these had a mobile arm, which competed with a third cellular operator, M1. Between them, these three companies dominated the local telecoms scene. To set up and launch a new, capital intensive island-wide operator from scratch was going to require a very substantial investment which, given its opening market share was zero, implied a substantial level of risk.

In recognition of this and to militate against it, the local telecoms regulatory and licensing body, the Infocomm Development Authority (IDA), was willing to pay the winning consortium a guaranteed but unspecified level of government subsidy. This was also intended to incentivise the competing consortia to meet the demanding coverage requirements and rollout timescales that the IDA would impose in its formal request for proposal document (RFP), which was to be issued in due course. It would be down to each consortium to propose in its bid submission their own detailed network coverage plans, the rollout and launch milestones, and the overall level of subsidy required. We would be shooting in the dark, and it looked a daunting exercise from the off.

★

We set up our project base in BT's local operational offices, on the first floor of a thirty storey tower, twinned with its identical sibling in the centre of the city's downtown business district. At the time there were around two hundred of BT's employees cohabiting in these chambers, providing a domestic and international telecoms service to local business organisations and global clients with a presence on the island.

There was a quiet but determined air about the place, borne of the unique Indo-Malayan fusion of cultural influences, which emphasised both hard work and social humility. Put simply, it felt like a nice place to work. And coupled with high-end infrastructural benefits of slickly silent lift services, smart marble-lined bathrooms, and the logistical benefits of a subsidised multi-ethnic food hall in the basement, this certainly had all the trappings of a place that was nice to work and I felt right at home from the very start.

I adopted the style of the former colonial masters and bought myself a couple of linen suits to see me through the raging heat. I couldn't fathom my British colleagues who favoured their regular wool attire, as indeed did many of the locals in what seemed an overly self-conscious effort to present what they felt was an appropriate professional look. It was odd to walk in the street under the burning midday sun in the company of our local banker, dressed to the nines in tailored pinstripe suit, buttoned-up shirt and tightly knotted club tie. Who was he trying to impress?

Now, it is a truth universally acknowledged, that even the most middle-ranking international business traveller assumes he has the inalienable right to a seat within the executive class cabins. A ticket in economy can only be the temporary outcome of a corporate squeeze on expenses, while a flight in first class would only be the peremptorily fortunate but nonetheless highly prized outcome of an upgrade.

My career in BT's international activities would afford me the opportunity to sample all three of these experiential options, and while long haul in business class is a splendid sensation of self-managed comfort, the acme of first class is a heavenly ritual of cossetted luxury. Suffice to observe that to fly in and out of South East Asia in the nose of a Jumbo is to cheat life itself.

★

As was often the case with an apparently straightforward project, there were various ancillary, even mercenary objectives lurking behind the decision to participate in it. First and foremost of course, it was about being part of a winning consortium which secured the licence to build and manage a new next generation optical fibre network throughout the island of Singapore. To make things more confusing, there could be more than one consortium, if partners elected to join just one of the new businesses to be created: the Netco, which would build, own and maintain the infrastructure, and the OpCo which would deploy and sell its range of communications services.

Secondly, it was about providing consultancy services from BT to the NetCo, regarding the design and management of the fibre network at the core of the bids. Thirdly, it was about providing specialist marketing and product capabilities into the OpCo to enable it to compete commercially. Finally, it was about providing and maximising regional and global connectivity for the winning consortium.

What had appeared from the outset as a simple network bid was rapidly evolving into a multi-dimensional, multi-headed beast that would create all manner of confusion and complexity for those of us on the project. I could already imagine how all this would play out back home when we came to ask for investment monies. The layering and de-layering of the various aspects of the project, in order to justify the business case for each of them, would surely prove to be a practical nightmare, both to present as an insider and to understand as an outsider; I did not exactly relish the prospect of that.

I had had an initial run in with a London-based finance analyst who was on point to police the project within his budgetary control ambit. Sadly, he personified the smaller minded, bean counting stereotype of his profession. Plainly, the days when central finance was home to champions of the wider vision were on the wane; it was increasingly the preserve of quibbling oiks with stunted ambitions merely to challenge and decline: the outriders of a new incrementalism. However, for now, I was getting ahead of myself, as was he. There was a project to run.

BT had been instrumental in bringing our consortium together and positioned itself as the technical partner. This was reflected within the BT representative team, made up of some fifteen people at its peak and dominated by technical experts in the luminous fields of fibre network design and implementation, network routing and switching, bandwidth management, network maintenance and customer service. They were a dour bunch, but we would permit them that provided they got the job done. But while we all loved the lifestyle and the working environment, there was a sense these guys were loving it all just a little too much; progress was slow, with a never ending cast of hangers-on shipped in and out for their fleeting contributions; it started to feel like a holiday camp. Compounded by a lack of formal project leadership, a culture of drift and listlessness soon began to take hold.

There were several of us functional heads, an account director who managed the relationship with the client, and a programme manager who corralled us into the office at eight in the morning (a challenge for those of us who never quite conquered the time difference and had usually not slept until four) but nobody provided overall shape and day to day drive. My boss was busy with several other projects going on across the region so he was rarely in town. His bustling presence, with his agendas and issue logs, would bring a temporary air of purpose which otherwise really didn't impinge too much upon our lovely island world.

Amidst the strutting concrete towers and the fluttering ribbons of colourful traffic there remained, in the rustle of the palm leaves, the embalming warm air and the purr of the canal boats, ghostly vestiges of the mystical East, an unhurried becalming sense of place and peace, and in the absence of effective management we took our lead from these instead.

As for the consortium itself, this had been settled prior to my arrival, through the offices of our local country management team. They had been involved in the liberalisation discussions with the IDA and from this had gleaned the optimal partnership to be formed of a major telco, the regional unit of a global investment bank, plus local players in telecoms service provision and the consumer electronics business. On paper this made sense, bringing together global capabilities with local market knowledge, a tried and tested formula. In reality, this meant all the pre-licence award work actually being carried out by the telco (BT), supported by the bank (HSBC), with our local partners simply kept up to date via very one-way monthly briefing meetings.

These partners had between them nominated an external consultancy to advise on the economic and competitive landscape, thereby getting themselves completely off the hook for resourcing the project. They just wanted to know the answers. It was a novel approach to partnership but it had the distinct merit of keeping them well out of our hair for most of the time.

My role as ever was to put together a business plan, in this case for each of the prospective businesses: NetCo, which would build the physical network assets, and wholesale its capacity to a series of existing and new operating companies; and OpCo, itself a new operating company which would purchase capacity from NetCo, dress it up as a portfolio of new wave communications services, and sell them on to consumers and businesses. It should have been a reasonably straightforward investment decision – what would the companies cost to build and operate, and what sales, margins and returns could we expect? – but with BT's machinations to consider, and in light of external developments within the market itself, it was to prove anything but.

For my part, the notion of designing and planning an island-wide optical fibre network conjured up images from German science fiction movies from the early twentieth century, of wild haired, swivel eyed boffins working through the painful calculus at scratchy blackboards, developing arcane prototype machines that hummed and growled in the dark, before the bulb on the Bakelite unit finally glowed.

The outer limits of telecoms were now coming to Singapore, only this time it was the early twenty first century, where the challenge facing BT's digital age boffins lay in negotiating the logistical tedium of plotting a network topology that took account of utility ducts, an intensive highway system, countless high-rise residential blocks and a rapidly expanding commercial and financial centre. The stark reality of building the new network: a study in mundanity and vermin containment. Digging up roads, laying fibres along ditches, nailing up ducting inside lift shafts; renting rat-infested warehouses and basements to house the routing and power equipment: a nexus of digital plumbing and tropical pest control.

★

Given the timescales of the project were likely to run for months if not years, if we won, we were offered an initial six month overseas assignment package. This amounted to an apartment to house your family, allowances for furnishings and fittings, regular flights home, an employment facilitating green card plus assistance with bills and in sorting out local tax arrangements. With a young family back in the UK, I initially elected not to take up the full benefits and resigned myself instead to an exhausting two-week-on, two-week-off arrangement.

This meant I was unable to participate meaningfully in the earnest discussions around the boardroom table on the merits or otherwise of the various ethnically styled furniture pieces on offer at the numerous discount warehouses around the island, where my colleagues would occupy the best part of their evenings and weekends. When they weren't debating these, it was only because their lady wives had shifted the focus onto curtains. It was a remarkable feature of island life; the shared detours of home furnishing. How we Brits like to put down our roots.

For myself, I was happy to spend my time at the smarter hotels around the central business district, which meant a fifteen minute walk to and from the office. I preferred to go around on foot. I had experienced the tropics before but this was my first real taste of a truly equatorial climate. I would spend evenings strolling to and from the canal side restaurants, dodging the scurrying bug life at my feet. But while I loved the heat and the food, I had nobody there to share it with. For all its sensual attractions, it felt empty.

Any misguided dreams of colonial entitlement I may have entertained as I wandered about the lushly planted squares and plazas were only enhanced by being ferried around the city from time to time by a local in his stylish 1970s Mercedes. Sat in the back, an elbow perched on the ledge of the open window, the warm air brushing across my face, it was too tempting to fantasise and drift back to another era. A time when my father had spent his overseas posting stationed there, one of the farthest flung corners of the Empire on which the sun never set.

I could imagine a life in its soothing embrace, embalmed in its blissful climate. I could imagine endless days steeped in oriental culture and the majesty of its natural world. I could imagine following in the steps of my mobile colleagues from a decade before and putting down roots there myself, perhaps never to return: unlike my father, who did, but never lost his sense of a place that had brought him an enraptured, metaphysical peace. I resolved to make a plan. With BT seemingly committed to the region, and the travelling beginning to take its toll, I too decided to bring my family out to Singapore for an extended stay.

*

Over the course of ten months, we were required to submit three detailed sets of plans, each in response to a specific market or network scenario that the IDA was exploring. The plans covered network design and rollout, marketing, sales and pricing initiatives, and financial projections that included specific details in relation to the subsidies, their timings and how they would be applied, overall funding requirements and outline plans for loan syndication. It was a bit like sitting university finals, simultaneously in four subjects, and then two sets of retakes, all in rapid succession.

With our technical colleagues weighed down by the grisly realities of urban network planning, the commercial planning activity boiled down to modelling a set of market scenarios: accelerating or slowing the rollout of the service; the rate of take-up by consumers and businesses; the range of services that would be made available; and the take-up rates for these. There was an infinite number of permutations, so we progressively closed down the options to match what we believed the market would withstand and welcome, based on the econometric statistics, the demographics and benchmark data on take-up rates for comparable network services.

In order to make the investment look credible, however, and to limit the level of government subsidy to a believable amount, we found ourselves having to make a series of critical assumptions regarding the behaviour of the existing operators and therefore, by implication, the regulatory framework. In short, to make the new venture a moderate commercial success and to generate a reasonable return for its investors, the existing operators would need to be constrained by the regulator from investing themselves in fibre networks.

In addition, they should be further constrained from offering a comparable portfolio of IP services for a fixed period of time, which would allow the new venture to gain its own traction in the market and begin to recover its investment. In absence of these two guarantees, there could be no new fibre network operator; the numbers would not work. It was a fascinating exercise in gaming our own set of requirements (market structure; subsidies; returns) in order to meet our client's own (coverage; speed; services; reliability) within a hypothetically workable framework. But in so doing, we were actually teasing out the flaws in the plan, the fault lines at the heart of the i2015 network vision.

A series of big questions were crystallising in our collective mind. How could the IDA conceivably prevent SingTel and Starhub from investing in fibre, in competition with the new company, or from launching IP services for which they had an investible business case? How, then, could a new business actually be a realistic possibility? Why would the Singapore government be prepared to spend hundreds of millions of dollars to sponsor BT – or someone else – to build a fibre network, which would in all likelihood ultimately fail commercially? Why didn't they simply enable or require SingTel and Starhub to do it themselves?

We tabled these at our third and final review session with the IDA. We sat either side of a long narrow table; the BT commercial team down one side, the IDA's i2015 steering committee on the other. They spoke eloquently of a new market dynamism, of innovative market structures, of their need to make strategic investments, and of the benefits their country stood to make as the vision was realised. They studiously avoided answering our central questions regarding viability and the alternative strategies open to them. Maybe they felt ambushed; maybe they were simply wedded to the dream and love is blind. Either way, they politely thanked us for our professional presentation, our arguments and our insight, and suggested they would respond to our specific points in due course.

Within days we received the IDA's anxiously awaited response. They had noted our observations and our concerns. These had been mirrored in presentations from other consortia. A number of internal working parties would now be set up to review all the work done to date, together with the critical views and concerns of the competing parties. A temporary cessation to the bidding process would be enacted forthwith, lasting several months. A summary of their internal reviews would be published the following spring. In the meantime we were roundly thanked for our interest and participation in the bidding process to date.

Without guidance of substance from the IDA regarding the fundamentals of the market or how the subsidy would operate, the business case for the project was crumbling in our hands. There was little we could present back into BT that would make a compelling case for continuing with the project as it stood, and there was little of substance that would change within the following six months. Even then we couldn't see how it could be made to work from our perspective; the circle couldn't be squared. The IDA was trying to build its house from the roof down. Most frustratingly, they had had from us ten months' worth of unpaid-for advice.

My plans to move out to the region were suddenly looking decidedly shaky. I got hold of Germon who told me to go out for a good dinner with HSBC, then "go back to Europe" (the UK not registering at that distance) and find another project to keep myself occupied. He would get back in touch when the time was right.

But the time would never be right. We had in effect made the case for saving our client hundreds of millions of dollars, by using the existing operators to realise their dream, with the whip hand of regulation to keep it on track and them onside. While there was no lasting role for us, we had done our consulting job, albeit involuntarily, and there would be other places for BT to build and run its networks. But none quite so enchanting as the island with the sighing breeze and the whispering palms.

13

Tower Record I

I had heard many stories of people returning to the UK from overseas assignments and finding they had nowhere to go and nothing to do and so it was with no great surprise that I learned that this was the precise fate that awaited myself. I was still notionally attached to Germon, but there was little I could add to his business from my home office in London, some eight thousand miles from his own. He was okay with me taking my time over finding the right sort of role for myself, but after three months of drift and frustration I realised I would have to broaden my search parameters beyond "strategic business planning" within the "global business".

This yielded a spectacular raft of unsuitable positions and I got to the point of pondering my very future with the company when my attention was caught by a finance role within the Global Media and Broadcast unit (M&B). I had been aware of this group for years and it had always been an ambition of mine to join it if the right opportunity should ever present itself. I pinged an email to its CFO and an interview was duly scheduled.

M&B was based at the iconic BT Tower in London's West End: not within the actual "stick" itself but in a standard-issue set of unprepossessing office blocks that gird its lower reaches. One of the attractions of this business was the co-location of most of its employees on this one site. For years I had endured the sometimes questionable benefits of "hot desking" and "flexible working" and longed for the affirmative sense of belonging that came with possession of your own desk. It also meant, at least in theory, that there would be little trouble getting hold of people who knew what was going on and who understood the detailed workings of the place, two invaluable sets of data in any job and without which you were always struggling to keep up.

Another attraction of M&B was its jealously guarded status within the wider business as a self-managed unit, meaning it had its own dedicated management team across all functions, reporting into a CEO who was responsible and accountable for its entire performance. This was ideal for the media industry, where relationships and dedicated teams of specialists are the natural means for getting things done. It also fosters a far deeper sense of team spirit and ownership than is to be found in modish flexible management models where, matrixed together temporarily into virtual teams, employees will understandably struggle to build a communal and heartfelt commitment. The twenty year history of "M&B Ltd" had knitted together the unit more tightly than any I had encountered since my earliest days in BT.

A final attraction of the role lay in the media sector itself, which I had had several tastes of over the years and where I was comfortable with the looser and more creative culture. I also felt, after my less than triumphant past experiences with BT Vision, Mediaset, Openworld and OnDigital, that I had some unfinished business with it.

I arrived at the Tower for my interview and was greeted at the door by Murray, the CFO. An affable chap on crutches due to a long term knee injury, he was a relatively new recruit to BT. He had plenty of telecoms experience but now he plainly had his hands full trying to get to grips with this media malarkey. He described the set of five or six sub-businesses and how they were so markedly different from other areas of BT's global activity, depending as they did on dozens of external suppliers, hundreds of freelance staff, and thousands of network and satellite circuits scattered around the world. For a second I thought he might burst into tears, so passionately frustrated and overwhelmed did he appear, although whether this was due to his experiences of BT, the media business or his physical incapacity, I couldn't say.

We chatted a bit about each business area and the ins and outs of the overall financial performance. The discussion then took a rather abrupt pivot when he asked me what I knew about television production. I waffled for a bit about my experiences twenty years previously on MTV but didn't actually succeed in convincing myself, let alone him. He then noted the scope and scale of my more general experiences in BT, before finally declaring me too senior for the role he had on offer. I thanked him for his time and left him with the retort that if he only came across people who were even more ill suited to the role than myself, he could always get back in touch with me, since he clearly needed the support. I hoped I had pitched it right.

To keep myself occupied and my face in the global frame, I contacted the BT Global Services (BT GS) head of business development to see if they needed any project support. I subsequently spent a month working on an acquisition project based in Amsterdam and a further month on an outsourcing project in Dublin. These were interesting enough diversions but I was really only keeping seats warm until others came along with more detailed local knowledge; I still needed a proper job of my own.

I set off on summer vacation not sure what I would be returning to. There were rumours of a final, hugely lucrative round of voluntary redundancies and this played on my mind as I flew out. I had been in BT for almost twenty five years: surely it was time for a change? Then, as I sat having lunch at a Greek quayside, my mobile rang. The screen bore the number of the BT switchboard and I was in two minds about answering, since it would surely be either a Dutchman or an Irishman in distress. My moral turpitude melted in the Ionian sunshine and I took the call. It was Murray.

He explained that things had moved on significantly since we had met, leaving him faced with a huge range of operational and financial pressures, and badly stretched on resourcing some major new investment projects, particularly in the priority area of digital media. Would I be interested in taking these on? Yes I would, as it happened, yes I would, and I raised my glass of Mythos to him.

*

I had naively envisaged the home of BT's media and broadcast commercial unit as a hi-tech, *outré* sort of place: web-centric, very IP, an app-ening environment, if you like. But it was altogether more prosaic in tone and nature, an entirely conventional set-up of fifty-odd sales and product guys sat in their austere, serried ranks. Mostly of a mid-years vintage, they looked rather care worn, and bored stiff. I wasn't expecting music and a dancing troupe, but some signs of life would have been nice. There weren't even any television sets.

The office itself was nothing to write home about either. Perched at the top of its nondescript block, it was the byword for utilitarian workspace. There were drawer-less desks, nose to tail like trestles at a school fete; creaky chairs with squeaky wheels; a shabby corner kitchenette featuring tubs of instant coffee and bags of maudlin tea; and a sixty foot long wall of tatty vertical louvre blinds, with all the warmth and charm of a sheet of tarpaulin. Nobody much cared for the view, apparently. It was pretty cheap and grim all round, but since it was only a five minute walk from my flat, I soon came to adore the place, and all and sundry therein.

Digital media was a catch-all term for a range of new wave products, services and development projects, which were aimed at the television broadcast, production and distribution markets. This part of the business provided playout facilities to local and international broadcasters, enabling them to upload tapes of broadcast programming from one central location, in this case the BT Tower, and reach destinations around Europe, America and Asia using BT's global satellite and fibre networks.

Separately it provided a production service, which would originate sports programming for broadcasters – about which more later – and post-production facilities, used to enhance pre-existing programming with content coding, audio tracks and transcoding into new digital formats. Finally, it was investing millions in an integrated production, post-production and playout software platform, which would be the networking hub for the digital file-based television content of the future. It was another dazzling assortment of novelty for me, and I felt pleasurably at ease from day one.

Television was a notoriously conservative sector and the logistics of the industry remained largely tape-based. As programming content moved through the production process, with the original footage being progressively enhanced into a broadcastable format, so the tapes (which still resembled ancient reels of film) would be schlepped around multiple urban locations by courier, since the work would be carried out by a series of specialist post-production houses. It was a monument to inefficiency.

The vision of the future was of file-based programming; digital files containing the audio-visual material. This would permit the transfer of programming over digital networks which linked together the various post-production facilities and companies. The BT media team wanted to go one step further, and build a virtual production facility housing the entire suite of software packages used in the post-production workflow. They felt, in common with so many of their predecessors, that they were making the future.

While ambitious and a substantial step into software development and integration, it was broadly in step with the latest BT GS mission, that of providing sector-based "ecosystems" of companies and organisations with sector-specific networking hubs. These hubs would bring together key processes and activities and realise them more efficiently and cost effectively through the use of shared resources. BT's right to play was in its IP networking capability and its ever growing data centre presence, while the fine line separating networking and data processing was gradually dissolving. It was already enjoying some success with similar initiatives aimed at financial services clients and within the broader telecoms sector itself; the media and broadcast market was the next in line.

I met the two guys who were the driving force behind the product strategy and the platform itself, known as Mosaic: Steve and Tom, an earnest, youngish, geeky pair. They talked me through their business plan for the product, which was targeting around a hundred million pounds worth of sales over the coming few years, based on a progressive build-up of contracted client sales and the numbers of "seats" they would rent in order for their employees to access the central production and processing capabilities.

Clients were bracketed as small, medium and large, with each segment showing an initially tentative, then progressively more aggressive upward acceleration in the volume of take-up. I had borne witness to many such profiles on paper before, and tended nowadays to take them with a pinch of salt. I was more interested in the inner workings of their business model and the drivers of value; how the costs and revenues, and hence investments and returns, were generated. In Blue Peter style, they proudly produced the Excel model they had prepared earlier.

I had seen many hundreds of spreadsheet models in my career and as a mathematician *manqué* I had come to appreciate the arithmetical labyrinths that some people were capable of producing as if addicted to the mind bending logic that flowed effortlessly through their fingertips. The Mosaic model, however, was of an altogether alien species, where the cells appeared not to contain an ounce of recognisably algebraic code. Instead, they were flooded with peculiar, hesitant, glottal-stopped assertions – "if sqrt is effect shift"; "gestep isblank and iferror not"; "choose floor or roundup" – which seemingly presented a torrent of conditional, anagrammatical angst.

I was utterly bemused by this and emerged from our two hour discussion none the wiser as to the attractiveness or otherwise of this business case. The question of whether I was losing my analytical prowess flitted across my mind; something in the weather had decidedly changed without my noticing, and for a dizzying moment I sensed tectonic plates shifting under my feet.

Of a more orderly and comprehensible nature was their schedule of development activities and the price tags associated with these. They had contracted with BT's newly formed Design function, a corporate-wide body charged with supplying all software developments required to deliver products and services over the global IP network. Sadly, its reputation was not yet up to scratch; contracting with Design, the BT-mandated default route for product development, meant a glacially slow, ruinously expensive and error strewn path to nerve shredding frustration.

The boys had listed out their thirty major development packages of which ten were complete, ten were in train, and ten were approved but awaiting resource. They had spent several million pounds so far, and were committed to spending several million more. This was for just the central hub and networking platform; the bolting on of the production workflow packages would be additional expense, driven by the volumes of anticipated seats. In all then, it was a mightily costly, not to say risky experiment. As I recalled "now diget complex imabs sum" from their model, I only hoped it was the profit maximisation algorithm, and not a prayer for the anguished from the Catholic liturgy.

One of the less attractive aspects of my role was acting in a financial control capacity across the digital media business. This led to great swathes of time being lost in examining and approving proposed expenditures on anything from edit suite upgrades and website click-through counters, to boxes of tapes and branded stationery. I eventually got used to these vacuous requests tumbling into my inbox daily by the dozen and simply shut my eyes and clicked "approve", although it had taken quite a while to achieve such a mellow state.

Further chunks of my life were saddled with reporting and forecasting monthly revenues and margins. There is a hermit-like form of human life that clearly enjoys undertaking these excruciating administrative minutiae but I am to all intents and purposes not a member of it. However, I would take hold of my nose and plunge into this swamp of recurrent financial reckonings, if only for the sake of form and to preserve what remained of Murray's fragile sanity.

One of the features in this regard was the opportunity to spend a couple of days every few weeks at one of BT's panoply of hideous bivouacs scattered around the M25 motorway, within the limits of such esteemed parishes as Croydon, Watford and Sevenoaks. Herein resided an army of mole-like wastrels charged with keeping the books of the business. From what I could discern, the quality of the financial records had scarcely improved one jot since I had first encountered them nearly twenty five years before, and I never ceased to be amazed at the alchemy of our fiscal fudge-packers in turning these uproariously illegible ledgers into a tome of vaguely sensible and useable management reports.

★

Back on planet Earth, a new strategic plan for the accelerated take-up of the Mosaic product was being developed, under the codename of Rocking Horse. Mimicking the growth model of the core global networking business, Rocking Horse was the launch and rollout of an outsourcing proposition. This would involve M&B taking over and managing broadcasters' internal "contribution" and external "distribution" networks for them, and progressively inserting our new production and processing platform into the equation.

This would deliver a "faster, richer and more cost effective network-centric solution"; I was getting the hang of this by now. Moreover, it sounded quite brilliant; but then our strategic propositions always did. It was unquestionably "on strategy", aligned with what all parts of the Group were doing. All it needed was a market.

And so once again we were sucked into a polarised, fractious, ego-driven debate which saw one side aggressively in favour of getting it all underway, sales resource put in place, budgets assigned and monies spent; and the other side aggressively questioning the very validity of the idea, the clients' appetite for change and our capacity to overturn market inertia. It was always thus, one extreme or the other; rarely was a toe or two dipped in to test the water, it tended to have to be the whole leg or nothing. In this instance, the whole leg was on the menu. But before we could even begin to pluck it and dress it and set it before our drooling clients, the latest financial meltdown to hit the company was being announced.

The abrupt departure of the BT GS CEO – the visionary behind the "software as a service" strategy and a big supporter of the media and broadcast business – headlined the company-wide email. It went on to describe the catastrophic performance of a number of big IT and network outsourcing contracts that BT had undertaken with several major UK and global clients. The financial implications were immense, requiring a write-down in profits of two billion pounds. Footage of the Group chief executive announcing the news revealed him ashen-faced and incredulous. Brought in as the company's finance director several years previously, to provide commercial and financial strictures aimed at precluding such disasters, he plainly took this latest failure personally. While some lamely tried to blame the economic crisis for this self-evidently self-inflicted disaster, it was clear he had been misled and let down shockingly.

And so, even within the confines of M&B, where financial performance was solid if underwhelming, we would feel the cold blast of yet another restructuring of the global business, as it sought once again to organise and style itself as an effective and profitable global IT networking powerhouse. It seemed wholly inappropriate that the M&B business should have been brought within the ambit of this review in quite the way it eventually was; maybe there was some pent-up historic resentment towards its self-managed status. Either way, we found our hitherto independent standing and all new business and investment initiatives suspended, as the latest strategic audit of the entire global operation was worked through.

When the time duly arrived for its spotlight to fall on M&B, a number of strategic variants were identified, which were boiled down to three main options: keeping everything unchanged; a wholesale sell-off; and a winding down of new initiatives and refocusing onto core areas. In the end, in a failure of nerve, the latter one prevailed, with the as yet uncompleted Mosaic platform, and the team working on it, put up for sale. And as if to rub salt in the wound, the remaining organisation would be thrown to the winds and split into four separate units, reporting into each of the main BT lines of business except, remarkably, BT Global Services. Somebody out there, for whatever reason, did not like M&B, let alone understand it.

The separation of the business along functional lines finally brought it into line with the operational model that BT had adopted across its main businesses several years before. There had been notional consideration given to its remaining intact: what had applied in the past was still applicable at this point; but the winning arguments at this time centred not on the industrial logic of growth, but on the capacity to deliver cost savings. There was deemed to be greater value to the Group as a whole from delivering synergies by placing the teams into functional homes. It was a classic short term solution, but given the relatively small scale of the M&B business nobody aside from its own employees saw fit to quibble with the outcome. The deal was done.

While the operational folks were bundled off into a couple of technical divisions, the bulk of the commercial activity was shifted, inexplicably, into BT's wholesale division. There was a story that the CEO of this business was rather taken with the sector, had experience of it and wanted to bring it under her wing, which also suggested it would receive a more than fair wind; that remained to be seen. However, the fact that she promptly left the company barely six months later rather pulled the rug from under that piece of delusional speculation.

Murray then triumphantly announced that he would not be joining us on the onward journey, he had cannily made himself indispensible to his own previous boss by displaying a penchant for working capital management which at the time had made the hair on the back of my neck stand on end, so crashingly dull did the entire chore appear. Still, it brought cash into the company and he was rewarded for his diligence with a further senior position from which to grimace at BT's lamentable financial processes assuming, that is, he was no longer getting twinges from his dodgy knee.

★

So I had another new boss, this time by the name of Andrew, a scholarly type with a quick and forensic commercial mind. He set me upon all of the M&B international business, which was to be the focal point of the unit's latest growth efforts. Rather than reach out along the broadcast value chain of activities to take on entirely new areas (such as outsourcing broadcasters' network management and production platforms) the unit would now concentrate on selling more of its existing product portfolio in new geographies, taking advantage of the presence overseas of employees in the BT GS country organisations. The main thrust of this enterprise would be sales of our newly completed global media network and a nascent broadcast satellite business.

Several years previously, in a bid to address one of the global division's regular bouts of financial incontinence, BT had sold off its broadcast satellite business to a rival operator, and signed commercial agreements which barred BT from competing in the sector for a specified period of time. That period was now up and at the drop of a hat a case had been made for re-entering the business, albeit on a small scale, incremental investment basis.

The product was being offered in conjunction with BT's global fibre network to broadcasters around Europe, the US and Asia to provide a seamless, cost effective alternative to its competitors. It was a sensible and pragmatic approach to optimising the network proposition. The global media network (GMN) product itself had for years been a product in search of a market. Now completed, it wrapped itself around the globe and linked the giant media centres of London, Amsterdam, New York, Los Angeles, Hong Kong and Singapore. To be precise, it linked the financial centres in those cities, as BT's global network rollout had been largely shaped by its significant legacy presence in the wholesale finance markets. This meant incurring additional costs to serve media clients, and this and the tentative speed of the GMN rollout had to date hindered its progress.

A new team was now pulled together to drive growth in India and China. It was managed by an affable Midlander called Andy. He had a completely shaven head, a lyrical Black Country accent, and a relentless line in salesmanship. I had not come across that particular mash-up before; I would have bottled it and sold it. Where had he been hiding all these years? He was unique. With a shared passion for football, pubs and the Welsh coast, we hit it off straight away. Now all we had to do was earn some money.

Clever new investment projects were pulled together and approved, creating more appropriately sited network gateways within the media clusters, which allowed new clients to be brought on to the GMN at a fraction of the cost previously incurred. These would be paid for by savings gained from re-routing existing clients through the same, shared gateways. The cost savings fed through to a more commercial pricing plan, and in rapid time we had the revenues on an upward trajectory.

This was a victory for innovative thinking by the product team and for the insightful support and slick approvals for which their newly installed financial management would be rightly applauded. In two years we grew the GMN business by almost thirty per cent and finally turned it profitable. There had been no great secret to it; we simply applied our creative cells, took a few well managed risks and, for once, screwed our suppliers.

It was in some ways as refreshing as any previous investment projects I had been involved with. Not only did it work, but I was actually there to quantify and report on the benefits of it. But the unreality of it – I was never physically to set eyes on any of the gateways or the network upgrades, it was all taking place on the furthest sides of the world from my desk – this affected me; it was all too remote. I was getting older, and I needed some sense that I was doing something tangibly worthwhile, something that was its own reward. And now this wasn't quite cutting it for me. It seemed I was going cold on globalisation, or perhaps it was going cold on me. Either way, the old love wasn't there any more.

14

Blurred Vision

I was to spend a year with a partial oversight of the operations and finances of the latest of BT's forays into the television market, BT Vision. An atavistic brandname for some of us, it inevitably conjured up memories of our earlier struggle to establish the company as a credible player in a market for which we were not truly cut out. In a similarly assertive move twenty years on, the company was using its newly acquired regulatory freedoms in the UK and its rapidly expanding next generation broadband network to launch an IP television service. This would enable users to view their own choice of programming over the internet, via their television set, as and when it suited them.

The product had been launched back in late 2006, some three years previously. Rather than position itself as a direct competitor to existing pay television players, it was a ploy to defend and expand BT's share of the broadband market. It was a bundling tactic, which is as strategically coherent to the market and financial analyst as it can be confusing to the layman, who simply wants to be associated with a successful product, and the humble employee, who will not necessarily know if his customer base number and usage rates are where they need to be or not.

As proof of its assigned role as a buttress to BT's UK consumer business, Vision was set up alongside other heart-fluttering products such as calls & lines and devices, as well as broadband and a minor residual mobile play, albeit with stentorian marketing and a budget worthy of Croesus. Initially established in splendid isolation at a dedicated site in Holborn, it was soon brought to heel at BT Centre. One way or another, then, it quickly came to know its place.

So I found myself briefly back at headquarters, for the first time in almost five years, and the place had a decidedly different feel to it. It had moved on. The atrium was rammed with people in dark grey suits, tapping away at dark grey laptops and barking into dark grey mobile phones. In place of the gentle chatter that once babbled around the café, there was a hubbub of voices that sounded driven and corporate. The queues at the tills were lined with unsmiling faces and newly polished shoes. Ties were back.

*

I wasn't entirely convinced by the Vision product nor by the way it was being managed. There were a number of good people involved who had plenty of television and media experience, but they were being hemmed in by the management strictures of the wider consumer business; manpower reductions, for instance, were already becoming a regular feature. Barely three years old, it was having to contend with operational pressures similar to those facing the legacy business. I was stunned.

That said, I found myself strangely unmoved by my own involvement in this initiative. While it was new, innovative even, the sense of it being a core UK consumer product brought me low, since in truth I was only truly inspired when looking globally, strategically, across a mix of business types and geographies. In relative terms, and notwithstanding its budget, it struck me as a sideshow. Stripped bare of its presumed frills and thrills, it was obscure, homespun knick-knackery and, by extension, rather beneath me.

The number of users signing up for Vision was inching slowly upwards. When I joined, this figure stood at around three hundred thousand. The year-end target was for some four hundred thousand. We ran a sweepstakes on what the final outcome would be, heady stuff for a core finance team. Looking at the monthly run rate of new additions to the network, a quick bit of basic arithmetic told me it would be three hundred and forty eight thousand. We each vouchsafed our gloomy estimates with the CFO, who remained remarkably sanguine at the portents of our forecasts.

When the year-end figures eventually emerged, remarkably at three hundred and forty eight thousand users, I was awarded the token prize, and thereafter regarded by my child-like colleagues as a witch. They were a simpleminded crew, and I secretly hoped I had really spooked them, since it might expose signs of life in their hitherto bloodless visages.

There did appear to be a lot going on; people were very busy with detailed business cases, closing endless content deals, developing new micro-propositions, building multi-dimensional management information systems (MIS); it just seemed to lack a big picture which would bring it all together and give it some cohesion, some purpose. It was never going to rival Sky with its ten million subscribers, but according to our management that apparently wasn't the point. But even if it wasn't, without greater and faster take-up it would look a relative failure in the eyes of the market, and since the market doesn't want to be associated with failure, it wasn't going to take it up. To my mind, in the absence of a game changer, it appeared destined for the same fate as BT's half-baked CATV interests and the unlamented OnDigital.

There was an indigenous unreality to Vision. For a start there were no clients to talk to and no in-house sales team to give feedback. This was a product group who were building a product to sell, that was true. But aside from the dismal sets of weekly performance data, there was a remoteness to the project, an air of detachment surrounding the people involved.

This was not a positive reflection of specific management policies, of empowerment or independence, which when successfully harnessed have the power to unleash proactive behaviour and create a beacon of entrepreneurial vigour. Rather, they were being moulded into another BT core business, and it didn't really suit them, but they didn't have the capacity to fight back, so they just looked lost, forlorn.

My first introduction to Mark, the Vision CEO, would therefore be an interesting experience. I had gone to meet up with him to discuss the post-production element of the digital media business at BT Tower and the work it was doing for Vision, where there had been some operational and relationship problems.

I made my way to the "leadership" floor, a conceit hung over from an earlier regime and which seemed ever more posturing the longer it was allowed to continue. I found Mark camped out in a side office; not for him the democracy of open-plan. I admired him for that. A colleague from Vision was on the speakerphone. We made our introductions.

Mark was clearly not a detail man and made no pretence of understanding precisely what the post-production unit did, either for his business or for our external clients. But he knew he wanted it done properly, efficiently and on time otherwise he would get someone else to do it. We assured him our teams were now working well together, the problems had been addressed systematically and all would be back on track in short order. He then demanded a couple of specific commitments, on costs, in return for which he would finance our plan to expand the production business at the Tower.

Introducing our wider ambition, which was not on the

agenda, and establishing his own pre-conditional support in this way, shifted the grounds of our discussion. It was a clever manoeuvre, with something in it for all of us. He was as smart and charismatic a leader as I was to meet in BT, more so than a couple of Group CEOs I came up against, and it left me wondering just why his wider team looked so fucked off.

★

Vision had for three years run a strand of football programming, having secured a block of English Premier League (EPL) matches. Unfortunately this had been the runt in the pack, a selection of "near live" games pairing up some of the less compelling clubs within the League. So not exactly a top-notch affair; rumours abounded that at times there were significantly fewer viewers tuning in to Vision to watch a match than there were attending the game itself. Either way, as a strategy for driving Vision sales, it had not quite hit the mark.

And so, in a move reminiscent of the earliest days of videotape, DVDs and the internet, Vision decided to follow the well trodden path to drive take-up of new technology, by loading up its platform with pornography. This didn't have a significant effect on subscriber numbers either, no doubt because of the proliferation of free adult content available elsewhere on the net. It did, though, make our monthly reviews of the media encoding operation at Tower rather more stirring, as we combed through the inventory of ever more lurid titles that passed through our doors. But it felt distinctly shabby. Was this really what BT was coming to?

I had been aware for some time of the ages of my various finance peers falling off relative to my own advancing years, and this was particularly so in this neck of the woods. Their inexperience was to be expected, but their growing lack of "office personality" was disturbing. There was a noticeable narrowing in the range of subjects and interests they would be comfortable discussing, or jokes they would understand, and a widespread reluctance ever to switch off and just chat. The new generation were fixated on their work, it was true, but also increasingly dull and characterless. They lacked a cultural hinterland, and I was becoming rather bored of them.

In an insane work-based variant of the dumbed down education mantra of "prizes for all", growing numbers of these cyphers were having to be eulogised and rewarded, pandered to for producing unoriginal and blandly average output and initiatives, in the name of victim-driven processes of "recognition" and quota-based promotions. Paul, a normal enough colleague, was bizarrely venerated for his breakthrough in the presentation of forecasting spreadsheets, remarkable apparently for having dates in the rows and volumes in the columns, a ninety degree pivot on the usual presentational method. Try as I might, I just could not fathom the significance. We all seemed to be walking on eggshells, trying not to upset anybody, making a show of being ultra-positive and ultra-supportive.

There were occasional highlights, whacky stories that came out of this tawdry excursion into pleasuring the British consumer. A favourite concerned an exception on a monthly MIS report, which revealed continual, exceptionally high usage of an on-demand sports programme. Closer inspection revealed this to be a football match from several years previously, in which Manchester United had secured an EPL title. The recording had been streamed nearly a thousand times during the latest three-month period, to the same IP address. It was assumed to be an error, either in the MIS or on the streaming platform itself; but it turned out to be neither.

When contact was eventually made with the actual customer, a lady from the north west of England, it transpired she was a dyed in the wool United supporter and this particular match was her favourite one of all time. Having chanced upon a recording of it on Vision, she had repeatedly viewed it day and night for almost ten weeks. It had cost her over a thousand pounds, and she was happy to pay it. If Vision could just find a few more nutters like her, then it was on to a sure fire winner.

BT then finalised a negotiation with Sky and the regulator which would permit Vision to purchase and resell Sky Sports programming. This had been viewed internally as a potential killer application since it would enable BT to offer the service at a discount, grow the overall market for pay television, and further raise the profile of its television business. It did indeed lead to a short term acceleration in the take-up for the service and by the end of the first season over seven hundred thousand users were on the platform. But it then plateaued more or less at that level, still significantly short of the two to three million subscribers originally targeted for the main service. BT would still need to take more significant steps to establish itself as a major player in the UK television sector.

The market was plainly still finding the basic premise of Vision at best confusing, or at worst underwhelming. It was now selling Sky programmes, but accessed via the Sky platform itself, or as top-up subscription channels run by BT on the terrestrial digital platform Freeview. People heard and read about on-demand programming, but nobody but a few geeks really got what that meant. It wasn't even catch-up television, not initially.

It seemed that, once again, BT had prematurely launched a product way before there was a real market for it. Of course, there are rich pickings to be made by market pioneers, but that only happens when the market fully materialises, and it did appear as if the market for online catalogues of historical television programmes was nascent at best. Amid competition from live sports programming, multiple minority interest channels and online catch-up television itself, together with boxed sets of DVDs, it was still finding the going very tough.

I was co-opted onto a working group that was minding BT's financial interest in a project that later launched under the name of YouView, a development of the free-to-air digital broadcast initiative but which would also deliver catch-up and on-demand programming over broadband and through the television set. The project was a partnership between BT, the UK's four main broadcasters, and a couple of other telecoms operators. The business plan was being finalised, and I was somewhat surprised to note that the plan offered only a one-sided view of the business, namely the investment required and the future cost base. There was no inclusion of the benefits, the revenues, the returns. When I asked why this was so, the reply suggested the consortium was not yet clear in its mind what exactly these would be.

When I then asked about how Vision fitted with YouView, I was told they were the same thing, or soon would be. I was sure it all made sense to somebody – I had seen a neatish Venn diagram which purported to explain it – but I pitied the poor would-be viewer sat at home trying to figure it all out. We really weren't making it easy for him.

With my temporary assignment with Vision drawing to a close, I worked on a management analysis of the organisation, looking at core purpose and resourcing. We discovered that of the notional eighty-odd people in the unit, over half of them spent the majority of their time dealing with other parts of BT. This meant less than half were spending a majority of their time actually building the Vision business. It hit me then, why so many of the team could look so downcast; they were spending way too much of their time chasing endless BT shadows; trying to work the matrix, with its casual, hollow commitments. A devil to make work, and a devil to fix; countless were those who had tried.

Of course, BT Vision wasn't really television at all. It was Blockbuster Videos, down a wire. The central proposition had never truly caught on, but over time it did at least establish BT as a media presence of some substance. Together with the sports programming that had taken up residence at the BT Tower, to say nothing of a willingness to spend large amounts of money in defence of its position in the UK broadband market, it now had sufficient leverage and credibility with the EPL football organisation for it to entrust BT with sharing the UK broadcast rights for its product for a second time, from the summer of 2013, when the company would launch its own television sports channels.

As I write it would appear the BT Vision brand is being consigned to the past for a second time. A puff of publicity is now gathering around something called BT TV, an umbrella marque which may yet bestride the new sports channels, the involvement in YouView, and the on-demand catalogues, at least while the latter survive in their current guise before, one speculates, they dovetail with and are then superseded by a broader concept of catch-up.

I was relieved to pass up my fleeting acquaintance with Vision and concentrate solely on my media and broadcast duties, a step back into a more familiar, simpler world. I assumed I was finally losing the appetite for experiment, but I was to have one final bite at the cherry.

15

Tower Record II

Back at the BT Tower, I had expanded my responsibilities to take in the financial and commercial aspects of the television production activities. This was the closest I would come to the inner workings of the media and was yet a further step away from the core business of the BT Group. It provided some of the most entertaining and eminently surreal experiences I would enjoy at the company, largely due to the mix of people involved and the nature of the work we would undertake.

Some background context and explanation for what this was even doing as part of BT is required. In 2006, in order to realise the television content for BT Vision, notably the sports programming, the Vision organisation had issued a request for tender to various production and media companies, including BT's own Media and Broadcast unit. Lo and behold, M&B secured the contract to produce the programming, in partnership with a major sports production company.

As part of the agreement securing this partnership, BT purchased a substantial amount of production equipment from the partner, sufficient to fit out two production galleries, four audio booths and eight video edit suites, in all accounting for some three thousand square feet of the second floor at the Tower offices. In addition, a presentation studio set-up was installed on the thirty fourth floor of the Tower, on the site of the once public restaurant. Separately, M&B also won the subsequent tender to process original on-demand content files into standardised formats, for loading onto the BT Vision content platform. The server farm required to deliver this was installed in the basement of the Tower, with online access available from desks within the newly established production facility. Within a matter of months therefore, the BT Tower had morphed from being merely the hub of the UK's terrestrial television distribution network, and that of BT's then-nascent global media network, into a fully fledged television broadcast, production and media services complex. With the advent of digital television, this placed BT in a commanding position.

In addition to producing television programmes on site for BT Vision, the production facility would be used to pull together a range of sports programming on behalf of the production partner as well. These were then distributed onwards to a significant number of territories around the world where the partner held local distribution rights. This would take advantage of BT's reach into vast tracts of Eastern Europe, the Middle East, India and South East Asia, and was a massive undertaking in its own right.

The full launch of the facility had taken place in the autumn of 2006, and by the time I arrived in mid-2008 the party was in full swing. The facility retained over fifty fulltime BT employees, supported in turn by a small army of freelance production and encoding staff; while not all on site at once, which would have represented a major health and safely risk, there were over two hundred of them named on the preferment roster.

The general manager of this shindig, a decent, raffish type with a finance background most recently applied in the issues of chocolate manufacturing at Nestlé, had his hands permanently full of personnel, operational and contractual problems. For the previous two years he had scarcely enjoyed any consistent, dedicated finance support, and now he had entirely lost sight, if he had ever enjoyed it, of the true financial performance of the unit; our priority was a major drains-up on the state of the books.

After a detailed, month long trawl through salary details, freelance invoices, maintenance contracts, network charges from around the world and asset depreciation policies as they applied to television production equipment, and taking account of the charges levied on BT Vision and bills sent to the production partner for programming and distribution services, we discovered the unit was losing so much money that by rights it should have been closed down there and then. Meanwhile, with issues over contractual commitments coming to a head, the relationship with BT Vision was in tatters, while the production partner was threatening legal proceedings. I had walked into yet another commercial catastrophe, only this time with absolutely no idea how to put things right.

By a miracle, this realisation coincided with the organisational upheavals within BT Global Services, which opened up the possibility of a complete change of management. The BT Vision initiative was a very visible and strategically important project to BT, too important to be put in jeopardy by messy internal wrangling and inefficient internal processes. It was therefore suggested, and rapidly agreed, that the BT Vision sports management team should take over running the facility, since they were the main clients for the production and processing services anyway, and they actually had experience of managing sports production companies.

Their objectives were clear: to redefine the hand-offs between the Tower and BT Vision, rebuild the relationship with the external production partner, and reengineer the entire business model of the facility. To start again from scratch; who knew where it might lead. The general manager was paid off, much to his obvious relief and, a confectionery man to his fingertips, he returned to his roots, television but a distant memory.

The whole sorry episode to date bore all the hallmarks of previous attempts by the company to casually step into new and uncharted territories as though money and naked ambition – with scant regard for professional courtesies of knowledge, experience and skill – imbued it nonetheless with a God given right to participate and to assume an indignant, high handed response to failure.

We were summoned to a presentation suite in the Tower by BT Vision's director of sport, Steve, who played it straight and, while claiming not to have all the answers to hand, clearly had a pretty good idea of what he thought needed to be done. After he had spoken, I went up and introduced myself to him. "Ah yes," he said, "I was hoping to meet you. We have a lot to talk about. Can we get together tomorrow morning?" We certainly did have a lot to talk about, and I went upstairs to spend the evening printing it all out.

The decision to undertake television production was not in itself blind arrogance, since the facility had been placed from the start in the hands of operational staff equipped with the appropriate skills. However, the decision originally to use BT's starry eyed satellite and broadcast network managers to actually run it, to make important investment and recruitment decisions, and to negotiate the original client and supplier contracts, had been daft. They were out of their depth, the basics of production and nuances of media hopelessly lost on them.

Added to that, a lack of financial support and meaningful reporting meant the poor hapless soul who ended up in charge was always on a hiding to nothing. The vast majority of the production work was competently done and completed on time, but had been carried out in the absence of proper controls to ensure it was done within appropriate cost and resource budgets, recoverable within the relevant charge bands. The commercial model was broken and we needed to start all over again.

I met up with Steve and his team to take them through the paperwork. Relaxed in their raiment of denim and fleece, their demeanour grew uneasy as I described the numbers of employees engaged in the most basic of tasks, and the freewheeling volumes of freelancers that whirled through the doors of the Tower on a weekly basis. It was like a nightmare social organised on Facebook.

Between the four of them, they brainstormed what a real life production team should look like; I sat, listened and scribbled. It had obviously been a bad decision to employ so many production staff on fulltime contracts, given the peaky and seasonal nature of the work. Where there was over fifty fulltime staff, the nature and volume of the work necessitated well under half that number, maybe as few as ten, and while the bulk of the work should be undertaken by trusted freelancers, there should be a far more tightly controlled number of them on the roster.

Given there was now less than a year remaining on the original Vision contract to broadcast EPL football matches, they would use that natural breakpoint as the driver for a restructuring of the entire unit that would begin straightaway, so we would be in shape for the future. And they would look for new business to fill the utilisation void created by the cessation of EPL programming. They had contacts; they would start to ring round; it was that sort of business. It was a good facility, and there were good people working there. It just required good management; appropriate, knowledgeable, fit for purpose management. No miracles.

★

As we sought to patch up the relationship with our production partner, we jointly bid for a series of contracts for sports programming which suddenly and magically appeared out of thin air; all of which, through a further twist of good fortune, we somehow contrived to win. We found ourselves with a healthy pipeline of business, which would credibly place us on the map of London's sports television production houses.

The first contract win was to provide a weekly highlights package covering all English Football League matches to be played over the coming three years. The fact this amounted to over one thousand matches, spread all over the country, didn't seem to faze anybody. The primary objective was to capture all the goals scored at each match, edit the footage at local BBC facilities and then transmit it to the BT Tower. Once there, the action from all the matches would be consolidated into a single package for onward distribution to the BBC, Sky and our production partner.

The BBC would use this footage in their newly planned Football League Show which would be put out late on a Saturday night after the flagship Match of the Day programme. While it didn't exactly make a great deal of use of our own production facility, it was a solution that deployed the strengths of BT's media networks and it put us in the shop window. Through televisual genius, our cameramen and editorial technicians managed never to miss a single goal out of over three thousand scored during the period of the contract.

On the back of this, we swiftly secured two more deals. The BBC wanted to mirror their broadcast football coverage online via their sports website. This would involve a swift edit of the footage and then transcoding the files into standard formats required to load video content onto the web; the challenge for our team was simply in meeting the strict deadlines for preparing and transmitting the material to the BBC.

The work we had long been doing for BT Vision provided more than sufficient evidence of our capabilities in this area, and since the original files were coming through the Tower anyway for the highlights programme, it would be a relatively straightforward procedure to provide a direct feed into the edit suites and transcoding systems. A three year contract was duly signed.

The Association of Tennis Professionals (ATP) organises the men's year long, global tennis tour. As part of its public relations activity, it had been producing in-house a weekly magazine programme which aimed to get behind the sporting headlines to reveal the lives of the players as the tour progressed around the world. They were looking to outsource the production and marketing of the programme and initially approached our partners who, having no spare capacity of their own, recommended our team.

After a quick spin round the facility, a glimpse at our early work for the BBC, and then lunch on the thirty fourth floor of the Tower, the deal was done. If the BT Group CEO had asked a few months later how we had contrived the rather bizarre situation whereby a BT employee was filmed interviewing Roger Federer in Miami on his accumulation of umpteen Grand Slam titles, it would no doubt have been an interesting discussion. But it happened, and he was very nice about it. Roger Federer that is.

One evening in an empty office, I heard some relentless muttering from a nearby workstation. Unable to tune it out, I listened in. The presenter on the ATP programme was sat in a nearby audio suite, recording his script over and over until he got the rhythm and inflection just right. I felt like joining in by the end: "Away from the tensions of the show courts and the rigours of the practice arena, Rafael likes nothing better than relaxing by the pool with a cold beer." He spoke for both of us.

I was continually impressed and affected by the sunny disposition of the overall team, from the executive management through the programme production staff to the facility administrators. They plainly all got on well and enjoyed their work. This was infectious and added to the general sense of pleasure derived from being associated with the activity. The team was a close knit community based together on one floor; the buzz was tangible and authentic. It was great fun working there, and with the new management team in place it had a clearer and more rounded sense of purpose too.

There was also a thriving social life, in which both the production team and the network and satellite mob were heavily embroiled. The local public houses were scarcely bereft of clientele during the weekday evenings, and doubtless over the weekends too once the last of the Saturday afternoon football footage had passed through the Tower. This was a profound change from many previous roles, where self-imposed long-hours regimes and a general unsociableness had left little time or inclination for interpersonal hospitality.

Here at the Tower, there was more of an objective-based culture, where the day was spent carrying out what needed to be achieved by the relevant production or process deadlines. You wouldn't invent any more work to do, so it was off to the pub. Not everybody, every day; but some people, on most days. You were never short of a drinking companion. It was a throwback to my earliest times in the company and would help to keep me in this neck of the woods for several years. I had missed this.

Another of the old style pleasures of working at the Tower was the presence of a staff canteen, one of the last of its type, a glorified tuck shop that also served glorious, hot comfort food. The functional appearance and heavy air of pungent gravy laden smells transported me back to Shaftesbury Avenue, and the simpler, more easygoing days I had spent there when work was just work, not a step in a career or a fork in the road. I would while away time on the post-prandial sofas, their yielding upholstery lulling me into mulling the carefree futility, the abandoned pointlessness of corporate life. All that time and effort. For what? I would shudder at the thought of it ending though, even as I acknowledged my growing detachment and my wearying efforts towards concealing it.

I delighted in taking advantage of the full range of minor perquisites available from being based in the Tower. In all my years in the company I had never actually visited the suite of viewing floors at the top of the stick. I had read of and passed over countless opportunities to participate in sponsored walks up its famed eight hundred and forty two steps. Now though, I just had to have a word with one of my colleagues who held the magic pass to the lifts and moments later I would be up in the sky, nose pressed to the glass, drinking in the magical views of central London, hundreds of feet below. Only when the floor unaccountably began to rotate did the magic wear off.

On one occasion, I accompanied various colleagues who had never had cause or opportunity to venture up there. We were ushered by our guide up to the casements, from where the street plan of the West End of London lay before us like a sheet of graph paper. The sunlight beyond the glass was hotting up the rather narrow segment of floor space into which we were all crammed, so our host sought to alleviate any mild discomfort caused by this – by throwing open one of the windows. Some of us gasped, one yelped and a couple screamed. I could not believe what I was seeing, and thought for a split-second that we would be sucked out through it.

An open window, the size of a small door, thirty three floors off the ground. The inward rush of cold air created a disorientating effect. It was something out of a nightmare. I stepped away to rest my back against the wall of the inner core, momentarily unsteady on my legs. This was horrible. Seconds later it was closed and we made our way down. I couldn't bring myself to think about reporting him for breaching health and safety regulations; I just wanted to forget the entire episode had ever happened. An open window four hundred feet up in the air? Don't try it.

One weekend I went along to the production facility with my sons and their mates to watch the team in action. I had never seen the facility in full swing like this, the screens ablaze with footballing vigour, the audio suites thrumming, the galleries as editorial bear pits, the corridors teeming with runners and overseeing it all was our production head Martin, as unruffled as ever. He simply had to give himself over to it and hope it all went well.

We then walked around to the media network management centre, a vast setup reminiscent of the Apollo spaceflight control rooms. The main room here was dominated by huge flashing electronic displays depicting the global network configurations, interspersed with dozens of LED screens showing the programming currently transiting its multiple circuits. The kids were struck dumb; it was a digital wonderland, and made mincemeat of their smartphones and games consoles.

Amidst this sparkling array of audio-visual splendour, it was easy to forget that one of the main functions of the Tower complex was as a plain old telephone exchange. But away from its glossier precincts, this soon became apparent. Floor after floor was rammed with ancient Strowger switching equipment, redundant early digital network kit, live "DSLAMs" carrying broadband services to the Fitzrovia community, server farms and IP routers forming a hub of the company's trumpeted twenty first century network. It was impossibly cramped. We once spent a surreal afternoon clambering amongst this stuff, searching in vain for a vacant space which might theoretically house a new television studio; for one fleeting moment, I had the glorious sensation of being lost.

★

Time was sliding past as sports seasons came and went. The underlying financial performance of the unit was improving all the time, as we continually edged towards the typical production house operational model, reducing overhead staffing and dipping into the vast pool of freelance television resource available across the capital. The range of expenditures I was called upon endlessly to approve never failed to leave an imprint on my mind, whether it was commissioning a renowned football commentator to provide a running commentary on a pre-recorded match using our audio suites, or wheeling in a former England international to sit alongside him and provide the expert summarising.

Then there were the exotic travel requests from the team covering the ATP tour. They were each of them covering over a hundred thousand miles in the air each year, and after a while they were beginning to look it, with the bags under their eyes almost too big to take on board as cabin luggage.

A couple of other noteworthy opportunities came our way. BT had signed up as a key sponsor of the London 2012 Olympic Games and was providing the telecoms infrastructure around the various locations where the Games were taking place. A feature of each location would be a network of video screens, which throughout the period of the Games would broadcast programmes relating to events taking place locally, plus a series of news items on the main developments at the various other venues. We were asked to pitch for the provision of this service. My colleague Tony, an industrious individual with a taste for sorting out knotty problems, took on the task of liaising with the client, the London Olympic Games' Organising Committee, unedifyingly known as LOCOG.

There followed the most dauntingly detailed and gratuitously painful bid application. It plainly wasn't enough for BT simply to be a key sponsor, a producer of original and related content, and the provider of telecoms grade communications infrastructure and services throughout the Games' estate. We had to evidence our proficiency in every conceivable politically correct compliance criterion, which the tender document had racked up in its horrifyingly cliché-ridden appendices.

For a matter of what seemed like months, Tony was immersed in the blinkered, brain numbing torment of the box ticker's guide to global, environmental and social betterment, with its kaleidoscopically sanctimonious agenda towards climate change, sexual diversity, disability and fair trade. His never-say-die attitude had met its ultimate foe, and he would not be cowed. He was a man transformed as he learned of and loudly proclaimed BT's multiplicity of earnest policies across these and other tenets of the slavishly championed ethical and inclusiveness prospectus; someone had actually sat down and written these. In the end, sadly, Tony's heroic efforts and jovial observance would count for nought, since the organisers were ultimately wary of granting more than a specific value of business to one pair of grubby commercial hands. They might have told him earlier.

We were then asked to support our networks colleagues in a bid to broadcast the world jujitsu championship. Originating in Brazil, where the sport has a cult status, this annual event had rapidly grown into a major global festival, with competitions being held across Asia and Europe, as well as South America. The initial bouts would be staged in a handful of locations across Brazil, and we were requested to provide a budgetary price for this opening phase of the tournament. I had never seen my colleagues move so quickly.

There were several unknowns as to the production levels required, so a series of scenarios were drawn up regarding the numbers of cameras to be used, the extent of production facilities provided on site and how much would need to be shipped in, and the availability of local technical and production staff. A comprehensive document was drafted which captured this matrix of possibilities, together with a pick'n'mix rate card of prices for the services on offer.

It was a stunning if surreal piece of work, requiring as it would the ability of BT to organise the transportation of cameras, portable mixing galleries, lighting rigs, and a team of twenty around the Amazon basin for three months. I could just picture the scene: a line of trucks stamped with the BT logo, winding its way through the steaming rainforests, followed by a coachload of our production team and cheery local hires, hanging from the windows of their charabanc and swigging from bottles of cachaca. Fortunately, I would never need to present the financials to the CEO on this one, since our opening bid was roundly dismissed on grounds of cost.

As well as pitching for work externally, we had had some success offering our services to other parts of the BT Group. There were always parts of the company commissioning training videos, client communications via YouTube and promotional footage, and we became the default supplier for these services, saving hundreds of thousands of pounds for BT each year. The looming arrival of the Olympic Games brought a deluge of work into the facility, in support of a major corporate marketing programme positioning BT at the heart of London 2012. One element of the project I had not yet been made aware of was the proposed use of the Tower in an event to mark the launch of the thousand day countdown to the start of the Games.

An expenditure request landed in my inbox, which sought approval to spend twenty thousand pounds to rent a fucking helicopter for an evening, in order for us to film a laser show due to take place over London. I honestly thought the sender was pulling my leg, so I rejected it on governance grounds, since he had plainly failed to furnish me with a detailed set of researched, benchmark data confirming this was unquestionably the precise fucking helicopter required for the task. Moreover, I suggested, he could borrow my own camera, and lean out of the Tower window which he had recently opened – causing me great distress – to film it himself, thereby saving us the cost not only of the fucking helicopter but of the cameraman's time as well.

Following a serious humour failure and in a mildly apoplectic state, he tore round to my desk and laid into me for jeopardising the highlight of the countdown event, now only days away: "I need a fucking helicopter!" But in all conscience, and as I explained to him in as even a tone as I could muster, there was no way I would ever authorise a fucking helicopter to buzz around the Tower of an evening. The military authorities would probably bring it down, and then where would that leave us; we might end up at war. I sent him off to liaise with the corporate marketing folk; they could organise and pay for their own fucking helicopter. They did.

★

As the summer of 2012 approached so our external contracts were coming to an end, and discussions were opened with the clients over renewing them. We had enjoyed positive relationships with each client and had established the BT facility as a high quality supplier of production services. Some of the equipment was starting to fray a little at the edges and elements of it were becoming technically obsolete. So in order to assist the contract negotiations and put the place on a sounder footing, a renovation and upgrade proposal was put forward.

While the facility was known to a section of the BT executive community, there was a sizeable majority who had never actually heard of it, or who would struggle to conceive of it as being a BT asset at all. The proposal to upgrade it, rendering it fully high-definition compliant, had to be couched in a detailed explanatory thesis of its provenance, rationale, object, scope and value. Even then, it would need to take its place in the queue of projects bidding for what was at the time a diminishing pot of investment capital. When its turn for consideration finally came along, the arguments were knocked down one after the other; above all, it was non-core and too small a business for the prioritisation of limited cash.

Contract negotiations were stumbling on grounds of price and technology; the writing was appearing on the wall. From left field, our sales colleagues inadvertently came up with an innovative solution. Given the dreadful prevailing market conditions, so desperate were they to hit their targets that they had given up all hope of making any significant product sales. Instead, they had furtively taken it into their heads to try to flog off parts of the business instead, and had received interest from a couple of parties in acquiring the production facility. We weren't sure whether to laugh or cry.

The potential buyers were shown around the place and in short order an initial commercial offer was received from each. Momentum was gathering without any real internal consideration having been made as to the attractiveness or otherwise of a sale. Senior executives were finally engaged, who then havered; nobody wanted to be the one to say "yes, sell". This was unsurprising, since BT was not at all, in the normal course of events, a selling company. It accumulated stuff, it didn't dispose of it; it was by nature a hoarder, a sentimentalist. But the failure to back the facility with new investment meant it could only depreciate in value; logic dictated a sale should be sought.

A formal disposal project was hurriedly concocted; lawyers and corporate financiers descended upon the place like flies. Documents were drafted; asset registers compiled; numbers crunched; prices set; letters dispatched. One prospective buyer pulled out immediately, baulking at the cost. The second proposed a series of due diligence meetings and review sessions, and I was duly carted off to parade the numbers before their CFO in his smart Soho office. If we were going to be bought out, it could have been worse.

At this point a classic intra-BT moment arose. Another line of business had for years borne the costs of housing and maintaining computing and air conditioning equipment that supported some of the activities within the facility. I was quite oblivious to this, since they had never bothered to charge us for them; they preferred instead to recover the totality of their operating costs, which dwarfed those incurred running our kit, from BT Group centrally, a far simpler exercise.

Now facing pressure to reduce the level of costs they recovered in this way, they saw an opportunity and decided to charge us directly with the full whack of these running costs. At a stroke, the reported profitability of our business was slashed. Sheepishly, I returned to Soho with the news that the cost of running the facility had suddenly spiked, trashing the profit margins. The value of the business plummeted and within days the deal was dead. The matrix had struck again.

An eerie calm settled over the Tower. As a team we engaged in half-hearted, quixotic discussions about taking it on ourselves either as a BT-backed venture or even as a spinout. But questions over reinvestment and client contracts rendered this unrealistic, plus the fact that we were at heart corporate citizens and not entrepreneurs; deep down we preferred the prospect of spending BT's cash rather than our own.

★

The external business came to a dignified close with all contractual obligations met and all payments banked. It had been a successful last twelve months and the production team had done their bit towards delivering the Media and Broadcast unit's best ever set of financial results. The residual team was now down to a bare handful of people, a timely voluntary redundancy package having been eagerly seized upon by most of the production staff, who were now looking to capitalise on their recent experiences outside of BT. In addition, the media processing activity supporting BT Vision was fully merged into their scheduling team. The facility now had a cold and empty feel to it.

Then, another classic intra-BT moment: in a bolt from the blue, it was announced that BT had bid for and won exclusive rights to broadcast a bloc of English Premier League football matches beginning in the summer of 2013. Steve, who had been noticeably absent for some weeks, had been busily advising the BT board on the rights auction, but for confidentiality reasons had not been able to share the news of BT's participation in it.

Over the coming months, as the plan for launching and running a new sports channel – BT Sport, the new vehicle for the programming – became clear, so the facility would be handed a lifeline as an operational backup to the main production centre, which would be based in the former Olympic Park media hub. The remaining production staff at the facility would be joining the team being set up to run the new channel.

This was deserved recognition for the work delivered over the previous three years in particular, and the qualities of the staff involved. While the production business had been an integral part of the BT Vision initiative since its inception, it had remained a relatively small affair, another cottage industry. To put a post-rationalising spin on it, it had been a five year testing ground, an experiment; and one which had turned out successfully. The reward for this was to be its direct involvement in the BT Sport initiative, a far bolder strategic bet and at the very heart of BT's consumer market proposition. The team had come a long way.

My own association with the production unit had run to almost four years, the longest period of time I had spent associated with one department, and I was now contemplating another change of scenery. While I might have liked to work on the new channel, the commercial challenge would require expert knowledge and experience in managing a raft of outsourced television supply contracts. A step too far, even by my standards of dilettantism. Besides, it was being made very clear to me that my skills and experience were now urgently required elsewhere, in an altogether different place.

16

Calling Time

And so it was that, twenty five years on, and by some strange and unaccountable force, I found myself back in the bosom of BT's core UK telephony business. My boss's boss, an affable chap also called Andrew, finding himself short of strategic commercial brain power, plucked me from the welcome obscurity of my BT Tower existence and thrust me into the relative limelight of a proper BT Wholesale headquarter role. Some nasty-sounding projects were looming and he needed to rebalance his team to make the most of the resources available. It all happened very quickly and delivered a sharp shock to my maverick mindset. My square peg was being forced into a gapingly open round hole, all smilingly done but going ahead whether I liked it or not.

The wholesale division of BT looked after the Group's relationship with other telecom operators and service providers in the UK, of whom there were several hundred. There were three main areas of activity: selling network circuits and "interconnect" services to the other operators, enabling them to build and run their own networks and interlink them with BT's own; selling white label products, such as telephone calls and broadband services, for resale to business and consumer customers; and running outsource contracts to manage and maintain networks on behalf of other operators. It was profitable and reasonably well run, but like the rest of the Group had been facing tough recessionary pressures which were now forcing it to improve productivity and reduce its operating costs.

My initial task was to join up with a working party looking at cost transformation, a function as leadenly uninspiring as it was central to the division's fortunes. With the combined pressures of recession, regulation and competition making their presence felt ever more acutely, the company's revenues had been declining for several years and were forecast to continue doing so over the medium term. This led to an inevitable emphasis on cost containment and reduction in order to protect margins and cash flows. And with the Group now in the combined clutches of its three leading accountants (as indeed the chairman, CEO and CFO all were) they saw and seized an opportunity to make levels of savings quite unprecedented in the company's history. Billions were to be delivered.

Our working party was set a target of removing one hundred million pounds in annual running costs from the wholesale business plan, and we fetched up in a meeting room: a selection of the smartest and most knowledgeable individuals from across the entire Wholesale management team, and me. They proceeded to brainstorm cost saving options for several hours, delving into the inner workings and cost drivers of networks, exchange buildings, call centres, field forces, product technologies, even electricity bills.

They certainly knew their stuff, which was just as well, since I didn't have a clue as to what they were talking about. What I did manage to glean, however, was that around ninety per cent of the division's cost base was not directly managed by it at all, but was in fact transferred in from other parts of the company. It would be my job to liaise with these other organisations, and firm up and agree with them the savings as identified by the working party. Gah: the dreaded matrix.

I went home that night, lay on the bed and stared at the ceiling: what on earth had I spent my day listening to, and what was I to do with my life? Then I was swept back over twenty five years to my original perceptions of my new employment. They had been wrong; maybe I was mistaken now. But faced with the clear prospect of weeks of mind numbing tedium, I reached for the survivalist's philosophical codes, about remaining strategic, and everything coming to an end; it was just a case of grinning and bearing it in the meantime. And so with gritted teeth and spasmodic effort, I ploughed on and somehow managed to bluff my way through six months of this merriment, stressing my own ignorance of operational detail and relying on others' expertise. I concentrated instead upon occasional analytical forays and presentational élan. Anything to avoid discussing the mechanics of delivering any actual savings, conversations I had no means of, nor interest in, either conducting or concluding.

★

The role was based in what would prove to be the final destination of my peripatetic time in BT, Faraday House, a bustling few floors carved out of an imposing former international exchange building set back a couple of streets from the River Thames, and a mere handful of steps down from St Paul's Cathedral. It looked like the headquarter building of a once prestigious, lordly corporation, and was thus the perfect choice to house the last vestiges of BT's unreformed legacy business. Its shabby exterior stonework brought to mind the local government seat of a former provincial power, laid low by the flight of capital and employment opportunities to the rampant south east. It had faded glory painted all over it, most notably in the branded signage of BT Wholesale.

Its sole redeeming feature was a splendid view, from a back staircase, of the emerging spear of the Shard building on the distant south bank of the Thames. I spent many aimless moments gazing at its climbing majesty, as it cast its lengthening shadow onto the predicament of my rapidly ailing BT career. I yearned to be plucked from this dusty hovel and propelled into a glistening tower of steel and glass, investing the roubles, reals and rupees of developing nations and their commercial investment arms; or maybe I just needed a change of scenery, fresh air and a new challenge. I was becoming too enclosed by familiarity and the contempt it was breeding left me nauseous and angry. It occurred to me for the first time that BT and I could be heading for separation.

Andrew was a decent, avuncular and highly intelligent chap who hailed from Yorkshire. He was one of the growing number of non-metropolitan envoys within the company's senior management who, alongside assorted foreign imports, second and third generation immigrants, and a visibly burgeoning cohort of women, were progressively transforming the make-up of the higher echelons within the company and bringing it into line with that of the wider workforce.

I had had a few arms length dealings with Andrew in previous roles in the global business, where he had run a financial planning team. On one occasion, he had turned down my request for clearance to submit a strategy document direct to a corporate unit, and with such high-handed pomposity that I had vowed at the time never to communicate with him ever again. I tried not to think of this as I sat opposite him as his new direct report. He came across as a model of pragmatic, helpful reasonableness. Well, I was getting him out of a hole, wasn't I, so he had to be nice to me. Soon after, I asked him to clear my sending a paper directly to the divisional CFO. "If you're sure, then go ahead." It was his new way of saying no.

He was one of a merry band of senior types who, no doubt on account of their generous share-based reward scheme, had taken to working all hours. I would regularly receive emails from him timed at six thirty in the morning, or after ten o'clock at night, to say nothing of his clearing of the decks on a Sunday afternoon in advance of our eight thirty Monday morning kick-off calls. His scheduler was always blocked out for weeks in advance, his days heavily bandaged in a recurring monthly binding of reports, reviews, meetings and conference calls that left him little time during the working day to sit at his desk and actually get on with some work; hence the evening and weekend slots. I have never known someone so busy, so occupied and so passionate about getting stuff done and done correctly. If we had been concerned with less mundane matters, I would happily have followed suit and sought to emulate him as the model employee. As it was, my own scheduler remained stubbornly clear, save for a smattering of appointments, like Band-Aids applied over a light rash.

I wasn't really involving myself in my new surroundings, and it showed. I was struggling to raise any personal interest in the matter of the wholesale business: it left me cold. Andrew chivvied me along with enthused insight and encouragement and could make it all sound plausibly interesting and worthwhile. Yet as he left me to it, so I sensed the fleeting moment of motivation and purpose he had engendered slowly ebbing away. Other people were complaining about their work-life balance, of working all hours, while I was managing to be out of the door comfortably before six o'clock.

Andrew was responsible for the product finances of the entire division. This effectively meant ensuring the entire business achieved its revenue, profit and cash targets, through working in association with the sales teams to deliver the top line numbers and with the product teams to deliver the net benefits to BT. Over time, he had brought in a number of improvements to the working practices of the unit, which meant a relentless focus was placed on to the operational processes.

Weekly calls were run with the sales director and his departmental heads, looking at deals which were imminent, and with the product director on the deal support work and what was being done to bring in contract profit margins. From these, a vast number of spin-off and follow-on calls and meetings were hurriedly organised and diarised to keep the pressure on the operational management. Numbers were reworked daily, and presented weekly, before further rounds of reviews and "interventions" were worked through.

I was now expected to lead on this activity for the core voice products. What I lacked in detailed technical knowledge I should apparently make up for in providing commercial drive and backbone. It was a one billion pound business and could not be left to itself; it needed direction and the teams needed to be leant on.

I took Andrew aside and confided in him: I had never run this sort of operation in my life. I was exposed by the shortfall in my technical ability, and above all, I had simply no desire to act as the CFO of a billion pound business. I was a fish out of water. He knew this to be the case, and offered mentoring and support. He needed an experienced hand in the role, albeit from a different background; he couldn't leave it un-managed. And there were some upcoming developments that needed a strategic perspective, which I could bring. He suggested we "give it six months and then take another look at it." He was an agreeable sort and I didn't want to cause him any problems, so we shook on the six months, time enough surely for me to cast around and secure another role.

CALLS OF DUTY

★

The voice services, namely the origination, carriage and termination of telephone calls, were still a major earner for the group and generated vast amounts of cash each year. The continuing dominance of BT in this market ensured it had remained squarely in the regulatory authority's sights. A continuing war had rumbled on for over twenty years since the privatisation of the company, occasionally blowing up in the faces of BT's generals, but otherwise it had consisted of relatively low level, minor skirmishes with few casualties on each side. Tensions, however, remained.

Wholesale retained a standing army of regulatory veterans within its ranks and in many ways they had been the unsung heroes of the company's privatised incarnation. They had held the enemy at bay in the face of potentially hideous odds, maximising the cash BT was still able to squeeze from its monopolistic assets, which in turn had financed its foreign and more exotic domestic adventures down the years.

I owed my career to these people, and I held them in high regard, but they truly were the last people I had ever dreamed of working with. It was nothing remotely personal, I simply had no taste for it. I felt I was now being made to pay for my part in our oft-failed experiments, the borderline squandering of the company's wealth, and for my long held, lofty contempt for the UK mother ship. *Honi soit qui mal y pense.*

I was given a team of two to help me in the broad task of maximising revenues and profits from the voice portfolio, with a vacancy for a third analyst which I immediately set about trying to fill. The more there was of them, the less there would be for me to do. It says much for the level of interest generated by the area when I say we received, from an internal population of finance staff seemingly in perpetual motion, the princely number of two applications. We rejigged the ad to lay greater emphasis on strategic development projects, and bolstered the figure to five.

A couple of young guns impressed at interview; I was astonished at their enthusiasm, and perhaps saw something of my younger self in them. I happily offered each of them the job, and they each in turn rejected it, in favour of more obviously commercial roles elsewhere. I tried in vain to stress the opportunity for advancement within our wider team, as an additional sweetener, but this only seemed to make them even more uneasy at the prospect.

Understandably, and without quite saying it directly, they saw it as a comparatively dead-end role in a dying product area. This was to understate the level of change being driven through by the product teams, and to underplay the level of satisfaction from working with them day to day as individuals. But in the end it was the sheer dryness of the subject matter that would work against it. I could see and understand exactly what went through their minds; it had been going through my own for twenty five years. So we three pressed on with the matters at hand.

Andrew's wider team was comprised of a handful of characters from around the UK who supported the rest of the product portfolio. This was roughly split between voice and data, with the latter embracing domestic broadband and high capacity corporate bandwidth services. He decided to bring us all together for a day's bonding at, of all places, the BT Tower. To kick off, each would take it in turn to explain their area of expertise, their experiences of BT, their ambitions for themselves and for their part of the business.

As their mouths opened and the words tumbled out, my mind wandered back to Holborn and Westminster Cable, over to Milan and Zurich, up and around the Tower complex itself and thence to New York and Washington, Hong Kong, Seoul and Singapore, and finally back to Shaftesbury Avenue. I had circumnavigated the globe and the world of telecoms, and had come back to rest on UK telephony. I made this the central theme of my own monologue, adding that my ambition was not to waste the knowledge and learning I had accumulated on the way. I'm not sure it quite answered the question but it kept us all entertained for five minutes. It also ensured the younger members of the group remained solicitous towards me, seeking out advice on how they too might enjoy a similar career profile.

I was positive and generous of spirit, but the reality was it had been an accident of time, while I had been merely sufficiently open minded to step into the unknowns as they opened up before me. Above all, I supposed, I had been intrigued, and had taken the opportunities as they had arisen. I had managed my own time, my own career, and they should try to do that too. It was unlikely anyone else would organise it for them.

We then split into two teams and spent the afternoon running around Fitzrovia, carrying inflatable monkeys (I forget why) and being photographed in front of as many famous landmarks as possible, securing one hundred points at each location. As I lived nearby, my team was at a slight advantage, and amassed over two thousand points to our opponents' miserly few hundred. My reputation was now assured. Maybe this wasn't going to be so bad after all.

Yet despite this, I found it difficult, approaching impossible, to form the sort of relationships with my new colleagues that I had so often forged in the past and which alone had, on occasions, provided the psychological foundations beneath the weather-beaten and occasionally crumbling edifice of my telecoms career. I searched largely in vain for like-minded, semi-detached fastnesses of irony and self-deprecation, which had so often proved a mainstay amidst the ebbs and flows of nebulous corporate and departmental concerns.

My immediate finance colleagues fell into neatly discernible camps. An old-school brigade, who clung to their personal fiefdoms, minding parochial concerns of regulatory decrees and their accounting repercussions. These would see them comfortably into their retirements, unfazed and untroubled by routine career pressures, since nobody could afford to lose their knowledge. In contrast to them, the younger, clear eyed new wave; suited and booted, and expensively recruited, with a keen sense of their own worth and their next career move. I may have been seen as one of these once upon a time, but now I had no time for their specious, sanctimonious presence, where performance meant as much about being seen at your desk at all hours as actually delivering anything of worth. The younger women were notably keen on this scam, garnering praise and recognition as if by right.

A lone soul bore an air of *ennui* and *chagrin* similar to my own, and we soon forged a loose affiliation: I had known Kam for years on the global business and were it not for his acerbic insights, caustic asides and cheery periodic accompaniment to local pubs and cafes, I would have found myself at the end of my tether long before I finally did so.

The voice product folk themselves broadly fell into two similar categories. On one side, the ageing technicians who retained unique insight and experience of the arcane regulatory and management practices that kept this massive cash generative machine ticking over. On the other, a supporting cast of one-time arrivistes who had rocked up with plans to revolutionise this dusty backwater and who now bore the scars and frowns of defeat and frustration, driven back by the endless lappings of bureaucratic tides.

These were people the like of whom had populated and dominated the BT landscape for decades. World weary, intelligent and with a command of detail that would shame a neurosurgeon, their corner of the office nonetheless wore a collective shrug of the shoulders, a "who knows?" to the endless speculation over the next tightening of the regulatory noose, the outcome of outstanding legal cases, or the likelihood of persuading the market ever to sign up for IP voice services. I was expected to force an answer out of them, where others for years had tried and failed.

I spent some time discussing these big, strange and unyielding questions, and never felt for a second that I was making any headway in understanding them, let alone resolving them. It didn't feel like a business at all; more like a casino. Over time they had learned to play the house and break even, and even win. But you could never be sure how the dice would fall. How these guys could stand all this was beyond me. If I had taken it at all seriously, it would have driven me insane.

I sat down with the head of the voice product portfolio, an amiable fellow called Tim. He had been into this type of work for a number of years and knew the subject inside out. He was a little taken aback when I explained I was a complete novice when it came to BT's core products, but professional to the fingertips, he set to with a pictorial guide to the components of the network, the interplay between BT's and other networks, the elements covered by regulation and those bought and sold at market prices.

I felt my head begin to spin but stuck with him as he talked through the various products that were formed of combinations of these network elements. My professional tenacity and intellectual grip were then run through the mill as he moved onto the pricing freedoms enjoyed by the company, and on-going debates and Court cases the company was embroiled in regarding the inclusion or otherwise of twenty year old equipment costs.

I hadn't anticipated a legal dimension to this commercial and technical nightmare, and felt the will to live seeping from my soul as he went on to outline the company's arguments presented throughout the legal process and the grounds for appeal that were still before the Court. The three hours simply crawled by, and as he looked at his watch to check the time before his next appointment, he made for the door. "Hope that was all okay. Call if you need any help." A lovely chap, he had effectively sealed my fate.

★

We were corralled by the divisional CFO to quarterly rah-rah sessions in efforts to boost morale and motivation and to widen interest in the general business of the organisation. There seemed to be a lot of these sorts of affairs taking place, which naturally led one to assume that there were problems with morale and motivation, a general sense of unease. This was borne out in periodic surveys of staff attitudes and concerns; nobody felt very loved-up and they were having to work too hard.

I had always associated these sorts of resentments with uninspiring places to work. While top management sensed it was a question of leadership, empowerment and recognition, the truth lay more banally in the dreary nature of the work itself and that, sadly, was never going to change. A merry cast of familiar executives would be wheeled out to weave their spells, ramming home the need for us to sit up front, drive and navigate the business, with "no room for passengers" the latest mantra to have found its way into the song book.

I suppose they had to say something, and it was achingly true that for years the finance population had hidden behind their spreadsheets and reports, pathologically ill-equipped to deal with their commercial counterparts. I had always found them an introverted function, resigned to their fate and glorying in their unhelpfulness; I sometimes shuddered at my association with them. My quantitative abilities and analytical strengths had once again snookered me into their lair, and it was going to prove difficult to break free. I was in a bad place, consigned to a finance role on core products in the UK wholesale business; it reeked of defeat.

*

I made tentative attempts to move back into the global business, a place I had for years thought of as my spiritual home in BT. It was a rather different beast (again) to the one I had left four years previously. A couple of specific opportunities presented themselves, although it transpired I could not be considered as they were now looking to redeploy hundreds of their own staff and not looking to increase their overall headcount with moves in from other parts of the company. Its contractual meltdowns in 2009 had left a gigantic hole to be filled, and much of it now contained the bodies of many of my previous contacts, colleagues and sponsors. I scoured the online directory in vain for names I recognised and whom I might have approached for a potential lifeline. But my heart wasn't really in it. BT GS was now in the hands of a new generation, and like myself and my peers of earlier years, they would be jealously guarding the territory as their own.

I tried sounding out the new BT Sport organisation about a potential position there, but this too came to nought with the key production and editorial functions outsourced to third party suppliers, and the commercial team a lean looking cadre of experienced television sports hands. Ironically, this was an approach I had long advocated – using professionals instead of poseurs – and which now left the gamekeeper in me without a poacher's role to play. Hoist by my own petard.

I tried to make a go of my role and there were moments when I appeared to be getting on top of some elements, most notably with regards to the newer, more abstract aspects. But the overhang of historic, arcane concerns and complexities, so central to the management of this cash rich legacy, was a barrier too high for my flitting attention. I was unable and unwilling to immerse myself in them. Brain said no.

As my attempts to engineer an escape to more engaging areas one by one proved unfruitful, so I became increasingly convinced that my days in this organisation were coming to a close. I sketched out in my mind how the next ten year cycle was likely to pan out, and didn't like what I saw. The upturn would feel like the downturn before, a grinding endless malaise.

The rulebook had moved on: it was about conformity and efficiency, with little or no room for maverick experiment; that era, my era, was at an end, and perhaps for the better too. The tide had turned and a generational shift had taken hold. I sensed I was no longer cut out for this, and that my face no longer fitted.

The business that would intrigue and entertain me was no longer there. I had seen it all in its cosmic prime, but that light was now fading. The radiant glows of focus and drive were the gleaming prerequisites now. A new model army had taken over and there was no place for me in it. I had sensed the changes taking hold for a few years and now the writing was finally appearing on the wall for me.

I was coming to loathe the journey into work in the mornings: the claustrophobic lift ride to the sixth floor, the slab of the office door, the self-conscious walk to my desk; a bilious distaste, that I felt for no person, rising with each alienating step.

It had the unwelcome equivalence of an approaching divorce, the sick and sorry awakening to another day in a failed marriage. I now knew from personal experience how that could play out, and had no desire for another protracted, grisly disengagement.

I unloaded my feelings to Andrew who listened intently and realised immediately there was no going back for me; I had reached the end of the road and he knew it. In some ways he shared my own frustrations, but he had a richer stock of skills and responses, a resilience with which to mask and overcome them. I guess I envied him that. Ever discrete and diligent, he organised the relevant paperwork.

He included me in the forthcoming departmental Christmas lunch, and the following day circulated an email announcing my departure. I returned early in the new year to hand in my equipment and building pass, the last material vestiges of my BT persona. I stepped out of the building, into the chilly January sunshine, wearing a cautious smile only; like a soldier returning to civilian life, I was neither aware of nor prepared for the adjustments that would be required of me. I simply marvelled at the huge clear sky over the river, took a deep lungful of cold city air, tightened my scarf around me and set off home.

Part Four

Perspectives

1984 – 2013

On Culture

Analysing the evolution of a company's culture, and then trying to write about it, is a tortuous process since it requires a questioning and understanding of so many capricious aspects of human, collective and organisational attitudes and behaviours. It becomes a sufficiently messy web of assertion and speculation, observation and grievance as to rival the outpourings of the psychologically challenged from an hour or two on the analyst's couch. There may be truths that lurk within the maelstrom of hypotheses, but spotting them is a rare gift.

Additionally, attempts to disentangle wider social pressures and developments from the picture, to reveal a purely localised tableau, introduce a further dimension of risk in efforts to understand the central and ultimately straightforward matter in question; what was it actually like to work there? A pragmatic solution is simply to concentrate on a handful of aspects only, which the layman would grasp as those which set the tone of the place: the people, the rules of the road and the atmosphere around the place, and a view on how these factors changed over time.

People

The BT of 1984 bore a remarkable resemblance to the Post Office telephone department of the previous thirty years. It had always been conspicuously progressive in its employment of tens of thousands of women (albeit assiduously restricted to traditional female confines of personnel, sales and marketing, clerical and secretarial assistance and, as this was a telephone company, operator services), while it maintained an army of almost exclusively white male telephone engineers, over one hundred thousand of them spread across the country, allocated by the score to some six thousand local exchanges. Over time, non-technical, white collar areas have grown as a proportion of the total, and women have extended their presence and influence into ever wider spheres. The engineering army has withered sharply, with self-diagnosing and self-healing networks just one driver of massive efficiency gains across the field force. With women therefore now accounting for roughly half of employees, and with a strengthening foothold in senior management too, their gender-based values and attitudes have progressively cast a spell over so many of the company's policies and approaches as to render the culture quite unrecognisable from its earlier form.

It is far less larky, lairy, bantering; less boozy, less dithery, less clubby. These were the underlying failings (there were others) that in many ways had led to the market's striking ambivalence towards the British Telecom of the early 1980s. Management had not only tolerated this, it had conspired in it. And while a dose of market commercialism has of necessity driven out some of these practices and behaviours, so the increasingly significant presence and status of women has had a similarly dramatic effect. Their patient, focussed, no-nonsense approach simply won't stand for them, and over time has largely forced them out. Playtime is over.

It is also a far more meritocratic place: way fewer Oxbridge graduates stalk the corridors of power (now the open plan "leadership floors", of course), preferring these days to pursue careers in the City or the higher-minded professions, while BT today stalks the provincial and newer universities for its latest waves of graduate trainees. It seeks out those with a keener commercial focus and ambition, as opposed to the smoother quasi-academics who formerly assumed what was then largely an administrative mantle.

Today's graduate recruits are a simpler, humbler sort, with a pre-disposition to learn and earnestly endeavour. A new model army, of compliant, even listless souls, who keep themselves to themselves and their nose to the grindstone. The eerie silence pervading today's general offices betokens their obeisance and relative characterlessness, even fear. And where did all the rare birds of yesteryear go? They left, chased out long ago, and have never been replaced.

The rules of the road

The earliest chapters presented a potent and portentous mix of maddeningly rudderless decision making, frustrated leaders and the sole purpose of some simply to meddle, glossed over by an assumed right to play in new and developing product markets. Time is a great healer and its sheer relentless passage created over three decades sufficient space and opportunity for both logic and experimentation to jointly forge a new, more productive and effective settlement. Built on ever firmer foundations of insightful research, shrewd analysis and a growing understanding of risk and its mitigation, the processes of issue resolution and authorisation, the critical lines of decision making, became infinitely clearer. They were increasingly pointed to nominated individuals, clearly identified and empowered owners of categories of problems, which were rightly seen as going hand in hand with the territory of their specific job.

In contrast to this raining down of operational responsibility, directional power was progressively being sucked up into far fewer hands: business strategy became the exclusive preserve of divisional boards, while significant cost commitments required far more elevated levels of approval as budgets were squeezed. The "top five hundred", senior staff at director or vice president levels, and above, became the true guardians of the business and its future, and were ever more handsomely rewarded for it. Where once a committee sat in judgment, so now the VP's email, the director's text, would seal the deal.

A formidable cadre evolved which operated as a collective, looked comfortable shouldering the yoke of accountability, and didn't mind getting its hands dirty. You would have put money on them delivering. They blended technical expertise and knowledge of day to day operational detail with clarity of thought and a desire, a drive to make a difference. If they lacked anything, and it was a widely held view that they did, it was an inspiring vision. Perhaps they were simply too ground down. Perhaps they were all of too similar a cast of mind. But at least the rules of the road, and who was sitting in the driving seat, or reading the map, were now clear to everyone.

Atmosphere

Americans, as was ever the way, had a pithy name for it. That moment when you're welcomed with open arms, addressed by your first name and shown to your desk by the window, amid the smiling terraces of glowing white teeth and where you now have everything to lose: you've been "grin-fucked".

While BT remained some way off of that eventuality, the direction of travel was clear; the sense of the company edging towards that type of snake pit, palpable. The pally emails from the knighted chairman or the ennobled CEO, from "Mike" and

"Ian", were the smiles and the matey backslapping, the fraudulent friendliness, the softening up. Behind this leaden bonhomie lurked a steelier mindset, one that increasingly sought to set colleague against colleague in a race to the line, to raise the bar of performance and demand ever more from an increasingly eviscerated workforce.

While power was drained up, and responsibility rained down, morale was confused: should it wax or wane with the increased challenge, and expectation to achieve more with less? The confident and capable would always see and seize an opportunity, but the remainder would see only threat. New leaders emerged, while the rank and file had no option but to fall in, or fall out.

*

That's what had become of it all; the same as everywhere else, perhaps even more so, as moments of change cause the pendulum to swing violently from one extreme to another before finally coming to rest. For now though, the Ealing comedy of thirty years ago, a sprawling, colourful, ungainly and characterful collection of villages, had been dragged and battered into today's psychodrama, a bleakly uniform, conformist and compliant wired world.

On Careers

My time at BT was spent in some eighteen roles, thirteen buildings and under thirty immediate bosses; veritably, I careered around the organisation like a rat round the sewers of London, chasing my next taste of life at the frontier. It became a habit: arrive in an emerging part of the business, stake out my territory, my area of contribution and set about it; make some progress, maybe pick up additional areas of responsibility; or alternatively, make frustratingly little progress, become disenchanted, then look around for something new to do.

Nobody stopped me, or suggested I should slow down, immerse myself in something, become a "subject matter expert". I had a knack of making an early positive impact, however marginal, of effecting some change or other, and having achieved that, would sense the clock had already started counting down to my departure. There was little in the way of structured management development to detain me. With an ever flourishing array of novelties to catch my eye, I was flitting my way through BT's plentiful orchard like some telecoms fruit fly.

The core of my being, which determined my own show, needed to be interested, entertained even; that was my driving force, to avoid the prosaic, to find something new to distract me and when the fun wore off, to move on again. Two years here, eighteen months there; a spot of foreign travel when it suited. I found myself doing the jobs that I wanted, as and when I wanted to do them. My crowning achievement over twenty five years or so was to have kept myself switched on. I took my work seriously, but more so its capacity for engrossment.

★

Notwithstanding the derivation or otherwise of pleasurable self-satisfaction, careers are assessed in relation to progress: visibility and seniority, whether actual or perceived, and across all these it would be fair to describe a near perfect parabola, peaking around the turn of the century after an uptick in my fortunes during the 1990s, before a steady relative decline over the subsequent decade as I embedded myself in my middle years.

Not for nothing do we fade at forty: family life takes its toll, its share of attention and priority; the mind and body begin to sense their destiny, the long and heavy deceleration; other interests accumulate demands on time and inner resource: the career then becomes just a job, the role just a part in a play, or a game, until it's time to bring down the curtain, to blow the final whistle.

★

The villages of our 1980s Ealing comedy had each had their own, localised personnel and operational requirements, and this quaint parochialism had ensured a great sweep of interesting jobs and experiences, unique to that particular geographic or business area. This phenomenon would drown in the inevitable upsurge of standardisation. A necessary evil as technological applications drove patterns of behaviour and work processes into ever greater realms of sameness and blandness, it in so doing also spirited away the sense of adventure, excitement and personal crusade.

The corporate sector is unlikely again to provide the opportunity for such self-realising indulgences. And as for clambering up its slippery pole: the trend for fewer decision makers means the path up is getting ever more crowded by the day. Those without sharp elbows need not apply.

On Crises

For sixteen years or so, from 1993 to 2009, and with daunting regularity, BT lurched from one serious financial crisis to another, the ruinous co-incidence of economic adversity and management ineptitude proving a lethal compound.

The opening episode of this sorry trilogy, in 1992/93, arose as the company clawed its way through the latter stages of the 1990s downturn still facing considerable pressures on its operating margins. It eventually countered these with significant downsizing programmes, a reactive but necessary measure which bought time and eased immediate pressures but which did little to address more fundamental commercial and operational shortcomings.

The second calamity, in 2000/01 was self-induced, borne of a rampant acquisition spree and a failure to manage the balance sheet dynamics, where spiralling debt, asset devaluations and margin attrition across the various divisions turned reported capital and reserves negative. A humiliation by any measure, this was especially so for a company formerly ranked number one for market capitalisation on the London Stock Exchange. This episode bore the hallmarks of a failed state, with multiple centres of power, poorly controlled, combining to debase the currency, in this case the BT share price which within the space of two and a half years tumbled from a high of fifteen pounds to barely two.

The reprise in 2008/09 began as another self-inflicted

catastrophe: poor financial controls, formidably over-ambitious contracts bristling with draconian terms of compensation, blindly signed up by starry eyed, deluded dreamers of the type who had given us Concert; it was a disaster just waiting to happen. That this misfortune should have elided with the wider global financial crisis meant the knife was driven in further, and a more protracted and fundamental programme of self-flagellation would be required for recovery fully to take effect.

★

Glaringly foolhardy and reckless: one is put in mind of the Greek economy, which during the same period, underwent a similar pattern of egregious and untimely mismanagement. The symptoms, and the underlying causes in each case, bore an uncanny resemblance, as did, superficially at least, the measures advocated to put the patient right, although to date with strikingly divergent outcomes.

In each case, a lack of competitive edge, inefficiency, sloppy controls, poorly maintained records and a blind ignorance of the true position, together with a wilful disregard (in some quarters) towards these facts and a long term failure to correct the underlying problems (as being just too deeply ingrained and difficult to put right) led to a tightening of liquidity and a threat to long term solvency. The measures latterly and urgently advocated, under new technocratic managements, would involve retrenched budgets and the proposed shift to a new, improved and sustainable business model. While Athens aspired to a "new national growth model", within BT the strategic cry went out for "a better business, a better future".

Greece remained in a five year tailspin to dystopia, locked into an economic model paralysed by political, social and cultural intransigence. By contrast, following five years of relentless painful adjustment, BT's balance sheet returned to a substantially healthier state, with the potential fruits of a longer term economic recovery still to come.

Fundamentally, BT reset its ambitions, raised expectations across all aspects of business performance, set tough financial targets, and imposed rigorous management processes to ensure their delivery. Not always popular, but unhindered by democracy, its own austerity programme has cleansed the internal operating model and rinsed out inefficiency.

★

The eight year pendulum would suggest another similar disaster is due to befall the company some three years from the time of writing. Outwardly, this appears unlikely to occur: the balance sheet is solid, debt is secured at low and affordable interest rates, the company's operations are running at healthy and sustainable levels, and the accountants' beady eyes have never been more closely applied. Any wrinkle to emerge is likely to be containable for the foreseeable future.

But the motto has to be "never say never": for while internal vigilance may preclude most self-induced problems of commercial mismanagement, it does little to withstand a pivot turn in the market, or a hell-bent economic slump, leave alone a yawning gap opening up in the company's pension scheme. Blighted by its historical crises and an understandably nervy and easily unsettled investor base, the BT ship must forever remain on watch for stormy weather, and refrain from seeding the cloudbursts itself.

On Globalisation

For twenty years, BT's global business has struggled to forge and maintain a consistent, coherent, focused and financially viable identity. It has moved from an international network-centric service provider, through an outsourcing and managed services phase, and evolved latterly as a supplier of networked IT products and professional services to globalised industrial sectors.

It has branded itself variously as Global Communications, BT Worldwide, Concert, Ignite and Global Services, while its strategic motif has wavered between multi-site global contracts and in-country domestic services. At times, Europe has assumed geographic centrality, at others the US. CEOs have come and gone, organisational units have been built and dismantled, acquired and disposed of. The whirligig has rarely if ever stopped spinning. Such transience surely betokens not simply flexibility, nor a prescient ability to engage with developing markets. It seems here to signify a fundamental question of rationale: what really is the point of it?

The initial strategic logic was to place a growing proportion of BT's capital under a spread of commercial and regulatory regimes in the interest of limiting risk, to protect and grow earnings. Early signs were encouraging: sales grew steeply, eventually to account for around half of the entire Group's revenues. However, profitability was slow to appear and only now, twenty years on, is it approaching the modest levels originally envisaged. There remains a way to go yet, and that is the central concern: that it has always been on a journey somewhere, or embarked upon another new adventure, and for all its client satisfaction ratings it has never actually arrived at any chosen strategic destination.

★

At one point the company had in excess of thirty equity partners in its various joint ventures around the world, and was simultaneously carrying out mergers and acquisition projects on all five industrialised continents. Building a global organisation had never been so hurriedly, so fissiparously carried out, and as a result it never quite gelled. There has never been a convincingly coherent and financially credible BT Europe in place, while BT America and BT Asia Pacific have always remained underweight. The early aspirational talk of Europe as BT's new home market has never transformed into reality.

There has been progress in rationalising the service portfolio and the multiplicity of networks, although in some areas this was but a gloss over a continuing ragbag of products and technologies. None of this would greatly matter, of course, if the financial performance had achieved the benchmark levels expected of it. But while the business evolved into a curious hybrid of capital intensive, technology-based telco, shrouded in a labour intensive wrap of IT professional services, it remained difficult to foresee how a significant upturn in its operating margins would materialise. A jack of all trades perhaps, mastering none.

And yet, and yet. It was always the place to work. It remained by far the most interesting and challenging division of the company, while also being the most complex, and at times frustrating to plan and manage. Where working on the company's

UK business could be a tiresome administrative chore, developing and growing the business overseas was an endless game of Grandma's Footsteps; a rush here, a step back there, hesitation, full scale retreat, a sidestep and then more tentative moves forward; a merry dance to the music of time, forever skating on very thin ice. Never dull.

Returning from holidays, it was uplifting to arrive back to discussions over the latest strategy for the US, the plans for launching new IT platforms across Europe, the investment case for the Hong Kong to Sydney media network upgrade. The sun seemed to shine on these deliberations; you brought your holiday destinations back with you into work. Or if fortunate, you actually flew back out to them. That is still happening, of course, if on a markedly lesser scale. Local teams are now in place around the world and in contact daily through a web of internal communications; there is less and less justification for travel. The magic and exotica has all but faded, although there are still seams to be mined.

A colleague spent a couple of years on assignment as CFO of a newly established South American subsidiary, before returning rather too promptly and resigning to join the Church of England. I am still quite unclear on exactly how the Latin hotspots managed to drive him to such a decision, but I was nonetheless gladdened he felt able to afford them the time and opportunity to do so.

It remains a big world with much going on within it, and it would be satisfying to believe BT has finally carved out a sustainable path to take advantage of it, before the allure of the dream finally fades for good. After all, twenty years is a very long time to spend stress-testing strategic logic.

V

On Television

The recurrent theme of a relationship between telecoms and broadcast media, and with the television sector in particular, has at times resembled an obsessive, mono-directional love affair. BT set its heart many years ago on a television "play", saw its passion initially quashed in law, then proceed unrequited, experience a subsequent teasing come-and-get-me phase, fall away for lack of mutual respect, then find itself rekindled and finally the basis for a hoped-for, life long companionship. With the 2013 launch of its sports television channels, BT and television finally got spliced.

They have plans for a long and happy marriage. But what was the basis for love in the first place? What was the spark? The last twenty five years witnessed three potent forces, each pitching our lovelorn luminaries into the throes of a tightening embrace; thus was it written in the stars.

Convergence

That both telecoms services and television signals can pass seamlessly together along glass fibre cables had been known and anticipated for many years. What had not been in place to permit this to actually happen was the economic model and cost base. These requirements have only effectively clicked into place in recent years, enabling the rollout of fibre to street cabinets, to the kerbside, and ever closer to our front doors and living room walls. The IP revolution, now some two decades old, has provided the switching, routing and streaming technologies that process all digitised content (voice, video, data) in one and the same transmission format. It has increasingly made economic sense to squirt it all down one tube. This inevitably changes business models and industrial models too: ISPs will eventually reach further into our homes to provide machine-to-machine household and personal networks that will make broadcasting a couple of football matches each week a mere sideshow. But for now, multimedia has arrived.

Bundling

The ability to market fixed line telephone, broadband and television services, and to charge for them all via one bill, had for years been a driving and defining vision for many within the consumer orientated telecoms universe. The lifting of regulatory restrictions since the turn of the century provided BT with a level playing field with its competitors, albeit it has taken over a decade for it to finally materialise as a broadcaster of some substance, having taken only tentative steps with the most recent BT Vision initiative. The acquisition of 4G mobile spectrum, while laying the ground for a bundled "quad" play, also offers the prospect of BT playing a central role in the development of the next generation of multi-access interactive content. So from zero to bundling hero in a single bound? Would that life were that simple; Google, Sky, Vodafone and others will be right in the mix for that too, but BT has finally positioned itself as a player.

Seduction

The world of telecoms is a dry and dusty place, a world of earnest engineering, soulless contact centres, and dependably featureless offices. For the globally minded, there has been an exotic gloss, an escape from the mundane, a cloak of excitement to wrap oneself in. For the UK domestic business of BT, however, there was no such inherent glamour which, for some at least, left a void. They craved their own veneer of pizzazz, which would have to be devised, manufactured and self-consciously applied. Instead of a naturally acquired tan, it would need a deep coating of slap. Television was the obvious source for this makeover, and stepped in as the assiduously courted, gaudy ageing vamp that would escort the tired old relic into the arc lights. Not to be spurned, he would shower her in expensive gifts and whisper endless sweet nothings; "You'll be the making of me, darling". How could she possibly refuse him?

★

So how do we rate their chances of staying together and making a go of it? Will it be happy ever after? Certainly there are offspring in mind: cute little bundles of apps and interactive programming. But successful marriages are built on affection, companionship, trust and mutual respect; two hearts beating as one. Is that what we have here?

Their mooted fusion could have come from either of two directions: from telecoms embracing television, or vice versa. It appears straightforward in principle for television to reach back along the value chain, to exert control over its own destiny and its cost base, and on its own terms. As a source of innately higher value, from content and prestige, it wields market power; its patronage will be highly sought after, its success encouraged and celebrated.

But when telecoms comes edging along the value chain, to drape itself in more seductive outerwear, it is likely to be viewed with suspicion and condescension: the crass outsider, the *arriviste* wheedling its way into the market's affections, its failure snobbishly and disdainfully anticipated.

Irrespective of this, one might nonetheless question their prospects; they are simply too different to remain close indefinitely, it will be too uncomfortable, even if they insist on their own space. For television is expansive, cultural and creative, where the focus is always proudly on the end product; it is at root an artistic process, a form of expression. Telecoms, in stark contrast, is commodity-minded, grubbily functional and utilitarian, endlessly chasing down the cost to serve; an efficient and effective platform for expression, to be sure, but there the synergy ends. Think of cars and roads: one cannot seriously imagine the Highways Agency running Porsche. The languages and cultures are alien to one another, and don't mention the dress codes.

So let them by all means remain friends and enjoy each other's company. But living together? Perhaps the honeymoon is not the right time to make harsh judgments; best to leave alone, and let nature take its course.

vi

On Networks

The privatisation of BT (British Telecom as it then was) was a remarkable event. It marked the transition of more or less the entire telecoms sector of the UK economy (then accounting for some two and a half per cent of the country's GDP) from the public realm into private ownership. There were a handful of other minor operators and suppliers but to all intents and purposes BT comprised, appropriately enough, the British telecommunications industry.

Over the past thirty years, hundreds of new entrants have sought to make their mark, some more successful than others in taking a slice of the ever burgeoning cake. Telecoms has retained its proportion of GDP, while BT has foregone rather more than half of its overall share, a gradual erosion from genuine competitive pressures and the vice-like grip of regulation. Notwithstanding the periodic bemoaning of its retail and wholesale rivals (and some customers), this has been a largely smooth and successful process and has resulted in one of the most competitive telecoms markets in the world.

A reasoned discussion about the UK network business requires clarification, and is defined here to include the following assets and activities: the managed copper and fibre lines that reach from households, shops and offices to the exchange buildings; the switching and routing equipment therein; the backbone networks that link all the exchanges, large and small; the data centres and server farms that sit within this mesh of transmission technologies, housing the intelligence and content; the software that defines and controls the portfolio of products and services, which in turn determine how voice, text, images and video are moved around the whole piece.

*

The UK network has undergone two significant technical upheavals over the past three decades: digitalisation during the 1980s and 1990s, followed by the shift to IP transmission from the early 2000s, which continues to this day. A visit to an exchange building (invariably the ugliest block in the vicinity) is a revelation. The endless rickety racks of wiring; the quietly humming, flickering computing equipment, under a film of dust; the thick black cables, like the tentacles of a stunned kraken, draped filthily and menacingly across the floor of the damp, dank basement cable chamber. This is the messy actuality, the guts of the modern network, and it remains to me an utter miracle that it still works.

The exchanges themselves have barely changed in thirty years. They have just got older and shabbier, more derelict, largely shunned by the commercial echelons of the organisation, who wouldn't be seen dead in one if they could help it. They are emptier now than they were, as the kit itself has shrunk and more centrally hosted services have been introduced. It is virtually impossible to get shot of them though: the cost of re-routing transmission is hideously expensive, while an abiding obsession with security means that partitioning and reusing spare capacity is mostly unwelcomed. And so entering most examples of the operational estate is like stepping back in time. Even the smell, the oily, sweaty effluvium of the engine room, hasn't changed.

What has changed is the presence, more specifically the absence, of humanity. Where once each exchange was crewed by some twenty engineers, they are now largely unmanned, periodically checked over by a peripatetic handful of multi-skilled yeomen, armed to the teeth with iPads and sonic screwdrivers. While their union organisation has sometimes sounded posturing and anachronistic, it has in practice adopted an overwhelmingly pragmatic approach to change, and has maintained its members' living standards and working conditions with alacrity and integrity. While it may occasionally represent a blast from the past, in fact it is fully resigned to the present.

★

And while the infrastructure, products and the workforce have been transformed, the money has kept on rolling in. The half year results at September 2013 revealed that over ninety per cent of BT's profits come from the UK network business units (Openreach, BT Retail and BT Wholesale), while a generous slice of the BT GS business is also UK generated. Fully twenty years after the launch of its global thrust, the UK network business still accounts for just about all of the company's earnings.

The guardians of the UK network and the business that it supports have done an extraordinarily effective job. Despite regulatory and competitive pressures it has grown by a compound of two per cent per annum since privatisation and still delivers today a combined cash margin of thirty per cent. Over the years, this has provided the company as a whole not just with cash to reinvest, but with its very lifeblood. It has kept it alive, seeing it through its various crises and laid open for it countless new opportunities. Its ability and willingness to change and evolve has ensured BT's very survival.

vii

On Management

While it is the mix of employees, the corporate personality of the general staff, that provides the tone and texture of daily working life, it is the character, structure and approach of the company's management that provides the score – the key, the notes, the rhythm – and harmonises the constituent parts. Thus it was with some avidity that corporate or groupwide emails were devoured as they dropped into the global inbox. News of the latest arrivals and departures, reorganisations and restructurings provide the high gossip and low rumours that unfailingly intrigue the contemporary corporate choir.

But this had not always been the way of things. Twenty years ago, it was rare indeed that the arrival of senior executives would spark the interest of the general staff; these people came and went with reasonable regularity and made little or no discernible impact upon our daily lives, nor on that of the Group. For the first ten years I was in BT I could not have named more than a couple of the executive board members; latterly, and not merely through a growing personal network, I could have named all of them, and most of their direct reports. These people today make it their business to be known. Rather than hide behind their grand job titles, they are aware of the need to be seen and heard; it bestows on them a legitimacy, influence and power. It means above all that they can get things done.

Their predecessors were a far more remote and obscure bunch, happy to remain in the executive suites and issue their occasional mandates from on high. Their only visible stirrings were the endless reorganisations and restructurings they put into effect as regularly as the planets spun around the night skies, in their own never-ending circles. In a more charitable vein, these shake-ups could be likened to visits to the gym, in that they never seemed to make any difference, but you couldn't be absolutely sure how bad it might have become without them. So they kept going with them, assuring themselves it was probably better than doing nothing at all. I believe I was affected directly by no fewer than sixteen "reorgs" and rejigs in twenty eight years; more than one every two years. I can still name the thirty individuals I reported to as a consequence of these constant upheavals; more than one boss per year.

Yes, the mantra of change was never more appositely applied than to the shape and structure of the management organisation around me, in how it attached itself to me and in how it would make use of my time and efforts. Often the restructuring would involve no direct change at all to my daily working life; I would be, in the parlance, as prevalent as it was prosaic, "lifted and shifted". In some, my role was "repointed" towards carrying out something broadly similar to what I had doing before, while in others I was "conditionally liked" (as in "we would like you…") to pick up additional or completely new areas of responsibility.

I was fortunate never to find myself without portfolio, nor was I ever plunged into a murky redeployee pool, there to await an unspecified, possibly grisly destiny. No doubt my bountiful salary package saw to it; they would always want their money's worth out of me. Eventually the Group settled into a handful of lines of business, each aimed at particular markets rather than geographies or specific product sales, and with this, the logic of endless upheaval was finally exhausted, or at least took an extended breather.

For the fad for management fads had finally faded. With markedly fewer staff on the books, and with ever more earnest and productive activity required to accrete market share and market capitalisation, there was simply no time for them. They had been squeezed out by the need for real work, and market forces had finally seen to that. They cleared the air of much totemic bullshit, blew the dust from the desks of the hidebound, and marshalled leaders and led alike into a clearer dawn.

Into a tougher fight, an endless and relentless battle, a bloodless war in the face of these forces. It was not really like going into work any more; it was reporting for duty, and the transition of BT's management, from sullen administration to proactive leadership, was finally complete.

On Bets

As even the most casual reader will have noticed, and contrary to general perceptions, BT has never been reluctant to take a strategic punt. True, it may have moved quite slowly, but it got around to it in the end, whether it was internet services in general, broadband in particular or the eventual rollout of optical fibre in the local loop, the last mile from the exchange to the customer's premise. It was in the vanguard of cable and satellite television, and mobile telephony; so too with globalisation. The recent foray into pay television was not of itself an innovation, yet it remains a bet: that pay television can be shifted from its twenty year home on satellite and cable, and find a permanent home on a terrestrial fibre telecoms platform. That in itself will be at least a ten year project.

The millstone around BT's neck has always been the need for scale. As a national operator, let alone brand, it simply could not opt for selective local investments; it had to plan on a national scale and so inevitably the numbers were always going to be big, and the risks concomitantly higher. Not the risks of success or failure, but the values at stake. It has never had the luxury of maintaining its cottage industries as micro businesses.

Once the trial was proven, it would have to be upscaled or industrialised; it had no place as a plaything, which would act as a needless distraction. Fewer and bigger, do or die were the unwritten rules, and try as they might to keep their own babies under wraps, the chiefs of these micro-industries were eventually made to fall in line. Sometimes I agreed with it, at others I had gone native and deplored it. But the logic was sound, if at times poorly applied in practice. There simply wasn't the room for all these experimental activities, and at some point they had to get off the pot. The process of renewal created its own trail of nostalgia.

★

At the time of writing, BT has entered its thirtieth year in private ownership. In that time it has incurred annual capital investment in the order of three billion pounds, excluding a host of major acquisitions. The network and system commitments have amounted to around ninety billion pounds, while the acquisitions have totalled in the order of twenty billions. The company has thus invested comfortably in excess of one hundred billion pounds since it was privatised. Was it worth it?

Market capitalisation has grown from eight billion pounds in 1984 to some thirty billion at the time of writing, an increase of twenty two billion pounds. Six billion pounds of this is accounted for by the emergency rights issue of 2001. This suggests that sixteen billion pounds of shareholder value has been generated through commercial activities, giving an average return across all investments of about fifteen per cent. Project and contract guidance was reset a few years ago to establish this floor and the improving operational performance has been growingly reflected in an improving share price.

The recent re-rating of the shares is better news for long term investors who have seen far better returns from other 1980s privatised stocks such as British Gas and BP, while BT consistently struggled to track the stock market overall, as the Financial Times noted in 2010. The recurrent financial crises took a lasting toll.

Recent investments have been as much about saving costs as increasing turnover and have arguably been as beneficial for investors as previous unremitting dashes for revenue growth. A bird in the hand, one might say.

★

The company is still making substantial investments: over one and a half billion pounds in cash to date on its sports television network, yet this is hedged at barely fifteen per cent of its free cash flow over the three years of the rights period. BT has managed to give the impression of significant expansion, while actually pulling in its horns. It is now taking more measured steps in its pursuit of transformation, and this will further reassure a fragile and wary investor base. It still likes a flutter, but its shirt remains tightly across its back.

As noted above, value is overwhelmingly generated by the UK business, and with the eurozone especially locked in dire economic straits, and conditions in key emerging markets noticeably tightening, this looks set to remain the case for several years. This imbalance in the dynamics of BT's internal investment portfolio has arguably been going on for too long now, with little early prospect of a meaningful geographic rebalancing, the key objective when the globalisation programme was launched twenty years ago.

In the absence of substantial improvement in the financial performance of the global business, investors are bound to ask the question of whether it could be better managed elsewhere, or by itself, or by someone else. What might this mean for the company: a spin-off for BT GS along the lines of O2? It would be perhaps the biggest bet yet, but it cannot be ruled out.

On Survival

"The verdict on BT plc must be that privatisation provided a route for the managed decline of a business whose historic purpose was disappearing."

Professor John Kay of the LSE, a notable long term observer of the UK economy, its key sectors and participants, writing in 2009 and quoted above, suggested the privatisation of BT was but the start of what would inevitably be a long and painful process (I am paraphrasing) driven by technological and investment priorities, which its then senior management caucus were ill-equipped to oversee and control.

This would lead in due course, following his logic, to the progressive fragmentation of the company and ultimately to its complete disappearance. Its role, he implied, was effectively that of facilitator for change: a nest of modest assets and limited human capability which, due to continual relative underperformance both operationally and financially, would over the course of time be broken up, absorbed into or displaced by new and more commercially adept market entrants, to usher in a modern industrial landscape for the UK telecoms sector. No timescale was set for this unfolding of events.

In part this has indeed occurred – he wrote with the benefit of some hindsight, of course – with the sale to private equity of the Yellow Pages classified business (now Yell) and the mobile business spun out as O2 (and subsequently subsumed into

Telefonica). As mooted above, it is quite possible the global business will eventually go the same way; its relative underachievement within the BT purlieu paving the way for its eventual disappearance in the wake of its notable predecessors.

Much of the core fixed network business as was privatised has indeed disappeared as well, in this instance not through corporate transactions, but following a process of internal renewal. A transformation in quality of performance, driven by self-interest and clever exploitation of its prized UK network asset. Never too big or too good to fail, it was nonetheless smart enough and fit enough to survive. One generation on, this historic purpose of BT has arguably never looked in ruder health, and is set to be with us for another thirty years.

Afterword

In 1996, William Strauss and Neil Howe published their seminal book The Fourth Turning: An American Prophecy, an acutely accurate foretelling of the crisis that was to hit the US (and the rest of us) early in the new century. Their work centred on historical study of generational changes which occur every twenty years or so, and which broadly coincide with, and explain, history itself moving into new eras. These historical shifts they refer to as turnings; the fourth turning (tagged portentously as "crisis") represents the entry into the final twenty year era of a four era cycle which endlessly repeats every eighty years or so, the average length of a human life.

This crisis turning also signalled the end of the previous, third era, known as an "unravelling", which in this latest cycle had begun in 1984. An unravelling occurs when the mid-life leadership and management cohort comes to be dominated by a generation of value-based visionaries (generically labelled as prophets) who relentlessly pursue individual fulfilment; most recently, the Boomer hippy-to-yuppy "me" generation behind the consciousness-raising revolution of the 1960s and 1970s. As they recede into retirement, they have arguably left a dubious legacy.

★

1984 also marked the first entry of a new cohort, Generation X, into the world of work. A tougher, more worldly and pragmatic group (generically labelled as nomads) noted for their resilience and survival instincts, their priority is to seek out safe harbours, and minimise risk. At any time, they have their hands full coping with the bequest left behind by their predecessors. It's grim work, but they are up to the job.

In 2008, as crisis struck, the first envoys from the latest generation to attain adulthood, the Millenials, came knocking on the office door. Generically labelled as heroes, they are collegiate and energetic team-workers, with an optimistic and outward looking drive for prosperity.

The fourth turning crisis period has a further fifteen or so years to run, before a climactic event finally buries the current cycle for good. As Generation X retires during the 2020s and beyond, exhausted and broke, so the leaders of the Millenial generation will increasingly take on the challenge of piloting us through the next turning and into the opening era of the next eighty year cycle. We will be fortunate indeed to be in their capable, concerned and willing hands.

★

I was born in the final few months of the Boom era. A classic inbetweenie, I was parented by representatives of the silent generation of pre-war conformists, schooled in the shadow of counter-culture, and employed amongst a growing band of lost souls. Never a hippy, I was nonetheless a child of alternative culture; I had a compromised vision, but I would work, on my own terms, and make it my business to survive and realise it. It wasn't too difficult, even with the unravelling that unfolded around me, and for that I am grateful.

Crisis eras ultimately spawn a regeneracy, a recharting and a rebuilding. These are the first tentative beginnings of the next cycle, the spring after winter. It is not so much a handing on of the torch, as the forging and lighting of a new one. Everything will change again, as it always does.

Acknowledgements

I should like to acknowledge a debt of gratitude to the people who assisted in the development and production of this book. They are: Tia Darik, for read-throughs and unstinting support; Joe Norman, for editorial input; Francois van der Langkruis, for creative management; Silvija Drazdziulyte, for photography; Edwin van der Langkruis and Dennis Meerhof, for artwork; and Troubador, for taking this project on.

And of course to the supporting cast, and others, who made it all an enjoyable and rewarding time; you know who you all are. Roger, Craig, Angie, Pat, Miriam, Glyn, Gary, Daksha, Dennis, Abdul and Dara (1984-1986) – Mike, Bonnie, Margaret, Peter, Tony, Bill, Ian, Mark, Katty and Sheila (1987-1988) – Simon, Ray, Diarmuid, Barry, Pat, Debbie, Katherine, Pete, David, Edwina, Meredith, Martin and Tony (1989-1990) – David, Les, Edward and Rajesh (1991) – Mike, David, Joe, Alan, Rob (1992-1993) – Andrew, Mike, David, Doug, Jackie and Kate (1994-1995) – Graham, Giorgio, Lorenzo, Alessandro, Paulo, Linda, Maria, Dave, Rob, Kevin, Donald, Maggie, Mike, Kail, Kieran, Sue, Nigel, Nick, James, Michael, Len (1996-1998) – Claire, Sally, Courtney, Sinead, Alan, Nick, Adrian, Dave, Jerry, Gail, Bruce and Ian (1999-2001) – Harry, Nick, Chris, Robert (2002) – Steve, Annie, Peter, Barry, Tim, Adam, Matthew and Michael (2003) – Paul, Colin, Gordon, Neil, Mike and Jeremy (2004-2006) – Germon, Uwe, Taleb, Anna-Maria (2007) – Murray, Keith, Daljit, Andrew, Simon, Tom, Steve, Andy, Tony,

Jan, Pete, Martin, Steve, Fergus (2008-2011) – Andrew, Kam, John, Tim, Theresa and Martin (2012-13). Thanks all.